ISBN 88-8398-022-0

©2003 by European Press Academic Publishing
Florence, Italy
www.e-p-a-p.com
www.europeanpress.it
Proprietà letteraria riservata - Printed in Italy

THE ATLANTIC PRIORITY

DEFENCE POLICY OF THE NETHERLANDS AT THE TIME OF THE EUROPEAN DEFENCE COMMUNITY

JAN VAN DER HARST

TABLE OF CONTENTS

6

General introduction

This book is a slightly adapted and updated version of the PhD thesis I defended at the European University Institute in Florence in 1988.[1] At that time the work was only printed in limited numbers, and ever since I have intended to write a commercial edition for a wider public, but never really got round to it, mainly owing to the usual teaching commitments and other more pressing research activities. When, in the year 2000, more than a decade after the happy Florentine event, the editor of the present volume hinted at the possibility of publishing a commercial edition under his patronage, I felt extremely honoured, but I also asked for time to screen the text, to adapt the parts in need of polishing and restructuring and to get rid of the parts which, for one reason or another, were no longer presentable. To be honest, it was a rather rude awakening to be confronted with the manuscript I had finished with so long before but, after a difficult start, I started to enjoy working again on this fascinating period and topic.

In this book, the debate in the Netherlands on the European Defence Community is set against the background of the country's defence policy in the period 1948-1954. These were the years that government, military and business faced the difficult challenge of rebuilding the national army and armaments industry after the morally and physically catastrophic period of World War II. Moreover, up to 1949 the country was undergoing the traumatic process of de-colonisation in the Dutch East-Indies, which led to the dispatch of large numbers of conscripts and professional soldiers to that part of the world. As a result, serious defence of the home country was hardly feasible, all the more so under circumstances of inadequate financial resources and a lack of commitment on the part of the international community to defend Dutch territory. This was

---

1 J. van der Harst, *European Union and Atlantic Partnership: Political, Military and Economic Aspects of Dutch Defence, 1948-1954, and the Impact of the European Defence Community* (EUI Florence, July 1987).

exactly the dilemma The Hague had to face in the early post-war period: why build up an expensive army against an unknown threat coming from the east, if the country was not assured of credible international security guarantees against such a threat? Because of initial US preferences for a peripheral strategy on the fringes of the continent, and because of the lack of depth in European defence at that time, the Netherlands was likely to be invaded fairly quickly and easily in case of a foreign - Soviet - conventional attack. To remedy that awkward situation, the Netherlands was one of the first European countries to start pleading for the allied defence line to be extended eastwards, resulting in a forward defence of Europe instead of a peripheral one. But forward defence - defence on the river Elbe in Germany - was impossible without simultaneously allowing a certain revival of the West German army. At that time, so soon after the war, German rearmament was understandably a highly controversial issue in the Netherlands, and large parts of the population were downright hostile to it, but with that in mind, it was surprising how easily the government succeeded in convincing the country of the need for accepting the return of German soldiers. Apparently, the communist threat was seen as far more serious than the German one, and the conciliatory stance towards Germany fitted in well with the more general government strategy of establishing solid relations with the eastern neighbour because of the indispensable importance of the German economy to post-war domestic reconstruction.

In its approach to the German question, the Netherlands differed from France, which, during the entire period under discussion, persevered in a much less compromising stance towards Bonn. It was not the only issue on which the French and Dutch governments held divergent opinions. The entire debate on the European Defence Community (EDC) witnessed an almost perpetual clash between the two, with few gestures towards compromise and conciliation. France and the Netherlands agreed on virtually nothing, as demonstrated both at the beginning and the end of the EDC: in 1950, when Paris launched the Pleven plan, The Hague was its fiercest opponent; but, in 1954, while the Dutch parliament was the first of the six to ratify the treaty, the French *Assemblée* stalled, and eventually decided to ignore the treaty and pass to other business, resulting in the end of the EDC. The details of this intriguing development will be dealt with in this book, written from a Dutch perspective with additions from French and other secondary sources.

The central research questions dealt with in this work are the following: How did Dutch defence policy evolve during the period 1948-1954, what were the government's priorities regarding defence and European integration, and to what extent did the proposals for a European Defence Community square or clash with these priorities? The study covers a historic-political approach to the problem, dealing primarily with policy-making by the government and the most relevant ministerial departments.[2] If and where necessary, economic (business) and military (General Staff) considerations have been taken into account but, again, the main focus is a political one.

A major motive for writing this book was to investigate whether in the early 1950s the Netherlands was really such an all-out, convinced supporter of European integration and federation, as has often been alleged in the historical literature on the topic. It is true that from the early 1950s the country became a fervent advocate of economic and commercial integration within a regional European framework, but to what extent did this hold true in the area of 'High Politics', covering foreign and defence policies? Based on the documents provided by the governmental and departmental archives for the period relevant to this book, it became apparent that, in the latter domain, The Hague's European fervour was highly moderate, not to say non-existent at times. The Atlantic link with the United Sates was considered sacrosanct and any European initiative aimed at

---

[2] For an analysis of the national parliament's position towards defence in the period around 1950, see J.W.L. Brouwer, 'Om de doelmatigheid van de defensieuitgaven, 1948-1951', *Politieke Opstellen* 10 (1990) CPG/KUN, pp. 85-108; J.W.L. Brouwer, '"De stem van de Marine in de ministerraad." Schout-bij-nacht H.C.W. Moorman als staatssecretaris van Marine in het kabinet-Drees-Van Schaik', *Politieke Opstellen* 9 (1989) CPG/KUN, 29-56.

interfering with this link was therefore condemned. The priority given to NATO at the expense of the EDC and other European political initiatives is one of the dominant themes of this study.

The book is divided into two parts and five chapters. Part I (covering the first two chapters) deals with Dutch defence policy in general in the period 1948-1954. The first chapter begins with the creation of the Western Union, which heralded the involvement of the Netherlands in an institutionalised security framework, soon followed by membership of NATO. Despite that, the government for quite a long time, until early 1951, hesitated in building up the country's defence. The reasons for this will be dealt with in this chapter. Chapter 2 starts in January 1951, on the eve of the announcement of a new defence programme which provided for a substantial increase in military expenditure and forced the Netherlands to comply with international demands for improving its military performance. The country had become a faithful partner to NATO, but even in that position uncertainties prevailed, mainly resulting from the perceived unwillingness of the allies, the United States, and France in particular, to come to the Netherlands' rescue in case of an emergency situation. German rearmament was the obvious solution to this problem, but for a period of four years France succeeded in delaying a decision on this issue. The second chapter, spanning the period 1951-1954, attempts to describe and explain how the Netherlands responded to strategic and other uncertainties and to what extent the country succeeded in achieving the goals set by the 'crash programme' of March 1951. It also aims at providing a background for the negotiations on the EDC, which took place contemporaneously.

Part II (chapters 3, 4 and 5) illuminates from three different angles the position of the Netherlands with regard to French proposals for a European army and a European Defence Community. Chapter 3 deals with the views held by government and the Ministry of Foreign Affairs, chapter 4 with the Ministry of Defence and the General Staff, and chapter 5 with the Ministry of Economic Affairs and the business community. Each had its own preferences and objections regarding the EDC, and the question here is to what extent these were taken into account by the top-level decision-makers in the government. Other questions to be answered include why was the Netherlands unwilling to become involved in the European army debate at the start of the Paris negotiations in January 1951, why did the government change its mind in September of that year and decide on full participation, and, finally, why was the Netherlands, after the hesitant start in January 1951, the first country to ratify the EDC treaty?

The final conclusions summarise the main findings of this study, and attempt to answer the central questions posed here. They also aim at placing the results of the present research against a background of the generally (in the literature) accepted traditions of the country's post-war foreign policy. What follows in the section 'archivalia and bibliography' is a survey of the archives and literature consulted for this book.

Compared to the original PhD-thesis (see note 1), the most important adaptations concern the division of chapter 1 in two 'new' chapters and the leaving out of the 'old' chapter 2 on the economic aspects of Dutch defence in the period 1948-1954. This was prompted by the publication of a thorough and elaborate study on this topic[3], which made the information provided in the 'old' chapter 2 somewhat superfluous and general. The other adaptations are, apart from the updating, mainly of a textual and editorial nature.

I would like to express my thanks and gratitude to the group of colleagues and friends who have helped me through the protracted process of writing this book, back in the 1980s and more recently. In the preface of my PhD thesis I mentioned many persons I felt indebted to and, while my gratitude to them has by no means diminished, I hope they take no offence if they fail to find their names on this page. I will make an exception for Prof. Alan Milward, my supervisor during the EUI years in Florence, who remains, even today, a continuous source of inspiration and erudition. I owe him a

---

[3] C.M. Megens, *American aid to NATO allies in the 1950s. The Dutch case* (Groningen 1994).

lot. The publication of this book is a welcome occasion to pay tribute to my colleagues of the International Relations department in Groningen, and to thank them for the invariably comradely atmosphere and stimulating working environment. Anjo Harryvan deserves a special word of acknowledgement, having shared with me so many professional experiences, including co-productions of articles and books. But this time I had to do it without his invaluable knowledge, humour and inspiration. I can only hope that his absence is not too easily visible in the quality of the work. I thank Margaret O'Connell and Julia Harvey for reading and correcting the final version of the text and computer wizard Bastiaan Aardema for helping me through the last stages of editing. The last word is always dedicated to one particular, beloved person, and I have no desire to make an exception to this tradition. Although China and the EDC have, at first glance, nothing to do with each other, the coming of Lijuan Yi into my life has certainly brought this study under special influence from the 'China connection'. I dedicate this book to her.

Groningen, December 2002

PART I

DEFENCE POLICY OF THE NETHERLANDS, 1948-1954

CHAPTER 1

Reluctance to build up the nation's defence, 1948-1950

Introduction

When the Netherlands joined the Brussels pact and NATO, the government had to adopt a defence policy that not only reflected internal views but also took the interests of the allies into account. In particular, during the first two decades of NATO's existence, Dutch defence policy gave priority to demands made by the alliance.

In the literature on post-war Dutch history, the common opinion is that, immediately following the foundation of the Western Union (in March 1948) and particularly of NATO (in April 1949), the Netherlands became a staunch supporter of military co-operation within an international framework, since such co-operation was considered the surest way of protecting the country against the - perceived - expansionist policy of the Soviet Union. It has also been assumed that the armed forces which had been sent to Indonesia (then the Dutch Indies), in an effort to restore colonial rule, returned in 1949 'to a peaceful climate, in which they could modernise their training with American and Canadian assistance'; moreover, 'for this task the government could count on a favourable public opinion, which was strongly anticommunist, pro-American and, much less anti-militarist than was usual in Dutch history, because of the war experience and the military threat from the USSR.'[4]

Although some of this is undoubtedly true, Dutch involvement in Western defence did not pass off as quietly as has been assumed. During the early years of membership of the Western Union and NATO, the government's position was rather passive and hesitant.

---

[4] J.J.C. Voorhoeve, *Peace, profits and principles. A study of Dutch foreign policy* (Den Haag 1979) p. 121.

This was mainly due to six factors: the priority given to domestic financial and economic reconstruction; the difficulty to incorporate military repatriates from the Dutch Indies in an army geared for modern warfare; the country's military-strategic exposure which was to remain as long as West Germany was not rearmed; the ambitious NATO plans emphasising the build-up of the Dutch army, instead of the domestically highly respected Navy (the latter had gained substantial prestige during World War II); the widely held belief that the Soviet Union concentrated on the psychological, social and economic subversion of Western Europe, rather than on military aggression; and anti-militaristic sentiments of the social-democratic Prime Minister Drees[5] who was reported to have an inbred suspicion of anything that wore a uniform.

We argue that in the period 1945-51, Dutch reluctance to build up their defence force in an international context constituted a late - rather spasmodic - attempt to cling to the traditional pre-war foreign policy of 'neutralist abstentionism', meaning a fundamental aversion to involvement in European power politics[6]. The government's initial unwillingness to comply with international requirements was severely criticised by the national military who blamed civil authorities for their lack of familiarity with the fundamentals of post-war world politics.

At the end of the 1940s the Netherlands was undefended except for a few thousand air-defence troops[7]. Tens of thousands of soldiers were sent to the Dutch Indies, which at the time received a higher priority than the defence of Western Europe. In 1949 and 1950 the government refused to worry about delays in implementing the provisions of the Brussels treaty and the North Atlantic treaty. The psychological boost given by a declared American commitment to the European continent was deemed more important than the immediate realisation of a transatlantic military organisation with a

---

[5] W. Drees, Prime Minister, 1948-1958.

[6] Voorhoeve, *Peace, profits and principles*, pp. 45-49.

[7] Until 1953, the Air Force did not constitute an independent service, but air force units were integrated in the national army and navy.

well-prepared standing army. Maintenance of good relations with the United States dominated the government's defence policy, not only then, but also later. With the Americans nearby, the Dutch were in a position to concentrate on improving the country's financial and economic position, so desperately needed after the war. In fact, the only facility the military could provide in an emergency situation was a precarious plan for evacuation.

After the first successful Soviet test with an atomic bomb (in August 1949) and particularly, after the outbreak of the Korean War (in June 1950), the American government put pressure on all the European partners, including the Netherlands, to increase their national defence efforts. From then on American dominance over Dutch military policy was beyond dispute. The US government - taking into account Congressional demands - pressed The Hague to improve and accelerate defence capacity; to let the importance of the army prevail over the navy; to rebuild the domestic defence industry, etcetera. The US administration regularly threatened to cut off the supply of economic and military assistance, if the Dutch government refused to comply with its stipulations. In the late forties/early fifties it was obvious that The Hague had little space to shape its own policies.

Because of the central position of the Dutch army in allied military programmes, this chapter focuses primarily on the problems concerning the build-up of the army in a national and international context. The position of the navy in the early post-war period is analysed expertly in other works[8], and will be only briefly covered in this chapter. The same applies to the development of the domestic defence industry in the period under review. Reference should be made here to the detailed research accomplished by Megens on the

---

[8] J.W.L. Brouwer, 'De stem van de marine in de ministerraad. Schout-bij-nacht H.C.W. Moorman als staatssecretaris van Marine in het kabinet Drees-Van Schaik, 1949-1951', *Politieke opstellen* CPG/KUN 9 (1989) pp. 29-56; J.W.L. Brouwer and C.M. Megens, 'Het succesvolle verzet van de Koninklijke Marine tegen taakspecialisatie in de NAVO, 1949-1951', *Transaktie* 21 (1992) 1, pp. 65-84; G. Teitler, 'De Koninklijke Marine en de komst van de NATO', *Marineblad* 99 (1989) 4, pp. 151-157.

impact of American aid on the Dutch army and armaments production.[9]

Chapter 1 focuses on the period 1948-1950 and on the problems experienced by the government regarding the build-up of the national army in an international framework. The second chapter deals with the later period, 1951-1954, beginning with the decision to agree on a multi-year programme for military expenditure, and subsequently surveying the impact of this decision on the development of the country's defence.

1.1 The Western Union, and Montgomery's requirements

In January 1948, British Foreign Minister, Bevin, launched a plan aimed at creating a military alliance consisting of five Western European countries: Britain, France and the Benelux countries. The response by the Dutch government to Bevin's initiative was positive, despite strong reservations about signing a treaty similar to that of Dunkirk (signed by France and Britain in March 1947) explicitly directed against Germany - as Bevin had proposed. The Hague - together with the Benelux partners - urged instead the need to refer in the contemplated treaty to the possibility of a regenerated Germany entering the European comity of nations. Moreover, instead of the proposed bilateral framework, the government preferred a multilateral regional agreement, based on articles 51-54 of the United Nations Charter, with an economic as well as a political and military character. For the rest, no qualms were ventilated, not even regarding the crucial Article IV of the treaty which provided that, should any of the contracting parties be the object of an armed aggression in Europe, the other signatories to the treaty would afford the attacked party 'all the military aid and assistance in their power'. This was an ambitious goal, and - at the time - hardly a realistic one, given the poor military position in which the member-countries, including the Netherlands, found themselves.

---

[9] C.M. Megens, *American aid to NATO allies in the 1950s. The Dutch case* (Groningen 1994).

For the Netherlands the Brussels treaty led to the implementation of a policy, which had already been presaged in the explanatory memorandum of the 1948 budget. This memo stated that an independent national defence could no longer be sustained and, that as a result, Dutch army units should be integrated into an international framework.[10]

It is generally assumed that with the signing of the Brussels treaty, the Netherlands sacrificed its traditional policy of aloofness or even neutrality in foreign affairs[11]; before the Second World War the Dutch government had preferred to abstain from involvement in regional military block-forming. However, although it is formally true that by entering the Western Union, the country relinquished its neutralist past, in practice the multilateral involvement had little significance, at least initially. In the first three years after the signing of the Brussels treaty, that is, from March 1948 till March 1951, the government refused to strengthen the national army in a Western European context because at first, priority was given to retaining the colonial position in Indonesia. In 1947 and 1948 the army attempted two *politionele acties* ('police actions', basically a Dutch euphemism for 'war'), in order to discourage the desire for independence on the part of the Indonesian republicans.

Although there were strong feelings of anti-communism within the Dutch cabinet an imminent Soviet invasion of Western Europe was not considered a serious danger. For a long time it was thought that the Soviet Union lacked the economic resources necessary to fight a successful war in Western Europe. Nevertheless, The Hague certainly feared subversive activity on the part of Western European communist parties, supported by the Soviet Union. Such subversive actions were directed supposedly against the social and economic stability of the Netherlands and its neighbours. In this respect, the

---

[10] Ministerie van Defensie (MinDef), Archief Kabinet Min./Stasvo geclass. (inv. 66) no.5, stukken memorie van toelichting, herziene begroting 1950, rijksbegroting voor het dienstjaar 1948.

[11] Campen, S.I.P. van, *The Quest for Security: Some Aspects of Netherlands Foreign Policy, 1945-1950* (Den Haag 1958).

government was particularly apprehensive of the political situation in France[12] and Italy where strong communist movements existed. Although in the Netherlands itself fifth column infiltration was not considered a real danger[13], the cabinet was convinced that priority should be given to the reconstruction of the country's financial and socio-economic stability[14], which had been seriously affected by the damages sustained during the Second World War. Because of the economic priority, the *Ministerraad* (cabinet) thought that military readiness could be postponed until a later date.

Apart from financial and economic considerations, there was widespread confidence in the country that American monopoly in the field of atomic armament, would function as a credible deterrent against possible Soviet aggression. Insiders knew that in reality the Strategic Air Command - the US organisation responsible for atomic weapons - faced critical shortages at this stage, both in terms of atomic bombs stockpiled and, the number of aircraft and men capable of delivering the weapons to distant targets. Gregg Herken wrote that it was only with the 1948 crisis in Berlin that,

> The bomb and America's atomic monopoly became integral to US war plans and to the administration's strategy for containing Russian expansion. But even then the shockingly small number of bombs in the US arsenal, and the continuing lag in adapting military doctrine to the atomic age meant that America's nuclear deterrent remained a hollow threat during the years that the United States alone had the bomb. And it is likely that the Russians, through espionage, knew well the emptiness of that threat. *(Herken, 1980: 6)*

---

[12] Fear of insurrection and/or coup d'état was a major preoccupation of the French government until the end of 1948. A concrete symptom of this concern was that the first significant decision to increase the size of the French army (80,000 reservists were recalled into service in November 1948) had been designed to provide the government with a means of maintaining law and order at home. J. Frémeaux and A. Martel, 'French defence policy, 1947-1949'. In: O. Riste (ed.), *Western Security: The Formative Years* (Oslo 1985) pp. 95-96.

[13] Also support for the Communist Party (*Communistische Partij Nederland*) soon dwindled after the war.

[14] FRUS (Foreign Relations of the United States) 1948 Vol.3, Telegram 1948 Van Boetzelaer, 03-04-1948, p. 35.

The Soviet preponderance in the area of conventional armament was enormous. The Soviet Union could mobilise about 175 divisions (more than 25 of these were elite troops on standby in the eastern part of Germany) against the paltry number of 16 divisions stationed in Western Europe[15], two of which were American. Moreover, formations were sited largely for administrative occupational reasons; many units were in barracks where they happened to be at the end of the war and in no sense were troops in an operational posture. The balance of air forces was also disadvantageous to the West: 6,000 Soviet aircraft as opposed to 1,000 aircraft in Western Europe. This situation was to remain unaltered until after the outbreak of the Korean War in June 1950.

It should be noted that several members of the Dutch government doubted the credibility of America's nuclear deterrent, although not because of prevailing shortages. After the 1948 coup in Czechoslovakia, Drees remarked that the US administration would not contemplate starting a nuclear war in Europe for fear of the complete destruction of Western European civilisation[16]. On the other hand, Foreign Minister Stikker[17] wrote in his memoirs that,

> In this precarious period it was only the existence of the American atomic bomb, combined with Truman's pledge of American determination to help Europe, which enabled us to survive. In this period there was no discussion of how or when the bomb should be used; we in Europe had only a verbal pledge from President Truman of American support. There was, however, mutual trust, and from that mutual trust there emerged the sense of unity. This unity, together with our joint determination during the period of the Berlin airlift [June 1948 - May 1949, JvdH], gave credibility to our stated intentions to defend our freedom. It is this credibility, which is, in the last analysis, the ultimate deterrent to war. And this credibility triumphed, in Russia's most aggressive years, when conventional

---

[15] Although these figures exaggerated the strength of the Red Army, the Soviet bloc was undeniably in a superior position vis-à-vis the West.

[16] Algemeen Rijksarchief (ARA), Tweede Afdeling, Ministerraadsarchief (MR), 2.02.05, West Europese Unie, 03-01-1948.

[17] D.U. Stikker, Minister of Foreign Affairs, 1948-1952.

Russian forces exceeded ours by far in numbers, in readiness and in equipment. *(Stikker, 1965: 283)*

From later research we know that at the end of the forties, President Truman's policy towards the use of nuclear weapons was one of extreme reluctance.[18] At the time, the Atomic Energy Act of 1946 forbade any dissemination of information on nuclear matters.

In the years 1948-50 Dutch army authorities had hardly one standing division available in Western Europe. What Holland actually did for its defence concerned the build-up of both the navy and air force, while the army was treated as Cinderella. One of the underlying problems concerned the geographical-strategic position of the Netherlands. In the event of a Russian attack - which, as noted before, was not in fact expected, since the government thought that the Soviets were more interested in expansion towards the East, that is, towards China[19] - the Netherlands would be exposed to the enemy's arbitrariness because it was virtually impossible to defend the country's borders without the presence of German army units.

At the time of the signing of the Brussels Treaty, Foreign Minister Stikker had already hinted - although not in public - at a future German contribution to the defence of Western Europe.[20] It was obvious however, that 1948 was too early for a proper national and international debate on German rearmament. Apart from the fact that a substantial proportion of the Dutch population still harboured doubts about the democratic development of early post-war Germany, the government reasoned that, for the moment, the allies, and particularly France, would be hostile to re-establishing a German army. Under these circumstances The Hague considered it advisable

---

[18] H.R. Borowski, *A Hollow Threat. Strategic Air Power and Containment before Korea* (Westport 1982) pp. 102, 103, 113, 126 *etc.*; M. Trachtenberg, *A Constructed Peace. The Making of the European Settlement, 1945-1963* (Princeton 1999) p. 90.
[19] ARA, MR, Het West-Europese pact, 01-24-1949. Eight months later, the People's Republic of China was proclaimed, after the defeat of the nationalists.
[20] Ministerie van Buitenlandse Zaken (MinBuZa), Code telegram 116 Van Boetzelaer aan Van Kleffens, 02-27-1948.

to suspend discussions on this controversial topic and to refrain from needlessly provoking the Soviets.

At the same time The Hague promoted the development of the navy and air force, not in the least because ships and aircraft were held to be useful instruments in the event of a possible evacuation. A secret army plan existed according to which some 10,000 nationals - the Royal Family, members of government and parliament, top civil servants and industrialists, army commanders - would be transported to safe territory in the event of a Soviet invasion. Given the Russian preponderance, a large-scale build-up of the national army was considered futile, even after the signing of the Brussels treaty in 1948. Accordingly, the Army emphasised the training of a small number of territorial troops and national reserves, which were assigned the following tasks:

    a)   Protecting airfields and other key positions
    b)   Dislodging hostile elements by local offensive action
    c)   Maintaining internal order
    d)   Giving assistance in a possible evacuation.[21]

This could hardly be called an ambitious posture. In January 1948, the announcement was made that only in case of a commitment from the allies to defend Dutch territory, the government would be prepared to consider the substitution of territorial troops by divisions and army corps troops.

However, during this period, with only a small number of Dutch soldiers under arms (about 48,000, air force personnel included, see also Appendix II), the international allies showed little interest in securing the country's defence.[22] Particularly the commitment of WU partner Britain left - in Dutch eyes - much to be desired. In January, despite the plea by British army chief Montgomery, favouring a continental strategy, London pursued a traditional maritime/air strategy based on small and highly mobile forces that could be deployed anywhere in the world whenever they were needed. Even

---

[21] MinDef, Archief Kwartiermeester-Generaal (KMG), 2e etage, Nota Doorman aan Fiévez, 01-19-1948.
[22] ARA, MR, Bijlagen 498, Nota Staf, 02-08-1954.

when it was announced in May - after the signing of the Brussels treaty - that Britain planned to fight a military campaign alongside its allies, it was not until March 1950, that the British defence committee finally agreed to send reinforcements to the continent in the event of a Soviet invasion of Western Europe.[23]

Meanwhile, the Dutch army high command knew they had to draw up a plan of action concerning the defence of the realm. With this in mind, they approached the colleagues in Belgium in an attempt to forge closer links between the two countries. On 10 May 1948, the two governments concluded a secret agreement regulating some technical defence aspects between them. A Belgian-Dutch staff committee was created which was scheduled to meet once every two to three months. During the inauguration, Lieutenant-General Kruls[24] (chief of the Dutch General Staff) stated that the agreement should not be regarded merely as a bilateral responsibility, but as an integral part of wider WU co-operation. Kruls said he hoped that the staff committee would not feel discouraged if its activities failed to proceed at the desired pace as a result of collaboration within the larger multilateral framework. Kruls's modest expectations proved realistic. At the meetings of the staff committee, discussions centred on: demolition of bridges and other objects of strategic importance; communication between the two headquarters; joint armaments production and joint procurement; joint use of training-camps and artillery ranges; participation of Dutch troops in Belgian manoeuvres and vice versa; closer co-operation between Dutch and Belgian military schools; mutual exchange of military trainees, etcetera.[25]

More substantial were the efforts made within the allied framework of the Western Union, where Holland and Belgium formed, together with the United Kingdom, one defence section. The northern part from the North Sea to Remagen in Germany fell under the command

---

[23] J. Baylis, 'Britain, the Brussels pact and the continental commitment', *International Affairs* 60 (1984) p. 623.

[24] H.J. Kruls, Chief of the General Staff, 1945-1951.

[25] MinDef, Archief Belg./Ned. Mil. Samenwerking, Benelux Stafcomm., doos 1, uit: bundel correspondentie 1948-49; en idem, doos 1, uit: bundel correspondentie 1950.

of a Rhine-army with British, Dutch and Belgian forces. The middle and southern part fell under French responsibility. Apart from army co-operation, Belgium and the Netherlands developed joint activities in the air sector. A proper case for Benelux air defence presented itself in the summer of 1948 when WU authorities approached The Hague and Brussels for the immediate preparation and deployment of six air squadrons each (one squadron consisted of twenty-four aeroplanes). This request encountered heavy opposition in the Dutch cabinet; Finance Minister Lieftinck[26], being the most outspoken critic. Lieftinck pointed out that the WU had spoken of recommendations, rather than obligations and that the Netherlands should promise a maximum of five, instead of six air squadrons. He indicated that, since the colonial struggle in Indonesia imposed such a heavy burden on the entire nation, it was impossible to find additional finances for a credible defence of the home country. In this way, Lieftinck received ample support from his cabinet colleagues: apart from extension of the skeleton-drill and some reinforcement of the army air force (as the air force was called before it was recognised as an independent service, in 1953), which could be utilised for evacuation and territorial defence, the national air command failed to obtain the desired means for expansion. Lieftinck declared that improvements could not be expected until the task in Indonesia was brought to a conclusion. A majority within the cabinet agreed with Lieftinck's objections to the supply of six squadrons, notwithstanding Defence Minister Schokking's[27] plea for compliance with the WU recommendations.[28] What prevailed was the traditional policy of concentrating on the country's financial and economic reconstruction along with maintaining the defence budget at a 'modest' level (NLG[29] 850 million for 1949, about 5.1% of GNP).

---

[26] P. Lieftinck, Minister of Finance, 1945-1951.

[27] W.F. Schokking, Minister of Defence (War and Navy), 1948-1950.

[28] ARA, MR, Behandeling begroting oorlog, 08-30-1948; idem, Begroting 1949 (Luchtstrijdkrachten), 09-02-1948.

[29] In this study the central currency unit used is the Dutch guilder (NLG) which was replaced by the single European currency (Euro) in 1999 and ceased to exist as a circulating medium in January 2002. 1 NLG = 0,45 Euro. To give an impression of

The word modest is placed between quotation marks, because the amount was probably higher at this stage than at any time since 1815. However, the national army hardly benefited from these measures, since the greater part of the budget made available was spent on the navy, as well as on the two to three infantry divisions fighting in the Dutch Indies.

In November 1948, Field-Marshal Montgomery - meanwhile installed as chairman of the Commanders of Chief Committee of the Western Union - visited the Netherlands and urged the Dutch military to stop dawdling over the build-up of armed forces within the allied framework. He asked for an army corps consisting of three divisions - one active and two reserve units - as well as a number of air force squadrons, some minesweepers and submarine chasers, to be available by the end of 1951. The Field-Marshal aimed to use these divisions during the early phases of the ground war. In the short run, with 'forward defence' still being unrealistic, the retention of some strategic strongholds by Benelux and French conventional forces constituted the maximum achievable result. The General Staff - under the leadership of Lieutenant-General Kruls - thought it possible to comply with Montgomery's request - and to do even more than that - by doubling the term of military service (twenty-four instead of twelve months, to enable the available conscripts to perform active duty), as well as increasing the defence budget for 1949 (NLG 1,100 million in place of NLG 850 million). Kruls - happy to see that Montgomery explicitly prioritised the army to the navy - fundamentally disagreed with the government's perception of the Soviet threat. In his view, the Soviet Union, fearing an atomic strike on its territory, would start the war suddenly and unexpectedly, with the aim of penetrating in the shortest time possible, the coasts of the North Sea and the Atlantic Ocean. Kruls added cynically that the Russians would not wait 'until such time as the Western European countries would be sufficiently armed' and he urged the government to make available well-trained and prepared

---

the NLG's value over the years: between 1951 and 1999 consumer prices in the Netherlands have risen with a factor 5.8.

troops, because 'only then could Moscow be dissuaded from launching a surprise attack on Western Europe'.[30]

However, within the *Ministerraad*, the prospect of a 'hot' war was deemed very unlikely. Instead, the fear existed of an intensifying 'cold' war, which the Netherlands would lose in the event of a further decline in living standards. The government thought the better of Montgomery's demand for more troops, the more so, as the Field Marshal had indicated the Rhine-Yssel (see Appendix VII) and - even worse - the Rhine-Meuse rivers as being the main strategic defence lines of the Western Union.[31] Such a strategy implied that, in an emergency, a substantial part of the Netherlands - and especially the northern and eastern provinces inhabited by 2.5 million citizens - would remain undefended. Mansholt[32], the minister of Agriculture, suggested incorporating Germany in Montgomery's schemes with the intention of moving the defence of Western Europe as far to the east as possible - along the river Elbe, in Germany. Without the Germans participating, Mansholt added, there was no guarantee of even a minimum protection of the Dutch population. Although the cabinet essentially agreed with Mansholt, in reality defending the Elbe was still not feasible, because of international resistance against German rearmament. Drees felt, that in the given circumstances, the Netherlands should not pitch its demands too high and added, that he supported the Montgomery plan, on two conditions: a serious allied

---

[30] MinDef, Archief Dir. Adm. Dienst Begroting 1950 2, Nota Kruls aan Schokking, 04-02-1949.

[31] Originally, there had been talk of a Rhine-Meuse defence, but in the course of 1948, the Dutch government urged the inclusion of the greater part of the country's territory in the joint WU strategy, by proposing the river Yssel as a new defence line, connected with the Rhine. Montgomery himself was very sceptical about the Yssel strategy, but after a brief visit to the eastern part of the Netherlands, he conceded the Dutch wish for political reasons, despite the unfavourable effect it was supposed to have on the Rhine defence. The Dutch immediately started building dykes, west of the Arnhem-Nijmegen road. Also in view of his WW II experiences Montgomery seems to have had problems with that part of the world all his life! H.J. Kruls, *Generaal in Nederland. Memoires* (Bussum 1975) pp. 181-183. See also Appendix VII.

[32] S.L. Mansholt, Minister of Agriculture, 1945-1957.

commitment to defend the river Yssel - and thus the greater part of the country's territory - and non-interference with domestic economic reconstruction and the task in Indonesia. At that time, The Hague worried about the aggravation of the British embargo on military goods to Southeast Asia. In order to cope systematically with the evolving defence problems, the government decided to re-activate the *Raad Militaire Aangelegenheden van het Koninkrijk* (Raad MAK). This sub-cabinet council represented the Prime Minister, the ministers of Defence, Finance, Foreign Affairs and Overseas Possessions, and the Chiefs of Staff. The *Raad MAK* set itself the task of drafting a comprehensive defence plan within the limits of what was financially possible.[33]

In March 1949, Defence Minister Schokking and the General Staff drafted a plan (called *Legerplan 1950*) including a projection for military strength, by 1956. Encouraged by Montgomery's recommendations, the estimates were as follows:

---

[33] ARA, MR, Bezoek Veldmaarschalk Montgomery, 01-18-1949; idem, Het West-Europese Pact, 01-21-1949.

Army
An army corps of four divisions
Territorial troops
Anti-aircraft artillery
Six infantry battalions per year, for substituting the troops in Indonesia.

Air Force
(planning for 1955)
11 squadrons of day-fighters   ⎫ Total   number   of
4 squadrons of night-fighters   ⎬ planes: 320
6 squadrons of tactical fighters   ⎭
9 bases (peace strength)
11 bases (war strength).

Navy
1 aircraft carrier (the *Karel Doorman*, acquired in 1948)
2 cruisers
12 sub-chasers
6 frigates
4 submarines
6 squadrons of aeroplanes
48 mine-sweepers
1 operational sea-drome and
1 operational auxiliary sea-drome.

A predominantly anti-submarine and anti-mine warfare fleet would replace the more traditional battle fleet[34]. It was estimated that after its build-up phase, the Navy contribution would account for about three percent of total North-Atlantic sea forces.
Total peace-strength estimates (for 1953) amounted to 103,000 men (of whom 38,500 regular soldiers).

Source: ARA, MR, Bijlagen 447, Defensieplan 1950, 04-14-1949.

---

[34] J.W. Honig, *Defense Policy in the North Atlantic Alliance: the case of the Netherlands* (Westport 1993), p. 13.

These rather lofty ambitions put forward by the military were criticised in the cabinet, where the target figure of four army divisions was reduced to three, in line with Montgomery's advice of November 1948. The large number of troops on standby was questioned. The *Ministerraad* further hoped to implement the *Legerplan 1950* without increasing the budget or extending the term of military service. Kruls and Schokking both claimed that this was completely unrealistic. Instead, they proposed reserving an extra NLG 300 million for defence, to be financed through a special government loan, and an increase in the period of service from 12 to 18 months (a compromise, compared to the 24-month term originally suggested by Kruls). The Chief of the General Staff reasoned that, since twelve months were needed for just basic training, an extra six months constituted the absolute minimum necessary for keeping one division on standby.[35]

These proposals were however, disregarded in cabinet, where the conviction prevailed that the money needed for the defence programme could be found within the existing budgets. Moreover, the development of the air force was made conditional on receiving lend-lease aid from the United States. The government urged a more efficient use of public money and - in April 1949 - appointed two State Secretaries (Fockema Andreae and Moorman[36]) to assist minister Schokking to conceive measures on economising on defence. Kruls was greatly disappointed with the government's unwillingness to act and, in April, he threatened to resign from the General Staff. Schokking strongly advised him not to do so and argued in cabinet that Kruls was irreplaceable because his opinion was so highly respected in international military quarters.[37] The Defence Minister's plea had the desired effect and even more than

---

[35] Megens, *America aid to NATO allies*, p. 69.

[36] Fockema Andreae was made responsible for the Army and Moorman for the Navy. For a detailed analysis of the appointment procedure, and the competences of both officials, see: Brouwer, 'De stem van de Marine in de Ministerraad', pp. 34-35.

[37] ARA, MR, Nota Generaal Kruls, 04-14-1949; idem, Maatregelen ter effectuering van Nederlandse deelneming aan het West-Europese militaire pact, 04-11-1949.

that: a few weeks later - on 1 May 1949 - the government promoted Kruls to the rank of General.

1.2 The start of NATO, and the pleas for German rearmament

Why did the Dutch join the Western Union and later NATO if they were not prepared to enhance their military efforts?

Initially, the government wanted to utilise the Western Union or Brussels Treaty Organisation (BTO) as a means to have a voice in the German question. Moreover, it was felt that the signing of the treaty would benefit the realisation of the Marshall plan, which had not yet been accepted by Congress in the United States.[38] However, the main reason for Dutch participation in BTO was an ardent desire on their part, that the United States would soon become actively involved in Western European defence. Washington had made a direct commitment to Europe dependent on the latter's readiness to take the initiative and, in the Dutch view, BTO's creation represented such an initiative. Apart from the expected military-strategic benefits of US involvement, the government calculated, Washington would be prepared to bear the greater part of the financial burden. This strong 'atlanticist' feeling was only temporarily called in question in the summer of 1948, when Lovink, the general secretary of the Ministry of Foreign Affairs, told the American ambassador in the Netherlands that it would not be in the interest of the Western Union, with its small military potential, to join the proposed Atlantic community. Lovink reasoned that the Soviets would interpret such a step as an offensive act directed against them. Hinting at the actions of the Soviet blockade of West Berlin, Lovink said that Moscow had not reacted against the creation of the Brussels pact and that it was therefore preferable to strengthen the Western Union first, before starting with a broader Atlantic union. Moreover, it would, in his view, be necessary to know more about US intentions before

---

[38] A.E. Kersten, 'In de ban van de bondgenoot', in: D. Barnouw, M. de Keizer en G. van der Stroom (ed.), *1940-1945: Onverwerkt verleden?* (Utrecht 1985) p. 111.

reaching any conclusions on extending the Brussels treaty.[39] This was in fact not the only jarring note during the Washington security talks on the creation of the Atlantic pact. Early in 1949, the Dutch government was highly angered by US policy regarding Indonesia, where Washington pressed for an immediate Dutch withdrawal and insisted that Indonesian republicans be granted their independence at short notice. The Americans, fearing that armament deliveries to the Netherlands would be used to suppress Indonesian nationalist forces, threatened to cut off not only military assistance to the Netherlands, but also that part of Marshall aid which was meant for Indonesia. The Dutch - and their partners in the Western Union - considered this behaviour as a form of 'unwarranted interference in their internal affairs, reflecting inappropriate interpretation of UN resolutions on the Indonesian problem'.[40] Nevertheless, at the end of the day, the North Atlantic pact and, particularly American membership hereof, was deemed so important that government and parliament pushed aside their indignation concerning Indonesia and welcomed the signing of the Washington treaty. Bilateral tensions were eventually pacified by a promise from US Secretary of State, Acheson, that the Netherlands would not be excluded from military assistance.

According to the government, American participation in NATO was more important as it was expected that German rearmament would become feasible in the near future. The assumption in Western Europe - and the suspicion in France - was that the United States would use NATO as an opportunity and an instrument to include West Germany in the defence of Western Europe.[41] The Hague more and more openly welcomed German rearmament and, hence, this was an extra reason to support US membership of NATO.

This did not imply that Dutch attitudes towards German rearmament were free from ambiguity. In January 1949, a few

---

[39] FRUS 1948, Vol. 3, Telegram Baruch to Acheson, 07-21-1948, p. 195

[40] L.S. Kaplan, *The United States and NATO. The Formative Years* (Kentucky 1984) p. 106.

[41] T.P. Ireland, *Creating the Entangling Alliance. The Origins of the North Atlantic Treaty Organization* (Westport 1981) p. 224.

months before the installation of the Federal Republic, Drees remarked that the first priority of the German government was the reunification of their country. If Moscow offered assistance to realise this aim, Drees continued, the Germans would not hesitate to accept Russian assistance.[42] In May, Hirschfeld[43] (Government Commissioner for the distribution of Marshall aid) pleaded in an advisory report to the government for an active West German contribution to West European defence, although he realised that such a 'contribution was possible only in the longer term'. In his view, Western defence authorities should first try to catch up arrears, because the Soviet Union would consider the military involvement of Germany 'a warlike deed'. He remarked that, four years after the war, a German defence contribution still had an unfavourable psychological connotation in the minds of Western European citizens. It was possible to soothe such negative feelings by 'prioritising the security guarantees of the Brussels pact and North Atlantic pact, and the organisation of the European recovery programme'.[44] The wording used in an official government memorandum in June was even more guarded, mainly as a result of the fierce criticism Hirschfeld had received on the first draft of his report from the more conservative sections of the Foreign Ministry. With regard to Germany, the memorandum mentioned three principles to be adhered to:

(a) The military occupation of Germany should be continued until Western Europe was considered strong enough politically and militarily.

---

[42] ARA, MR, Bezoek Veldmaarschalk Montgomery, 01-18-1949.

[43] H.M. Hirschfeld, Government Commissioner, 1945-1952.

[44] ARA, MR, Bijlagen 449, Nota Hirschfeld betreffende de Geallieerde en de Nederlandse Politiek ten aanzien van Duitsland, 05-12-1949. The report was named after Hirschfeld, but written by his assistant Max Kohnstamm, who proved a fervent advocate of strengthening post-war Germany - especially economically - and integrating this country into a solid Western European framework. For a more detailed description of the Hirschfeld-Kohnstamm report and the reactions to it, see: J.W.F. Wielenga, *West-Duitsland: partner uit noodzaak. Nederland en de Bondsrepubliek 1949-1955* (Utrecht 1989) pp. 84-88.

(b) Germany should not be allowed to have armed forces.
(c) Production of war materials in Germany should remain prohibited.

It was added that 'at the same time Western Germany ought to be integrated as closely as possible in Western European organisations', politically and, more especially, economically.[45] As far as defence matters were concerned, the official position, as reflected in the memo, was more cautious than individual opinions ventilated by government members and high civil servants.

During its first year of existence, NATO failed to meet the high expectations of those Europeans who had hoped for a fundamental change in US military strategy. The Americans continued to promote their global interests and to develop their own national strategic plans without serious consideration of allied concerns. This was made possible by a deliberately vaguely formulated provision in the North Atlantic treaty: unlike the WU guarantee of automatic assistance with all the available means in the event of aggression against one of the members, NATO's only explicitly expressed requirement was that signatories should consult together, if the territorial integrity or political independence of any member was endangered. In other words, there was no obligation to send troops to the territory of the member-state under attack. Hence, even with NATO in place, Europeans feared that American strategy for Europe was still a so-called 'peripheral strategy', meaning that, in the event of an attack on Western Europe, the US army - having only two divisions stationed on the continent - would beat a hasty retreat in the direction of the Pyrenees, Egypt and the United Kingdom. This was a warranted fear: according to the American strategic plans of 1948 and 1949 (called *Halfmoon* and *Offtackle*) the heart of Western Europe - including the entire territory of the Netherlands - was still indefensible and, defence operations on the Rhine or in the Alps would be possible at the earliest in 1957. In the short run, in case of an attack on Europe, a greater or lesser loss of territory had to be taken into account. Apart

---

[45] Ibid., Memorandum of the Netherlands government, 06-16-1949.

from Canada and Great Britain, the partners were not officially informed about strategic conceptions held by the US. Greiner wrote that 'this attitude was quite understandable, as disclosure would have severely shocked and demoralised the European allies'.[46]

Although not officially informed, the Dutch government was aware of American intentions, as witness a lively discussion in the *Raad MAK* following statements by US Secretary of Defence Johnson and Senator Tydings that, in the event of war, occupation of a large part of Western Europe was unavoidable and that a serious defence of Western Europe was impossible for the next 15 years.[47] The United States urged Europe to do more for its own defence rather than to keep waiting for American support. Johnson even suggested that NATO membership would enable the US government to reduce defence expenditure.

Civil authorities in The Hague refused to worry publicly about American aloofness. In the meantime, they could and did, proceed with their country's socio-economic and monetary recovery. Initially, the political and psychological importance of an alliance with the United States prevailed. Drees felt that for the time being the formal link with the US was sufficient to prevent the Soviets from attacking Western Europe.[48] Concerning the value of the North Atlantic treaty, the American General Bedell-Smith, indicated his surprise at the importance the Europeans attached to 'what the Americans would have regarded as simply a scrap of paper.'[49]

After the creation of NATO the deterrent provided by the atomic weapon became the key to US guarantees of European security. With it, the United States was in a position to offset Russia's military manpower. The bomb was in fact all that protected the people of Europe from another war. And although the possibility of using

---

[46] C. Greiner, 'The defence of Western Europe and the rearmament of West Germany, 1947-1950'. In: Riste (ed.), *Western Security*, pp. 151-152.

[47] Ministerie van Algemene Zaken (MinAZ), archief Raad Militaire Aangelegenheden van het Koninkrijk (Raad MAK), Notulen 10-24-1949 and 01-09-1950.

[48] Ibid., Notulen 10-24-1949.

[49] M. Howard, 'Introduction'. In: Riste (ed.), *Western Security*, p. 16.

nuclear weapons in a European war was seriously questioned in military quarters in the US - and elsewhere - nevertheless the American atomic umbrella provided at least some relief for the ill-defended countries of Western Europe. On both sides of the Atlantic, but especially in Europe, there was an atmosphere of wishful thinking that nothing serious would happen.[50]

The peaceful climate could not last long however, and in August 1949, a new situation emerged when the Soviet Union managed the first successful test with an atomic device. The explosion occurred much sooner than many had expected and sent shock waves throughout the United States and Europe. Shortly afterwards the communists under Mao, completed their conquest of China. Suddenly the balance shifted in a dramatic way. A final American victory in a third world war could no longer be taken for granted. With the US nuclear monopoly broken, it was obvious that Western Europe had to be defended on the ground. But at that moment conventional forces were almost absent and their build-up would require ample time.

In the NATO Council, Foreign Minister Stikker wondered whether all NATO territory would be defended should the policy of nuclear deterrence fail. This was a rhetorical question but also a sign that even Stikker, with his declared trust in Atlantic unity, now came to doubt American willingness to support Western Europe.[51] Dutch army officials entertained similar doubts. General Kruls criticised the government for making the build-up of the national army dependent on agreements made within international organisations. Until the Netherlands could rely on foreign aid, Kruls felt that defence of the homeland was purely a national concern - in fact, in his view, the only concern. He therefore rejected the Rhine-Yssel strategy, because of its inadequacy to protect a substantial part of the Dutch territory and population. He also rejected the evacuation plans of

---

[50] Trachtenberg, *A Constructed Peace*, p. 91.
[51] Militärgeschichtliches Forschungsamt (MGFA) (ed.), Anfänge westdeutscher Sicherheitspolitik 1945-1956; Band 1: *Von der Kapitulation bis zum Pleven-Plan* (München 1982) p. 242.

Drees and Lieftinck considering it absurd to evacuate a small group of prominent people and expose the remaining 10 million to the 'enemy's arbitrariness'. According to Kruls the Netherlands should raise armed forces to such a degree as to have a minimum chance of defending its own territory. He asked for a serious and immediate implementation of *Legerplan 1950* which called for, to begin with, the creation of four divisions.

Kruls' suggestions were not realistic, because in the given circumstances, a Soviet attack on Netherlands territory was thought to be unstoppable. But the population needed a psychological boost and the General felt he had to take some form of action. Moreover, he expected that foreign pressure on the Netherlands was starting to increase and, it would therefore be useless to postpone action. As in November 1948, Kruls asked for an amount of NLG 1,100 million, to execute his plans.[52] Hereby he anticipated that the colonial struggle in the Dutch Indies would soon come to an end, which enhanced the possibilities of a strong defence of the home country.

Once again, Drees and Lieftinck refused to go along with the Chief of the General Staff, pointing to the danger of financial and monetary instability in case of a substantial budget increase. Lieftinck stressed the point that the Netherlands had to deal with fixed high expenses such as interest payments, the discharge of debts and war-damage indemnification. And, as if these were not enough to contend with, Lieftinck remarked, in the near future more children would have to receive primary education, a direct consequence of the post-war 'baby-boom'. Moreover, he expected that the end of the commitment in Indonesia - eventually granted independence in December 1949 - would lead to considerable problems in 1950, because of the repatriation and demobilisation of about 95,000 soldiers. This figure concerned not only the two to three conscript divisions which in 1946/47 had been sent to Southeast Asia, but also part of the Royal Dutch Indies Army (RDIA) which had collaborated with the conscript divisions in the struggle against the Indonesian republicans.

---

[52] MinDef, Archief Verenigde Chefs van Staven (VCS), Concept Memorandum betreffende doelstelling en opbouw van de Nederlandse krijgsmacht, 01-05-1950.

In 1949, the RDIA - incorporated into the Dutch army since the early nineteenth century - consisted of 15,500 Europeans (mostly regular personnel) and 50,500 non-Europeans (Amboinese, Menadonese, Javanese etc.). The expectation was, that after the transfer of sovereignty to the Indonesian republic and the subsequent dissolution of the RDIA (in Dutch: *KNIL*), the soldiers would be either drafted into the new Indonesian army, or dismissed, with or without a claim to retirement pay, or (as far as most of the regular soldiers were concerned), drafted into the Dutch army with the aim of strengthening the army's cadre. It was feared that the stability of the national labour market would be severely affected after the homecoming of such a substantial number of conscripts and professionals. Some 15% of the repatriates were considered for employment in special government workshops.[53]

To cope with all these problems, Lieftinck urged reducing the defence budget to NLG 800 million, by a retrenchment on demobilisation benefits, on public funds which were still not committed (particularly in the textiles sector) and, on the maintenance and enlargement of military buildings.[54] This was all the more necessary because material support from abroad did not live up to expectations. Lieftinck complained that the delivery of military equipment from the United States - following the signing of the Mutual Defence Assistance Act in October 1949 - left much to be desired. He thought it also unfair that in international quarters the Netherlands was expected to build up both its army and navy and air force, whereas Belgium did not have a navy and Britain abstained from building up an army. The Finance Minister referred to a comparative survey, which indicated that the Netherlands spent 28% of its budget on defence, the UK 20%, France 17% and Belgium only

---

[53] ARA, MR, Bijlagen 456, Rapport Joekes betreffende scholing van gerepatrieerde militairen, 01-03-1950; ARA, MR, Het defensiebeleid, 05-02-1950.
[54] MinDef, archief Dir. Adm. Dienst Begroting 1950 2, Nota naar aanleiding van Ministerraadsvergadering van 03-20-1950.

12%.[55] Drees supported him, contending that Holland should restrict its activities to what was absolutely necessary for obtaining American support and nothing more. He still refused to believe that the Russian military threat was pending; instead, he felt that the Soviets would try to dislocate - by political means - the social and economic stability in France and Italy. On the other hand, *if* the Russians decided to take the offensive, Drees felt that credible resistance was illusory, because of technologically advanced and highly destructive 'V-weapons' targeted on Dutch cities by the Soviet military. Drees considered France - with three divisions in West Germany - the pivot of Western European defence, but considering its domestic problems, he did not nourish great hopes of this country.

Stikker agreed that European defence was entirely inadequate, but, unlike Drees and Lieftinck, he preferred 'not to wait with folded arms' but to do something about it. Early in 1950, he demanded attention to be directed towards the risks for the West by Soviet infiltration in Yugoslavia and in March, he noticed that the allied negotiations with the Soviet Union had come to a halt and that a war between East and West could no longer be ruled out. He was not certain of the scene of the battle: the Far East, Middle East or Western Europe. Stikker feared that continued passivity would keep Western defence ineffective for the next fifteen years and he therefore urged rapid improvements after the termination of the military task in Indonesia in December 1949. He even threatened to disclaim all responsibility if the suggested improvements did not occur in time.

Defence Minister Schokking shared Stikker's apprehensions and claimed that the army was treated as the Cinderella in Lieftinck's budget-proposal of NLG 800 million. He calculated that the build-up of the navy and air force required a fixed expenditure of NLG 325 million respectively 160 million per year, leaving the Army only 315 million. Schokking regarded this amount as entirely inadequate - it

---

[55] J.W.L. Brouwer, 'Om de beheersing van de defensie-uitgaven, 1948-1951', *Politieke Opstellen* CPG/KUN 10 (1990), p. 90.

would yield only two highly simplified infantry divisions and not include territorial troops and anti-aircraft artillery. He also warned that American military assistance - which had finally started off - would be halted if the Dutch performance failed to come up to expectations. Both in cabinet and in the *Raad MAK*, the defence minister urged a substantial increase in financial means, also needed for a 'decent demobilisation' of the Indonesia repatriates.[56] Like Kruls, he pointed to the psychological importance of the military effort: neglect of the army was not acceptable to that part of the population 'which was not over-pleased with the idea of holding a post-mortem in Siberia about the utility of evacuation forces'.[57] Schokking asked for an increase in the defence budget to NLG 1,085 million, with 600 million earmarked for the army. The latter's build-up required unique additional expenses which should, he argued, be chargeable to the capital service - by means of creating a special fund - instead of to the budget. Minister of Economic Affairs, Van den Brink[58], objected that the creation of jobs for the growing labour force in the Netherlands absorbed nearly everything that was done in the field of capital formation and that extra funds for defence should be ruled out. He added that the government had recently begun to deal with the 'inescapable consolidation of the public debt' and that, in the given circumstances, it was inconceivable to reserve extra money for the defence sector.[59]

Notwithstanding Stikker's and Schokking's opposition, the policy of Lieftinck, Drees and Van den Brink carried the day. The latter carefully ensured that the budget for 1950 did not surpass the amount of NLG 850 million (5.1% of GNP) and that the size of the army remained relatively stable: 52,000 men (as compared with 50,000 men in 1949).

---

[56] Brouwer, 'Om de beheersing van de defensieuitgaven', p. 90.
[57] MinAZ, Raad MAK, Notulen 10-24-1949, 01-09-1950 en 03-09-1954; MinDef, archief Kab.Min/Stasvo geclass. (inv. 66) map Herz. Begroting 1950, Nota Schokking aan Drees, 04-22-1950.
[58] J.R.M. van den Brink, Minister of Economic Affairs, 1948-1952.
[59] MinAZ, Raad MAK, Notulen 01-09-1950.

Early in 1950 this number even dropped to 30,000. In order to facilitate the transition from British to American equipment - until then the army had focused almost exclusively on the British system, both in terms of equipment and training - national army authorities not only sent parts of the second draft of 1949 on long furlough but they also refrained from calling up the first draft of 1950 (except for the conscripts considered for skeleton service). In their view, a fresh start should be made with the second draft of 1950, to ensure optimum efficiency. Despite the reduction of available manpower, the government demanded urgency in the delivery of military ordnance from the US, in order to equip at least a part of the conscripts who returned from Indonesia. However, in the given circumstances, additional action should be avoided; Lieftinck proposed to inform the allies that the Netherlands was unable to reach the appointed targets.[60] With the greater part of cabinet against him, Schokking considered his resignation in May 1950, but eventually decided to stay in office, arguing that the Netherlands was 'one of the few stable elements in the Western Union'.[61]

There was one logical outcome to the Soviet nuclear test - the call for German rearmament became louder particularly in military headquarters on both sides of the Atlantic. Civil authorities continued to be sceptical. The US State Department played down the need of an urgent German remilitarization and, in Europe, priority was still directed at social and economic reconstruction. Some also said that rearmament might have a detrimental effect on the development of West Germany as a sound democratic state - following its creation in September 1949.

Likewise, the Dutch government still harboured doubts. In January 1950, Drees and Stikker raised objections to remobilization of the German army, but immediately added that in the near future, they might have to reconsider their position.[62] Their caution was prompted by speeches by former French prime minister Leon Blum

---

[60] Ibid., Notulen 03-09-1950.
[61] ARA, MR, Het defensiebeleid, 05-02-1950.
[62] MinAZ, Raad MAK, Notulen 01-09-1950.

and Federal Chancellor, Konrad Adenauer, who had both pleaded - in December 1949 - for German participation in a federal European army, under the authority of supranational institutions. Unlike several members of the Dutch parliament, who ardently welcomed this idea, the government rejected federalist solutions for political-military problems. The Hague obviously waited for a change of opinion in the State Department in favour of German rearmament within NATO. Stikker suggested that, in the meantime, prior to NATO membership, Germany could make itself useful by furnishing defence materials to its European allies.[63] This idea was elaborated in a government memorandum, which suggested lowering Germany's occupation costs in exchange for an indirect German contribution to European defence, in the form of delivery of materials and semi-finished goods.[64]

Early in 1950, the United States, frightened by the loss of their nuclear monopoly, developed a new strategic plan designated NSC-68, which, among other things, emphasised the strategic importance of Western Europe for both the US and allied security. The plan was so framed that the United States and Europe would jointly start with the build-up of their conventional forces, supplemented and assisted by nuclear and thermonuclear weaponry of American produce. NSC-68 proposed increases in military spending which President Truman had successfully fought to curtail since World War II. In mid-1950 the Americans looked for an opportunity to bring their new strategy into practice. This opportunity was presented in June 1950 with the outbreak of the Korean War, seen in the United States as being instigated by the Soviet Union. Although historians have raised questions of Stalin's approval of Kim-Il-Sung's attack, the presence of Russian tanks with the North Korean forces was apparently enough evidence for the American leaders to define their position. And then, of course, there was the obvious parallel between the two

---

[63] FRUS 1950 Vol. 3, Telegram US delegation at the Tripartite Foreign Ministers meeting to the acting Secretary of State, 05-13-1950, p. 1056.
[64] ARA, MR, Bijlagen 458, The policy to be adopted with reference to Germany in the future and the problem of German rearmament, 05-13-1950.

divided countries, Korea and Germany. Would East German forces be used as the spearhead of an attack on West Germany?[65]

To cope with these problems, the United States proceeded to increasing defence expenditure and, also, considered the stationing of an extra four divisions in West Germany. Moreover, in August, the State Department announced that German rearmament had become indispensable for a credible defence as far to the east - of Central Europe - as possible. Consequently, the allies in Western Europe were pressurised to renounce passivity and start immediate action. The Dutch response to the outbreak of the Korean War was rather calm, however. Stikker refused to believe that the Soviet Union planned to launch an attack on Europe - instead, he presumed, Moscow would try to infiltrate in the Middle East, in countries like Iran and Turkey. Holding these views did not reduce Stikker's concern about the state of military readiness in Western Europe. He repeated that something had to be done to break the deadlock.[66]

Notwithstanding Stikker's concerns and the pressure exercised by the US, the government once again refused to boost defence efforts. Unlike the British, who immediately took action, the Dutch government adopted a wait-and-see attitude. In July, Stikker confided to the US authorities that he was a 'voice in the wilderness' with his pleas in cabinet for stepping up the defence programme. He complained about 'violent opposition to his proposals' by Finance Minister Lieftinck and the other members of the 'apathetic cabinet' and about Schokking's 'feeble support'. Indeed, at the cabinet meeting of 24 July, the battle-weary Schokking made no reference to the need of extra military efforts - instead, he reiterated, that the Dutch population saw no reason to defend the country without German involvement. American authorities in the Netherlands had another impression, namely, that the greater part of the Dutch population showed more genuine concern for the necessity of strengthening the armed forces than 'such officials as the Minister of

---

[65] T.A. Schwartz, *America's Germany. John J. McCloy and the Federal Republic of Germany* (Cambridge 1991) p. 125; Trachtenberg, *A Constructed Peace*, p. 99.
[66] ARA, MR, De West-Europese defensie, 07-17-1950.

Finance'. In London, Stikker suggested a conversation between Drees and the British Foreign Minister, Bevin, because he believed that 'the only person who could fully convince Drees of the necessity of prompt action was another socialist'.[67]

International pressure eventually produced results. Early in August 1950, the government decided to increase military expenditure (NLG 850 million) by 10 to 15%, after a US promise of additional deliveries of Marshall aid to the Netherlands. This increase led to a total budget amount of almost NLG 1 billion. Moreover, those conscripted to the second draft of 1949, who had prematurely been sent on long furlough, were now recalled into the army for a period of three months. Another decision concerned the creation of two new divisions, made up of conscripts who had served in Indonesia; the three 'authorised' divisions were now planned to be ready by the end of 1951. And, last but not least, in sending a volunteer unit, the Netherlands became one of fifteen countries that joined the US in the UN forces to help South Korea repel the attack from the North.

In August, the government started to speak publicly in favour of German participation in the defence of Western Europe. It is interesting to note that the Dutch government, like the American, used the Korean War as a favourable opportunity to formalise a policy developed at an earlier stage. A rapid build-up of German armed forces was welcomed for military-strategic reasons (defence on the Elbe instead of the Rhine), as well as financial reasons (the availability of German troops reduced the need of having an expensive standing army in the Netherlands). However, international resistance to German rearmament was still strong. Early in August, Schokking said he was disappointed that the ninth conference of foreign ministers of the WU-countries in The Hague had 'not taken a positive decision' on the involvement of Germany in Western defence. As long as German remilitarization was not feasible the Dutch advocated a substantial increase in allied forces in Germany. In an *aide-mémoire* to the US government it was said that:

---

[67] FRUS 1950 Vol. 3, Circ. Tel. Acheson to Cert. Dipl. Offices, 07-28-1950, p. 151.

According to available information the allied armed forces stationed in Germany now total approximately 8 divisions. As the strength of the armed forces of Belgium, France and the Netherlands increases, the inadequacy of the military forces now maintained by the three major Atlantic nations in Germany will become more apparent. The present military forces in Germany should therefore be increased as soon as possible by stationing along the borderline a sufficient force drawn from contributions by all Atlantic nations to meet the first onslaught of an aggressor. (ARA, MR, Bijlagen 459, Nota Stikker, 08-02-1950)

At the *Raad MAK*-meeting of 31 August, the discussion centred on the strategic dimension of West European defence. Should Western Europe be defended on the Rhine or the Rhine-Yssel, or was it possible to move the defence line eastward into Germany? In Drees's view, the Yssel-line was indefensible: the river itself was not a credible hindrance and the hinterland lacked the required depth. To remedy the situation, military operations should be conducted as far to the east as possible, preferably on the river Elbe. According to Kruls, this could be realised by an increase in combat-ready troops and by immediate involvement of German units. It seemed that finally the time was ripe for such an involvement. In Stikker's view, the ongoing resistance to German rearmament by France, had to be overcome by means of international consultation and pressure. Drees added that German remilitarization had certain risks, but there was no other choice in the post-Korea constellation.

An important question raised at the *Raad MAK* meeting was whether or not the United States and the United Kingdom would come to the rescue of Western Europe if the Soviet army mounted an attack. It was especially important to know to what extent Washington was prepared to abandon the peripheral strategy towards Europe. His Royal Highness Prince Bernhard (Queen Juliana's husband), who, in his function as Army Inspector General, regularly attended the *Raad* meetings, knew that General Bradley (US army Chief of Staff) considered the preservation of Western Europe to be of crucial importance to US security.[68] Stikker added, that in the opinion of the American military, the industrial potential of Western Europe was the decisive factor for supporting their NATO partners on the continent. On the other hand, political circles in both the United States and Britain looked askance at France, the core country of allied defence. Stikker said that the British government was hesitant about sending troops to France, for fear of communist infiltration. Kruls, who was well informed about the French position, argued that Paris - in its turn - had serious doubts about British intentions. The French were obsessed with suspicions originating from World War II (and before), believing that if an attack *did* occur, British - and American - strategists would be content to conduct the defence of Europe beyond the continent or behind the Pyrenees. To remedy these suspicions, Paris urged the UK to increase the number of British divisions on the continent from two to five. At the time, France had three of her divisions stationed in Germany, and two on home territory.

Concerning the role of the atomic bomb in European defence, Kruls said that during a recently held WU manoeuvre, Montgomery had simulated the use of the bomb as a tactical weapon. It was difficult to judge its value however, because the Americans were highly reticent to disseminate information about atomic armaments.

In NATO's Medium Term Defence Plan (MTDP) of April 1950, the Netherlands was requested to provide six divisions to be ready by July 1954.[69] The subsequent debate in the *Raad MAK* went along established lines. Drees and Lieftinck complained that the development of six divisions was too much to ask from a small country, the more so as big powers like the US and Britain had each

---

[68] A few months before, on 5 April 1949, Bradley had said: 'It must be perfectly apparent to the people of the United States that we cannot count on friends in Western Europe if our strategy in the event of war dictates that we shall first abandon them to the enemy with a promise of later liberation'. Quoted from: Trachtenberg, *A Constructed Peace*, pp. 101-102.

[69] With the initiation of MTDP the US abandoned short-term planning in favour of a four-year programme, to be completed in phases by 1954. The first phase lasted till late 1951.

only two divisions stationed in Western Europe. At the time Holland had about one and one-third of a division at its disposal. Kruls replied that the gravity of the international situation required a maximum effort and he warned that the Rhine would continue to be the main defence line as long as MTDP - projecting a total of 90 standing and reserve divisions - was not fully realised.[70] Drees noticed that the plan did not make allowances for German and Italian participation; in terms of manpower and organisation, Drees thought it possible to execute MTDP, but the financial and economic consequences of the plan were 'incalculable'. In his view, MTDP represented a rather theoretical exercise and, as long as the necessary budgetary foundations were lacking, no firm commitments could be accepted.[71]

The general opinion at the meeting was that the build-up of Western European forces was necessary to take away every temptation on the part of the Soviet Union to launch an attack on Western Europe. Apparently, views had changed as compared with previous discussions, when such a build-up was still seen as provocative regarding the Soviet Union. It was felt that without a convincing military commitment, West Germany could easily drift off in an easterly direction. In conclusion, the *Raad MAK* decided to strive for a defence in depth, conducted as far to the east as possible. To attain this, a serious start would be made with the build-up of the required land and air forces, on the premise that the financial and economic consequences would be acceptable and that the greater part of the required equipment would be obtained from abroad, viz. the United States. For the moment, the *Raad* refused to consider an increase in the term of military service, opposed to the decision taken at that moment by the British army.[72]

---

[70] The MTDP provided for three strongholds to withstand a foreign attack: the Rhine-Yssel in Western Europe, the Kiel canal and Northern Norway in the North and the Italian-Austrian Alps in the South. Megens, *American aid to NATO allies in the 1950s*, p. 89.

[71] *Ibid.*, p. 91.

[72] MinAZ, Raad MAK, Notulen 08-31-1950.

Military plans appeared in many different forms. On 5 September the WU defence committee met in London to discuss a plan, outlining that Belgium and the Netherlands should each provide seven divisions, (two of these armoured) to be ready by 1954. In this plan financial and economic considerations were not included, the physical potential being the only thing that mattered. The government's response was, predictably, negative and Minister Schokking was explicitly instructed not to make any far-reaching commitments in international negotiations. General Kruls, also present in London, was not impressed by these instructions and tried to convince his Belgian colleagues, who had no naval obligations, of the need to supply eight divisions, so that the Dutch share could be lowered to six. However, Belgian army authorities replied that this exceeded what they could physically cope with. As far as aircraft was concerned, both the Netherlands and Belgium were asked to provide 450 planes, which was in line with the targets formulated in 1948.[73]

In the late summer of 1950, Western Europe experienced a time of great suspense. Stikker pointed out to Katz, the US special representative in Europe, that both BTO and the Council of Europe had failed in their job and that NATO was still in a 'talk stage', with hardly any accomplishments. He lamented that the US waited on the Europeans to act and that the Europeans waited for the US while 'leaving matters at dead centre'. He repeated the Dutch government's conviction that Germany should be brought effectively into Western Europe defence programmes, and expressed concern at French slowness to face this need. He was relieved in noting that the British government was gradually moving toward recognition of it. Finally, Stikker said that a unified command of the western forces was essential and, that 'such a command could only be American'.[74]

---

[73] MinDef, archief VCS (zeer geheim), Verslag van de WU Defence Committee vergadering van 5 september j.l., 09-09-1950; idem, Stukken WUCOS dd. 29 september 1950, 09-28-1950.
[74] FRUS 1950 Vol. 3, Tel. US Special Representative in Europe (Katz) to Acheson, 09-06-1950, p. 269.

Mid-September 1950 brought the long-awaited breakthrough in the deadlock when Secretary of State Acheson pleaded openly for German participation in an integrated Atlantic force. The Dutch government's immediate response was positive and, from then onwards, The Hague ardently supported Germany's admission into NATO. It was felt that German rearmament could be monitored more easily within NATO - with American and British participation - than within a continental European construction under the leadership of France.

1.3 Unwillingness to increase defence efforts

At the outbreak of the Korean War, the defence of the Netherlands was still in a deplorable condition, despite the end of Dutch involvement in Indonesia by late 1949. The army was completely disorganised, the air force had hardly begun to function as an independent service and only the navy - with 23,000 marines in its ranks - was reasonably equipped. Military commanders, having about 45,000 men at their disposal - including the conscripts of 1949-II who had been recalled into service - were unable to draft this manpower into two proper divisions. The Indonesia veterans had returned to their home country demoralised and ill-equipped; most of them unwilling to be re-educated in the techniques of modern warfare, an attitude encouraged still further by the lack of training facilities and equipment. General Kruls therefore refused to develop a proper (re)mobilisation plan for these soldiers.

In 1950, the General Staff decided to standardise and train the Army along American lines of combat, using modern American weapons. After the signing of the Mutual Defence Assistance Agreement[75] between the governments of the United States and the Netherlands in January 1950, this decision seemed to take extra

---

[75] With the initiation of the Mutual Defence Assistance Programme (MDAP), US aid to Europe became more militarily than economically motivated. In the period 1945-51 military aid averaged just 9.4% of total US aid; from 1951-1957 this figure increased to 56.3%.

shape. In Washington's view, countries receiving military assistance should integrate their armaments industries and standardise their weapons - as far as practicable - to US accepted types.[76] However, the supply of American equipment, which already left to be desired, encountered even more problems after the outbreak of the Korean War. The army was forced to accept obsolete weapons from Canada and the UK, which further delayed the implementation of modernisation plans.

Nevertheless, had the will be strong enough in government circles to re-organise the army adequately, it seems that most of these problems could have been solved. But in 1950 this will was lacking, firstly, because of the priority given to financial-economic recovery and secondly, because of the country's strategic position which was still highly delicate. According to an Atlantic strategy paper drafted in mid-1950, defence on the Rhine-Yssel was, in the short term, the maximum NATO could offer the Netherlands and even this defence line was considered practically untenable. Apart from the fact that in the event of war the North-eastern provinces had to be abandoned, the plan called for (a) the evacuation of large numbers of Dutch civilians into Germany, (b) the transit through Holland of British forces' civilians from Germany and (c) the rearward redeployment of allied divisions from the forward part of Germany back behind the Rhine-Yssel line, to areas freed by evacuation. As a finishing touch, all these actions would have to take place simultaneously. In September 1950, at the North Atlantic Council meeting in New York, Stikker said that the Atlantic strategy paper was 'sheer unacceptable nonsense from start to finish'. Instead, he - once again - advocated a forward strategy, implying a defence as far to the east in Germany as possible (as was discussed and propagated during the *Raad MAK* meeting of 31 August). This required either a substantial increase in American, British and Canadian soldiers in West Germany, or the rearmament of Germany. Stikker was strongly in favour of the latter; five years after the end of the war German

---

[76] Megens, *American aid to NATO allies in the 1950s*, p. 40.

rearmament was hardly a controversial issue in domestic political circles. The Foreign Minister told his colleagues in New York that 'in spite of the atrocities inflicted by Germany on the Netherlands, some 80% of the Dutch parliament would probably accept the proposals' made in this direction.[77] Stikker found Acheson on his side. For some time already, the Secretary of State was convinced of the need of rearming the Germans, but he had waited for the appropriate moment to make his ideas public. This moment was the New York summit where the Council in essence accepted Acheson's plan for a forward strategy.[78] It was obvious however that implementing such a strategy demanded forces far exceeding the numbers then available. Moreover, it was difficult to catch up arrears as long as the French government persisted in its opposition to German rearmament. French authorities were certainly less concerned about military-strategic considerations than their Dutch counterparts because they could still feel themselves relatively safe behind the Rhine-Meuse rivers.

The third reason for Dutch reluctance to strengthen their defence concerned the traditional position of the Navy as the most important service of the country's defence machinery. The Netherlands had always concentrated on building up and maintaining their naval forces, which were far ahead of the army, in terms of public esteem. The national parliament absolutely refused any spending cut that might affect the position of the navy.[79] Navy authorities thought it of the utmost importance to be represented in naval operations in the Atlantic, for the benefit of the home country, the overseas possessions and the merchant fleet, as well as of NATO's joint maritime defence. However, according to new American strategic plans, which were based on the concept of 'balanced collective

---

[77] Quoted from L.S. Kaplan, *A Community of Interests*, p. 115.
[78] Stikker, *Men of Responsibility*, pp. 297-299.
[79] Brouwer, 'De stem van de Marine in de ministerraad', pp. 50-53.

forces'[80], the Dutch should begin to improve their land defence and refrain from developing their popular navy. This was another matter of concern to the government, the more so since the navy placed very lucrative orders with the national shipbuilding industry.[81] Hence, it was feared that an increase in the army budget at the cost of the navy would be detrimental to the country's economic and employment situation, because in 1950 a domestic weapons industry was nearly non-existent.

Kaplan has written that,

> Despite the obvious fact that the Dutch could not really afford to maintain a large Navy the propitiation of their amour-propre required something better than the avuncular approach of Johnson [the American defence secretary, JvdH], who 'clapped' Mr. Schokking on the shoulders and said that the US Navy would be able to take care of Holland's defense. *(Kaplan, 1980: p. 93)*

As a result of the balanced collective forces initiative, the Dutch navy was initially confined to coastal defence duties in the North Sea and was only given a minor position in the North Atlantic Ocean Regional Planning Group[82]. General Kruls welcomed the strong emphasis Washington placed on the development of the national army, but it deeply worried the government and parliament in The Hague.

Strained relations between civil and military authorities hardly helped matters and in the course of 1950 the government began to lose confidence in the officials responsible for the reconstruction of the Army. In June, it was discovered that army authorities had deliberately overlooked a substantial stockpile of British weapons, which had been left behind at the end of the Second World War and

---

[80] The objective of the 'balanced collective forces' concept was to limit the military effort of each (smaller) country to the type of service it could perform most efficiently, while leaving the bulk of the burden to the larger partners.

[81] The four most important firms were RDM, NDSM, *Wilton Feyenoord* and *De Schelde*; responsible for the construction of cruisers, destroyers, minesweepers and submarines.

[82] Honig, *Defense Policy*, p. 17.

which could be used for the equipment of several army units. This was partly the result of organisational shortcomings, such as an apparent lack of co-ordination between the departments responsible for planning and implementation. Also the army's personnel policy was heavily criticised, as well as the lines of accountability within the military organisation. After an organisational reshuffle both the Quartermaster-General (QMG) and the Adjutant-General had officially come under the Chief of the General Staff, but they also maintained a direct line with the Ministry of Defence, as the ties with 'The Hague' were not entirely cut off. This led to embarrassing misunderstandings and duplications, partly resulting from the QMG's inability to co-ordinate his department in an adequate manner. Moreover, State Secretary Fockema Andreae reported that certain miscalculations had been made in the Army's budget proposals; peacetime operating costs had been overestimated by 20 to 25% (equalling about 100 million guilders).[83] The government held Kruls responsible for the chaos in the army organisation and blamed him for the weak financial foundations of his plans, and in June it decided to get rid of the General. This decision met again with heavy opposition from Minister Schokking who argued that Kruls was not only irreplaceable at home, but also an eminent representative abroad whose opinion was highly esteemed in international headquarters.[84]

Kruls saw the storm coming and on 10 July he wrote the government a letter explaining that it was in the country's interest that he remained in office. Kruls' letter consisted of a curious mix of arrogance, self-confidence and naiveté. He wrote that:

a) His organisational skills were exceptional
b) The army's ill-foreseen estimates of required equipment were due not simply to him, but also to the Minister and the State Secretary for Defence
c) He occupied a leading position in international military circles. This was illustrated by: the established position of the

---

[83] Honig, *Defense Policy*, p. 25.
[84] ARA, MR, Bijlagen 458, Nota Schokking aan de Ministerraad, 06-21-1950.

Netherlands in Western European defence, due to his prominence in the group of allied commanders-in-chief; US support for his initiative to create a strong NATO institution charged with implementation of the balanced collective forces concept; the eminent relations he entertained with Field-Marshal Montgomery and Generals Bradley and De Lattre de Tassigny; and wide-spread admiration for the manner in which he presided over the meetings of the WU chiefs of staff

d) He had taken successful initiatives towards intensifying relations between the army and public by supplying the latter with adequate information on the country's defence.

In conclusion to his letter, Kruls sharply criticised the cabinet's lukewarm defence policy, both nationally and internationally. In Kruls' view, the deplorable state of national defence was caused partly by the country's financial problems but for another substantial part by the government's irresolution. He urged the government to start clarifying its defence policy and to carry on with the present chief of the General Staff 'because the latter's resignation would be to the detriment of both army and country'.[85] In July, oddly enough the government dropped its intention to dismiss the General. The feeling in official circles was that a summary dismissal of the country's highest officer at that particular moment would make the Netherlands even more vulnerable for criticism from abroad.

On the other hand, it should be said that Kruls had valid reasons to criticise the - vacillating - defence policy of his government. Notwithstanding fierce American objections, the government decided to keep the 1951 budget under the ceiling of NLG 1 billion. This was a remarkable decision because, in the Atlantic defence committee, Dutch authorities had promised to have three divisions ready by the end of 1951, according to the terms of NATO's Medium Term Defence Plan. It was obvious that the development of

---

[85] Ibid, Nota Kruls aan Drees betr. positie CGS en defensiebeleid, 07-10-1950.

these divisions would be a costly affair thus far exceeding the funds available for 1951.

Schokking, the minister of defence, who was generally seen as an amiable person but weak politician, was bitterly disappointed with the government's frugality towards military affairs. He argued that the Netherlands would never be able to meet its international obligations under the prevailing circumstances. The problem with Schokking was the enormous lack of confidence in his ability to lead the department and the defence apparatus in an adequate manner. The lamentable defence minister was criticised from all sides: government, parliament and army. Repeatedly, Schokking reversed decisions and budgets, which he had earlier defended with firm conviction; for example, the conscripts of the second draft of 1949, who had been prematurely sent on long furlough, were a few months later, already recalled into service. Another complaint was that the army staff was over-organised, with too many high-positioned officers relative to rank and file. But the main criticism concerned Schokking's lack of authority over Kruls: it was common knowledge that Kruls negotiated with military authorities abroad without or regardless of ministerial instructions.[86] For example, during a discussion on the term of military service at a meeting of the WU chiefs of staff (in September), Kruls' position deviated from official government policy. In the *Raad MAK*, Drees argued that such a solo performance was simply unacceptable: he insisted that the chief of staff should strictly obey the instructions formulated by the government.[87]

During internal discussions at the defence ministry, Schokking complained that he was unable to make a coherent policy because of the contradictory advice he received from his military consultants. He explained that this obstructed him in his main duty, the promotion of defence interests within cabinet. Schokking acknowledged that army authorities sometimes disregarded his instructions and he was

---

[86] MinBuZa, DMA 00 inv.nr. 1, doos 1, Aantekening Van der Beugel voor Hirschfeld, 09-25-1950.
[87] MinAZ, Raad MAK, Notulen 09-21-1950.

furious about the regular leakage of confidential military information to the press. The criticism of his policy in the national press 'undermined his ministerial authority and was harmful for the army as such'. In mid-September Schokking made known that he was heartily sick of the whole concern and that he was considering his resignation.[88]

The severest critic of Schokking's policy was the *Ministerraad* and Finance Minister Lieftinck in particular. In October 1950, when the cabinet once again discussed the possibility of increasing the national defence effort and budget, Lieftinck (Labour party) bluntly said that Schokking, member of the protestant CHU - before the war Lieftinck had been a member of this party - was not the right man in the right place. He believed that the money appropriated for defence matters was not spent to the best advantage while Schokking headed the ministry and, he was therefore, reluctant to agree to any further boost in expenditure as long as the latter stayed in office. In October 1950, disagreements between the two ministers eventually resulted in Schokking's forced resignation. He was succeeded by 's Jacob[89], a former confidant of Lieftinck at the Ministry of Finance, and since early 1950 acting Government Commissioner for the Economic and Military Aid Programme. It was said that Drees had not got the nerve to tell Schokking the news of the dismissal personally and that he left this unpleasant task to deputy-prime minister Van Schaik.[90]

In retrospect we can say that, although Schokking was a weak politician and tactician who lacked the confidence of parliament, army and - most importantly - government, he was not the only official to blame for the chaotic state of national defence in the autumn of 1950. The chaos was caused also by the effects of Drees' and Lieftinck's austerity policy, their uneasy relationship with US

---

[88] MinDef, archief KMG (2e etage), Nota Schokking en verslag van de verg. m.b.t. de maatregelen welke moeten worden getroffen voor de verhoogde militaire inspanning, 09-18 resp. 25-1950

[89] H.L. 's Jacob, Minister of Defence, 1950-1951.

[90] H. Vuysje en J. Jansen van Galen, *Drees, Wethouder van Nederland* (Alphen aan den Rijn 1986) p. 144.

military authorities and, the mismanagement of the army by Kruls and his General Staff. In fact, Schokking's removal from office served as a temporary feint for the procrastinating defence policy of cabinet, because in the first months after his departure, nothing really changed. Until March 1951, Lieftinck - after Drees, the most influential member of cabinet - succeeded in maintaining the defence budget at a stable low level. The new defence minister 's Jacob proved to be a reliable ally of the finance minister.

This did not mean that, after the cabinet-reshuffle, the peaceful climate returned. US authorities continued to worry about the lack of willingness on the part of the Dutch government to proceed to action. On 2 October 1950, Senator Connally commented at a press conference, that 'Holland was one of the countries that should be put under pressure by the US government in order to insure that it armed itself in a correct way'. The senator added that 'Holland should entrust its naval defence to the United States and Britain, and supply itself land forces and materials'. Subsequently the *Daily report of foreign radio broadcasts* reported that 'political circles in The Hague were surprised by what had been said by Senator Connally'.[91]

US authorities emphasised that, in comparison with other NATO members, the Dutch effort lagged behind. In August, the UK had announced a three-year defence plan, increasing expenditure to a new high total of 3,400 million of British pounds, as well as an extension of the period of national service from eighteen months to two years. The French government also raised defence expenditure and contemplated an extension of conscript service from 12 to 18 months. If thus implemented this would mean an increase of fifteen in the number of their divisions available for Western defence. Belgium and Luxembourg also announced a longer conscription period and proposed a plan for spending more money on the army. In September, President Truman announced not only an ambitious defence programme but also a substantial increase in the strength and

---

[91] MinBuza, 921.10 NATO inv. nr. 67, Brief Van Roijen, 10-02-1950.

size of American forces stationed in Western Europe. Would the Netherlands follow suit?

General Kruls was eager to proceed to action and, early in October, he urged an increase in regular personnel and an extension of the term of conscription. Kruls said he based his case on the obligations formulated in the Medium Term Defence Plan (MTDP), which required the build-up of a total number of 56 divisions - of which 6 divisions would be American, 6 British, 14 Benelux and 27 French; a German contribution was still excluded. Kruls expected that some 6 or 7 of the 14 Benelux divisions had to be provided by the Netherlands (to be ready in 1954) and he felt this was a feasible target.

On the eve of the meeting of the Atlantic Defence Committee in Washington, starting on 28 October, the *Raad MAK* discussed Kruls' recommendations. Stikker was of the opinion that the forthcoming conference in Washington should deal with purely military aspects, free from financial and economic considerations, just as the MTDP was aiming for. In his view, two matters would be of particular importance in Washington: (a) the rearmament of Germany and (b) the incorporation of the national navy within the Atlantic framework. He considered German rearmament not only a strategic necessity, but also a welcome alleviation of the military burden of the allies. As far as the Navy was concerned, he had the impression that at least two members[92] of NATO's Standing Group - consisting of the 'Big Three': United States, United Kingdom and France - would make out a case for consolidation of a strong naval force in the Netherlands. He hoped that, as a result, Holland would be allowed to supply fewer army divisions than Belgium. Stikker's plea for an international role of the navy was not entirely unrealistic. Paradoxically, despite Washington's initial emphasis on balanced collective forces and a low-profile for the Dutch navy, the 1950 US military aid programme

---

[92] The third member was probably Britain that during the preceding months had made clear that the Dutch navy should relinquish its aircraft carrier, stop the construction of cruisers and concentrate, instead, on the production of minesweepers.

contained significant items of military equipment for the Netherlands, including destroyer-escorts and minesweepers.[93] This certainly helped to make the navy eligible for an Atlantic role, and boosted the government's efforts to defend the position of the national Navy. At the *Raad MAK* meeting, tentative mention was made of an increase in the defence budget by NLG 500 million a year, deemed necessary for the execution of General Kruls's plans. However, as always, Drees and Lieftinck strongly objected to Stikker's attempt at de-coupling military objectives and financial consequences. They indicated that the defence effort required either a tax-increase or a special government loan, both having high risks for the country's financial stability. They also rejected an extension of the conscription period, arguing that since France and Belgium had still not made a final decision on this issue, it would be pointless to act unilaterally. Drees and Lieftinck further felt that MTDP's lack of financial specifications - even of rough estimations - made it difficult to come to conclusions. Starkenborgh, permanent representative to NATO in London, urged the *Raad MAK* to supply the delegation in Washington with concrete figures and sound instructions because, in his view, the Netherlands should finally make a serious commitment and not run away from drafting a detailed programme on national contributions. Following Starkenborgh's intervention, the discussion centred on the number of divisions to be mentioned by the Dutch delegation at the Washington meeting. Opinions varied between five and six, with Drees commenting that the Netherlands could not even afford five. He was furious about Kruls's hinting at the possibility of supplying even seven divisions. Starkenborgh re-emphasised the importance of a serious role for the national navy and the involvement of Germany in allied defence, and stated that, subject to compliance with these particular requests, the delegation in Washington should be instructed to promise six divisions - one of which a standing division, to be ready by 1954. To attain this, the increase in the yearly contingent and regular personnel and the

---

[93] Honig, *Defense Policy*, p. 20.

lengthening of military service, needed to be realised as soon as possible. Lieftinck urged instead a development in three stages: a speed-up of the three divisions already promised to NATO, to be ready by October 1951; the build-up of one active, combat-ready division; and a further extension of the number of divisions, somewhere in the future, without further specifications.

At the end of the *Raad MAK* meeting the delegation in Washington was given the following directives:

a) The Netherlands promises to develop three army divisions to be ready by 1952 at the latest, provided that the US delivers the required equipment in time.

b) The Netherlands is prepared to contribute one active, combat-ready division, provided that this division is stationed in Germany and that other countries supply combat-ready forces in a reasonable proportion to the Dutch share.

c) The Netherlands is prepared to prolong the term of military service, at least as far as the agreements made under (b) necessitate such a prolongation.

d) From 1952, the Netherlands will continue to build up army divisions in reasonable proportion to the Belgian contribution, maintaining account of the country's substantial naval efforts. If precise figures are required, the delegation is authorised to mention a total amount of five divisions, as presumably feasible.

e) If the pace of the allied army build-up requires it and if other countries make a similar effort, the Netherlands is prepared to accept an increase - to be announced - in the contingent, provided that a solution is found for the shortage of training facilities and barracks.

f) No time should be lost in allowing West Germany to provide armed forces for allied defence.

The *Raad MAK* made the above promises dependent on an acceptable solution for their financial and economic implications.[94]

---

[94] MinAZ, Raad MAK, Notulen 10-13-1950.

The offer of five divisions mentioned under d), as well as the cautious wording of the instructions, implied a victory for Drees and Lieftinck. Starkenborgh's plea for six divisions was ignored, as well as Stikker's attempt at de-coupling finances and army-divisions.

Late October 1950, at the Washington conference of NATO's Defence Committee, the target for the Dutch contribution to the allied forces was set at three divisions by the end of 1951 and five divisions by 1954. This was in line with the instructions formulated at the *Raad MAK* meeting and somewhat less than individuals like Kruls and Starkenborgh had asked for. But even this negotiation result failed to satisfy Lieftinck. He thought it impossible to have three divisions ready by the end of 1951 - instead he proposed two. He also - successfully - blocked an increase in the period of military service that thus remained fixed at twelve months. Despite Stikker's concern that non-compliance with the three-division plan for 1951 would result in a delay or reduction in equipment deliveries from the United States and Canada, the government once again refused to proceed to action.[95] Stikker's concern soon proved justified: the US took immediate steps to cut military aid for 1951 by $ 45 million.[96]

At that time, the Ministry of Foreign Affairs made an inventory of the country's military capabilities in 1950 and, demonstrated that - compared to Belgium - Holland spent the bulk of public funds on military affairs, but the actual impact hereof was inadequate. Belgium's defence efforts totalled 11% of the total budget (2.8% of GNP) the defence of the Congo not included. The Belgian defence force comprised about 74,000 soldiers - nearly all drafted into the army, the Belgian navy and air force playing no significant role. At the time, Belgium had one combat-ready division at its disposal (stationed in Germany), while the build-up of two other divisions was in an advanced stage. Holland on the other hand, had no complete division: General Kruls even said cynically that he disposed of only 150 well-trained soldiers. At the time, the availability of a combat-ready division was merely wishful thinking.

---

[95] Ibid., Notulen 11-07-1950.
[96] Honig, *Defense Policy*, p. 27.

Nevertheless, the national defence budget was relatively high: the NLG 800 million budgeted for 1951 formed about 23% of total government expenditure (5.0% of GNP). This amount was divided as follows: NLG 325 million went to the navy, 325 million to the army and 150 million to the air force. As far as the army was concerned, the memorandum indicated that the Netherlands failed to get good value for its money. The British newspaper *Manchester Guardian* had calculated that the British government spent an average of £ 743 (= NLG 7,000) a year on a national soldier. Starting from the same amount, the Netherlands could raise an army of more than 46,000 soldiers, but the real size was much smaller. Foreign Affairs concluded that the national army was presumably top-heavy with relatively too many servicemen in high positions.[97]

Although this was certainly true - especially after the return of a great number of officers and non-commissioned officers (NCOs) from Indonesia - the main problem was the effective incorporation of available personnel in well-trained and homogeneous divisions. For example, General Kruls initially refused to admit Indonesia-repatriates into the army because these soldiers were only trained in guerrilla-fighting and had no experience with modern warfare and weaponry. Moreover, he thought, it would be useless to build up the army with British and Canadian materials because it would hinder standardisation along American lines.[98]

Early in January 1951, the Dutch government stubbornly attempted to withstand increasing American pressure for a rapid build-up of the army, arguing that there could be no talk of a defence budget higher than the estimated NLG 850 million (which was a slight increase as compared with the originally budgeted amount). One of the main reasons for US-Dutch controversies was a different assessment of military dangers and a different analysis of how to counter these dangers. By the end of 1950, American (and British) authorities, both civil and military, considered the risk of war very real. They felt that the great crisis was 'no longer two or three years off but that things

---

[97] MinBuZa, 921.10 NATO inv. nr. 67, Memorandum DEU/WS, 03-25-1951.
[98] ARA, MR, Het bezoek van Generaal Eisenhower, 01-15-1951.

might come to a head rather quickly'. Hence, it made sense for the western powers to build up their strength first, before they decided to rearm Germany, 'something which might well provoke a Soviet attack'.[99] The Dutch government, on the other hand, was far less aroused by imminent military dangers, postponed the build-up of the army, and kept prioritising German rearmament on a short-term basis.

The US State Department took the view that the NATO countries of Northern Europe - including the Netherlands - could do much more for their own defence, because these countries,

> Have only small communist parties, and therefore have to deal with a relatively minor internal communist threat. These countries are law-abiding and have sound governmental structures, with the result that they are in a better position to establish the controls necessary for an all-out defense effort. In general, their public credit and internal financing is good, or at least sufficient to permit sound financing of a considerable part of their defense effort. They have been reluctant to make an all-out effort because their policies have heretofore placed greater emphasis on social advancement rather than on security. While it has thus far been difficult to get them to undertake as affective programs, it is believed that they are now prepared to face up to reality. *(FRUS 1951 Vol. 3 (1), Memorandum State Department, 01-05-1951, 398)*

In January, NATO published some figures on the defence budgets of the member countries.

---

[99] Trachtenberg, *A Constructed Peace*, p. 111.

	FY beginning: (in mlns. of $)			Percent of GNP		
	1950		1951	1950		1951
	Pre Korea rate	Post Korea rate		Pre Korea	Post Korea	
Belg.	187	187	250	2.9	2.9	3.8
Lux.	4	6	NA	3.5	4.5	NA
Den.	53	75	75	1.8	2.6	2.6
Fr.	1,640	1,640	2,451	7.3	7.3	9.7
It.	515	595	915	4.0	4.5	6.4
Neth.	*307*	*307*	*263*	*6.2*	*6.2*	*5.0*
Norw.	48	63	80	2.6	3.6	4.5
Port.	41	44	NA	1.8	1.9	NA
UK	2,237	2,380	3,108	6.4	6.4	8.0
Can.	493	950	950	3.3	6.3	6.3
US	15,124	25-30,000	NA	5.5	8.7-10.5	NA

Source: FRUS 1951 Vol. 3 (1) NAT European Defence Budgets, 6

Compared to other smaller countries like Belgium and Denmark, the Netherlands still spent a substantial amount on defence. The main reasons for American dissatisfaction concerned the army's lack of efficiency and the country's persistence to invest in the navy rather than the army.

Washington wished to see concrete results from its assistance to Europe. In March 1951, Congress was to discuss the continuation of the European Co-operation Agreement and the Mutual Defence Assistance Programme. In order to placate Congress, Van Roijen[100], the Dutch ambassador to the United States, urged his government to clarify its defence policy, because just at that moment the State Department contemplated the recruitment and training of significant additional forces to be sent to Europe. This roused considerable political conflict in Washington, with the Republican Party, led by

---

[100] J.H. van Roijen, Dutch ambassador to the United States, 1950-1964.

Senator Taft, stipulating that the US contribution to Europe would continue to be primarily through air and naval forces. Officials of the Truman administration thought this would be inadequate and held a brief for additional ground forces. The ultimate persuasive testimony was supposed to come from NATO's Supreme Commander Europe (SACEUR), General Eisenhower, who decided to make a rapid tour of NATO capitals in January 1951. Van Roijen recommended The Hague to use Eisenhower's visit to 'repair the damaged national image abroad'.[101]

Conclusions

Just after the War, The Hague came to the conviction that the United States, with its enormous economic and military resources, was the only power capable of defending Europe against possible aggressiveness on the part of the Soviet Union. Not that a Soviet invasion of Western Europe was seen as imminent - during the period under discussion the outbreak of a 'hot' war in Europe was considered very unlikely - but the government felt that the existence of firm Atlantic ties would dissuade the Soviets from contemplating aggression in the short, medium or longer term. It had therefore no serious qualms about abandoning the pre-war foreign policy of neutrality and aloofness, and becoming involved in western military alliances like the Western Union and NATO.

At the same time, The Hague was reluctant to spend any more guilders on defence than was absolutely necessary. Priority was given to the country's post-war financial and economic reorganisation, which by the late 1940s, was well under way but might be threatened by additional expenditure on army and armaments. Dutch authorities carefully ensured that they paid just enough to be assured of American involvement in the defence of Western Europe. This was not easy because, from the summer of 1950, Washington called for a substantial effort on the part of the

---

[101] MinBuZa, DMA 01 inv. nr. 2 doos 1, Brieven Van Roijen, 06-05-1951 and 06-08-1951.

allies and did not shun methods of unprecedented pressure to reach this aim. During the period under discussion, the Netherlands balanced between domestic reluctance and foreign persuasiveness concerning defence. In reality, in an ever more dangerous Cold War constellation and with a dedicated 'group leader' breathing down its neck, the country had very little room of its own for manoeuvre.

Prime Minister Drees and his coalition government attached considerable value to the protection provided by the American nuclear umbrella, and realised that the Netherlands had to make a certain contribution - in terms of conventional troops and arms - to secure a US commitment to the European continent. This did not imply that Drees believed in the practical usage of nuclear weapons in a war situation, but he considered these weapons crucial for their deterrent value and attractive for their implicit effect of slowing down the build-up of conventional forces. An atmosphere of wishful thinking prevailed, whereby people just hoped that nothing serious would happen. Hence, the fact *that* Holland participated in NATO was deemed more important than the question of *how* it participated. Top civil servant Van der Beugel has argued that Drees saw NATO membership as an insurance against Soviet expansionism, for which a certain - preferably modest - premium had to be paid.[102] This did not restrain the Prime Minister from being highly critical towards demands made by the North Atlantic alliance. He complained not only about rising expenditure, but also about the refusal of the 'Big Three' to take account of the position of smaller countries. He was, for instance, annoyed that US authorities attached so little value to the navy and the country's territorial troops.

Retrenchment policy played an all-important role during the years that Drees led the government, and even the end of the colonial presence in Indonesia - a relief for the treasury - failed to produce a change herein. On the contrary, the homecoming of so many ex-colonials reinforced the prime minister's zeal to control public expenditure. His main ally was the influential Finance Minister

---

[102] E.H. van der Beugel, 'Drees als minister-president', in: H. Daalder and N. Cramer (ed.), *Willem Drees* (Houten 1988), p. 156.

Lieftinck, who carefully ensured that military spending was kept within bounds, for fear of negative effects on the national balance of payments position and the process of economic reconstruction. Unavoidably, such an attitude led to regular clashes with US and NATO authorities. Priorities in Washington and The Hague diverged substantially: the main problem for the United States was the immediate threat to collective security posed by the Soviet army, while the main problem for the Netherlands was the immediate threat to the country's standard of living. This was also one of the main reasons why The Hague advocated German rearmament: the more Germany became involved in the defence of Western Europe, the less the Netherlands needed to reserve for the development of national forces. Drees and Lieftinck attempted to escape from military obligations by all means open to them, even if this led to vicious confrontations with dissenters like Foreign Minister Stikker, Defence Minister Schokking and Chief of the General Staff Kruls, who all pleaded for a more indulgent policy towards the United States.

Apart from financial arguments, German rearmament had a dominant military-strategic rationale. During the years 1948-1950 the suspicion prevailed that in a crisis situation the allies would resort to a peripheral strategy, leaving Dutch territory open to foreign invasion. In other words, The Hague was not convinced of NATO's will to defend the country on the Rhine-Yssel line, let alone to proceed to a forward strategy on the river Elbe in Germany, at least for the time German rearmament remained forthcoming. The result was a classical deadlock: Holland waited for the allies to provide external security while the allies waited for the Netherlands to step up military activities. This situation was to remain unchanged until the start of the year 1951.

CHAPTER 2

The fixing of a defence ceiling and the development of the army, 1951-1954

Introduction

During the years 1948-1950, the Dutch government refused to build up the country's defence capabilities in proper accordance with international standards, because it doubted allied commitment to the protection of domestic territory in case of emergency. Under such circumstances, as was illustrated in chapter 1, the centre-left coalition preferred to concentrate on rebuilding the economy and improving social welfare in the country, and to keep military expenditure at a relatively modest level. Dutch lack of enthusiasm for defence increasingly annoyed policy-makers in NATO and the United States. The US Congress pressurised their own administration to stop the supply of defence equipment and other aid to Western European countries if they continued to prove unwilling to do more for their external security. Following events like the Soviet nuclear test and the start of the Korean War, American authorities were convinced that the threat posed to western civilisation was real and had to be taken seriously. They could not understand why such a loyal and diligent country like the Netherlands, with which it maintained a close and harmonious political relationship, now proved so stubborn in its lack of compliance with allied requirements. In January 1951, in a final attempt to convince the allies of the need for action, Washington sent Europe its most prestigious representative, General Dwight Eisenhower, recently appointed Supreme Allied Commander Europe (SACEUR). Because of his impeccable war record and personal charisma, Eisenhower was considered the ideal person for the difficult job of changing European minds. When he arrived in The Hague, the Dutch government was close to total chaos, partly as a result of the domestic defence debate (relations between civil and military authorities had reached an all-time low), and partly because of the problematic situation in the colony of New Guinea, which had remained under Dutch rule after the decolonisation of Indonesia. The impact of Eisenhower's visit on national policies will be covered in detail in this chapter. The central question is how The Hague finally responded to foreign pressure, which concrete measures it took concerning domestic defence, and which further problems the government and army encountered during the period 1951-1954.

2.1 Eisenhower's visit, and its immediate aftermath

On 10 and 11 January 1951, General Eisenhower, together with General Gruenther, visited The Hague, where he had conversations with Prime Minister Drees, Foreign Minister Stikker, Defence Minister 's Jacob - Schokking's successor - and the Chiefs of Staff. Talking to Stikker, Eisenhower stressed the point that maintaining adequate military strength was manageable only if all the countries 'put their hearts into the job' and 'started to take the necessary steps to translate plans into action'. Referring to the Chinese intervention in Korea in November 1950, the threat from the *Bereitschaften*[103] in East Germany, and a possible Soviet or satellite attack on Yugoslavia, Eisenhower thought it high time to increase the pace of defence preparation. Although Stikker agreed with Eisenhower's plea for action, he remarked that additional Dutch efforts would be futile without German rearmament. In this respect, he criticised the Council of Foreign Ministers of the 'Big Four' (France, the United Kingdom, the United States and the Soviet Union), indicating that the Soviets were trying to use this Council to demilitarise Germany. According to Stikker, this appealed not only to the large sections of the French population opposed to German rearmament, but also to 'those elements in Germany who wished to stay neutral or aimed at reunifying East and West Germany'. As an alternative, Stikker

---

[103] Paramilitary groups.

underlined the importance of binding West Germany closely to the West. He preferred that Germany join NATO at once, but realised that preference remained premature, given French opposition and their proposal to create a European army. On the important issue of raw material prices - which had risen steeply after the start of the Korean War - Stikker was unhappy with the plan to convene an International Materials Conference, to be composed of the United States, Britain and France, with powers of recommendation and decision-making. For the Foreign Minister, this was a particularly urgent matter because of his chairmanship of the OEEC. Since price increases in raw materials had such a serious impact on the national balance of payments, Stikker urged Eisenhower to take full account of the interests of the smaller countries, which 'should be given the opportunity to voice their opinion prior to decision-making by the 'Big Three''.[104]

At his meeting with Drees, Eisenhower reiterated the urgency of the defence programme, but according to Eisenhower's spokesman MacArthur, 'Drees listened but did not react with enthusiasm'. As for the German problem, Drees expressed his concern that allied policy towards Germany had placed the Germans in a position where they could blackmail the allies. MacArthur wrote to Washington: 'Drees's stolid complacency contrasted unfavourably with the attitude of the other officers. Mr. Drees gave the impression of an exceedingly amiable individual who was, however, unwilling to grapple with the urgent problems of this era with determination and energy.'[105]

During Eisenhower's visit the press reported some minor communist demonstrations in The Hague and Amsterdam, but these failed to result in a serious disturbance.[106]

Directly following Eisenhower's departure for Copenhagen, the next stop on his itinerary of the NATO capitals, Defence Minister 's

[104] FRUS 1951 Vol. 3 (1), Telegram Anderson to Acheson, 01-11-1951, pp. 413-414.
[105] Ibid., pp. 414-415.
[106] Ibid., Telegram Chapin to Acheson, 01-11-1951, p. 413.

Jacob met with the American ambassador to the Netherlands, Chapin, and informed him of a new government plan to increase the defence budget by NLG 150 million within the following three weeks. Over a period of three months, he intended to ask for two additional sums, the size of which he did not state. Chapin wondered why the Defence Minister had not mentioned his plans during his talks with Eisenhower. According to Chapin, Eisenhower's visit had been most helpful in that 'it would very likely give an extra stimulus to the Dutch defence efforts'. Eisenhower's view was shared by the Dutch chiefs of staff who told the ambassador that the 'citizens of the countries of Western Europe, as well as the chiefs of staff, were more aware of defence necessities than their governments'.[107]

On 13 January, Eisenhower wrote Chapin a letter, meant for distribution in the Dutch cabinet. Eisenhower complained that his visit to The Hague had been disappointing: the Dutch government did not seem to have a clearly defined goal commensurate with the obvious, pressing needs. The General added that 'no description of the current programme would convince his government that The Hague was showing a sense of urgency, a readiness to sacrifice and a determination to pull its full share of the load'.

Eisenhower further touched on two sore spots: standing army units and the period of conscription - he considered a twelve-month period of service entirely unsatisfactory. He finished his letter by writing that he had no intention of interfering in the internal workings of any North Atlantic Treaty nation or to advise directly on the methods to be used,

Eisenhower's complaint about the 'struggle for efficiency' in the Dutch army obviously alluded to Kruls's reluctance to incorporate Indonesia veterans in the army, and to accept second-hand British and Canadian equipment.

Stikker said that he was very impressed by Eisenhower's letter and, although he thought the letter would cause an enormous shock within the cabinet, he added: 'personally and very confidentially I will be

---

[107] Ibidem.

indiscreet enough to say that I liked the letter.' Chapin wrote to Eisenhower,

Specifically, Stikker mentioned an initial increase in defence expenditure of NLG 150 million - the amount 's Jacob had promised - and a proposal to build 48 minesweepers at domestic shipyards.[108] Tactically, this was a smart move, because apart from its economic importance, the minesweeper plan suited the allied preference for speeding up the process of clearing the North Sea of dangerous sea-mines. NATO was deficient in minesweepers at that stage.

Starkenborgh, permanent representative to NATO, also appreciated the tone and content of Eisenhower's letter. During a conversation with Spofford (US deputy representative on the North Atlantic Council), Starkenborgh said that Eisenhower's visit had been 'most timely' and he hoped it would soon prove effective. He fully agreed with Eisenhower's criticism of public and official complacency in the Netherlands: there had been too great a desire to relax, to lick the Indonesian wounds and to hide behind the view that not only would France and Belgium not really do what they promised, but also, that the United States had exaggerated its contribution. Nevertheless, in Starkenborgh's view, 'influential groups' in the Netherlands made good progress in 'developing a sense of urgency in the government'. France and Belgium had woken up to the necessity for full-scale action[109] and the magnitude of the defence effort by the United States was obvious. 'Holland was lagging behind' and Starkenborgh hoped that the next meeting of the national defence council (the *Raad MAK*) would produce concrete results.[110]

---

[108] Of the total of 48 minesweepers 12 were destined for the Dutch navy, 24 for the United States and and 12 for other European countries. MinAZ, Raad MAK, Notulen 01-19-1951. In the autumn of 1951 these ambitious figures were brought back to the total of 32 minesweepers to be built at Dutch wharves. See also Megens, *American aid to NATO allies*, p. 164.

[109] France had presented a three-year programme, which would increase its defence budget approximately 18% over that of 1950. Belgium had even proposed a 55% increase in its military expenditures for 1951 by allocating an additional $ 100 million to defence.

[110] Ibid., Telegram Spofford to Acheson, 01-17-1951, p. 431.

A great deal of fuss and furore was created by an article in the American newspaper the *New York Herald Tribune,* which mentioned (on 14 January) that Prime Minister Drees, 'an old-time doctrinaire socialist', was not prepared to take any effective action on rearmament because he 'was uninterested in the whole defense program.'[111] On the same day the influential *New York Times* published an article with similar contents. According to Ambassador Chapin, Eisenhower's letter of 13 January had been leaked to the American press and 'there seemed to be only little doubt that this leak was caused by a Catholic member of the cabinet defence council to embarrass Drees [member of the Labour party, JvdH]; likewise, the Dutch General Staff had collaborated in the *New York Times* article.'[112]

The *Raad MAK* discovered that the leak of Eisenhower's letter was due both to the indiscretion of the chief of the news service of the Defence Ministry, and to the American embassy (Chapin himself!).[113] Stikker told Chapin that Drees was 'deeply hurt' by the two articles and that he had even contemplated his resignation, stating that it was 'tempting for the Labour party to leave the government coalition now, because in the opposition they could be sure of a much better showing at the next elections'.[114]

Although 'in some ways regrettable and definitely coming at an unfortunate time for Drees and his coalition cabinet' (consisting of two secular parties, PvdA and VVD, and two denominational parties, KVP and CHU), Chapin was convinced that the affair would have a positive and beneficial effect on Cabinet thinking concerning defence.

On 18 January the Second Chamber (Lower House) of the States-General debated the country's defence policy. In his introductory speech, Stikker said that absolute priority needed to be given to the

---

[111] Ibid., Telegram Chapin to Embassy in Portugal, 01-16-1951, p. 426.

[112] Ibid., Telegram Chapin to Acheson, 01-19-1951, p. 436.

[113] MinAZ, Raad MAK, Notulen 01-19-1951.

[114] FRUS 1951 Vol. 3 (1), Telegram Chapin to Embassy in Portugal, 01-16-1951, p. 426.

build-up of the army since the 'safeguarding of national existence was at stake'. He warned that in the near future, important decisions had to be taken and that such decisions 'would have far-reaching social consequences'. In the same debate, even Drees stated that any unwillingness to support Atlantic defence would be 'absurd'. Drees added that the entire Cabinet supported the North Atlantic pact and the Dutch responsibilities entailed in it.[115]

At its meeting on 19 January, the *Raad MAK* retrospectively reviewed Eisenhower's visit and the General's letter. The prevailing opinion was that Eisenhower had been indiscreet in venting his criticism; he had not even taken the trouble to consider the country's domestic problems in depth. Drees regretted that Eisenhower had hidden behind a written expression of his criticisms, instead of coming out verbally. There was a shrewd suspicion that the General had deliberately chosen this method in order to put the *Ministerraad* on the spot. Drees disagreed with Eisenhower's paragraph on the duration of conscription in the Netherlands. In his letter, SACEUR had mentioned an overall term of twelve months, but Drees indicated that several categories (officers, NCOs, technicians, marines and air force personnel) served eighteen months or even more. Likewise, Eisenhower's assessment of the lack of an organisational framework for the build-up of new divisions was considered faulty. Drees thought it a matter of great importance to correct the misimpressions which were the cause of Eisenhower's dissatisfaction. 's Jacob observed that Eisenhower had already formed his opinion before the consultations in The Hague had even begun, and he estimated that SACEUR attached more value to the full utilisation of the contingent than to an extension of the conscription period. According to the Defence Minister, the main problems hindering full utilisation were the existing shortages of drill-sergeants, weapons and equipment. Stikker was annoyed that the *Raad MAK* had not anticipated Eisenhower's visit to The Hague, and he reproached his colleague 's Jacob for having regarded the visit as an internal military event, and

---

[115] Ibid., Telegram Chapin to Acheson, 01-19-1951, p. 436.

for having underestimated the importance and publicity value of the visit. An additional complaint was that the wording of the memorandum presented to Eisenhower on his arrival had been too vague; for example, the recall to service of the second draft of 1949 had not been mentioned at all. Starkenborgh said that what Eisenhower needed from the European governments was a 'demonstration of energy and mentality', because under the current circumstances these qualities were more important than drafts and plans. In reply to Eisenhower's letter, Starkenborgh urged the *Raad MAK* to take full account of the 'psychology of the recipient'. Co-operation was needed to appease Congress, and he added that this time, complaints about all manner of financial and economic problems were best omitted.

Ironically, at the same time, the *Raad* refused to discuss a memorandum drafted by General Kruls (on 13 January) on the army's future, because of an alleged lack of financial data. It was decided that reading the memo would be deferred until the *Raad*'s next meeting, scheduled for 25 January.[116] However, it would never be discussed, as in the intervening period the government decided to sack the General.

Kruls's dismissal came as a surprise to nobody. The refusal to discuss his memorandum in the *Raad MAK* was just another sign that the relationship between the government and the Head of the Chiefs of Staff had become untenable. In his criticism of Dutch defence policy, Eisenhower had found the army staff on his side. It is easy to assume that, during SACEUR's visit, Kruls had missed no opportunity to strengthen American doubts about the government's dedication and commitment, which naturally infuriated the government. One of the underlying problems was that the headstrong Kruls abhorred civil involvement in military matters, and openly complained about 'departmental ignorance' in The Hague. His personal relations with Minister 's Jacob left much to be desired, with both officials quarrelling about which task fell under whose

---

[116] MinAZ, Raad MAK, Notulen 01-19-1951.

competence. Although 's Jacob tried to trivialise existing tensions, saying that personal relations between him and Kruls were excellent, he showed no inclination to defend Kruls's views in cabinet ('because he was always hunting', as a bitter Kruls wrote afterwards in his memoirs[117]). Kruls further complained about the lack of a standing army in the Netherlands: he needed as much as 72 hours to mobilise troops, which was in his view 'unacceptable'. To improve this situation, an increase in the term of conscription was needed, but the government refused to accede to this request. Obviously, the distrust was mutual. The government in its turn lacked confidence in Kruls's ability to steer the army build-up in the right direction. It was, for instance, annoyed at the abstruseness of the system used for calling up reservists. As a result, concrete measures were avoided as long as General Kruls headed the army.

Mutual irritation culminated in Kruls's admission in the national newspaper, *De Telegraaf,* that he fully agreed with Eisenhower's criticism of the government's defence policy. For the government, this was the last straw: Kruls was dismissed on 20 January, just over a week after Eisenhower's visit.

In his memoirs, Kruls wrote that he suspected the Defence Minister of 'premeditated murder', and that he was convinced that 's Jacob, before his appointment in October 1950, had been forced to accept a list of desiderata, one of which concerned the replacement of the chief of the General Staff.[118]

Be that as it may, Kruls was doubtless a curious character, whose unpredictable and headstrong actions were always highly mistrusted within the cabinet. Drees, who was virtually allergic to military influence on his policy, had never been on good terms with the General. Their discord dated from the end of the Second World War, while the government was still in exile in London, and while Kruls was the head of a military authority that ruled rather arbitrarily over the liberated southern provinces of the Netherlands. Ever since, Drees feared that Kruls would take matters into his own hands and

---

[117] H.J. Kruls, *Generaal in Nederland. Memoires* (Bussum 1975) p. 203.
[118] *Ibid.,* pp. 208 and 212.

enter into international commitments without the government being properly informed. Also, Kruls's neglect of the provision of reliable financial data was a thorn in the side of the Prime Minister. In view of this, it was highly peculiar that in July 1950, the government gave up its plan to get rid of the general.

The eventual dismissal was put off till January 1951, and this confirmed the impression that the cabinet's defence policy was on the brink of chaos. In its efforts to deny such an impression, the government placed the blame on someone who had recently (in May 1949) been promoted to 'full general' (by the same government!). After Kruls' dismissal, the British ambassador in The Hague wrote that 'the unfortunate general' had been 'severely blackened by his government'.[119] The foreign press initially reported in a similar way.

Despite Kruls's removal from office, victory for his views was near. The United States had had more than enough of Dutch procrastination, and on 19 January (the day of the *Raad MAK*-meeting), Washington decided to interfere in the country's defence affairs by means of an *aide-mémoire* stating that:

The American government made the following suggestions for the utilisation of the said $ 170 million:

- $ 60 million should be spent on the training of troops and organisation of divisions, and

- $ 125 to $ 150 million should be spent on domestic production of military equipment.

In a telegram to Secretary of State Acheson, Ambassador Chapin proposed 'to follow up this *aide-memoir* with joint discussions on a working level to get the Netherlands over the hump'.[120]

The Hague was clearly not amused with this direct manner of American interference, and calculated that the Americans wanted them to raise the budget to a total of NLG 1650 million net, consisting of NLG 850 million (already reserved for the year 1951) + NLG 150 million (additional expenditure announced by Stikker and

---

[119] Brouwer, Politiek-militaire verhoudingen', p. 85.
[120] FRUS 1951 Vol. 3 (1), Telegram Chapin to Acheson, 01-19-1951, p. 437.

's Jacob after Eisenhower's visit) + NLG 650 million (the amount referred to in the *aide-mémoire*). Starkenborgh felt it irregular that the US administration not only ordered a foreign government to spend more money but also indicated precisely how the extra amount had to be divided. He said 'it was a pity that the American note came at a moment when the Dutch government was just giving serious consideration to extra measures for the benefit of its defence'. Mutual friction grew even further, when the government discovered that without prior announcement officials of the US Embassy had visited the Fokker and Philips factories, where they discovered that 'in both cases production lagged behind capacity'.[121]

Kruls was succeeded by Lieutenant-General Hasselman, previously inspector of the cavalry (as a lieutenant-colonel). Although Hasselman was universally admired as an outstanding officer, his appointment provoked many negative reactions because of the allegedly dubious role he had played during the Second World War. It was said that Hasselman had collaborated with the Germans in arranging the dissolution of the Dutch army in 1940. Moreover, immediately after the country's occupation, he had added his signature to a summons by the Dutch army command calling on Dutch officers to report to the German authorities. After liberation in 1945 Hasselman had been forced to resign, but within two years he had been rehabilitated and reinstated in his military duties. One of the leading officers of the Dutch General Staff referred to Hasselman as 'a fighter, as hard as nails'.[122]

By the end of January 1951, after the resignation of both Schokking (in October 1950) and Kruls, Dutch civil and military authorities felt compelled to reconsider their army policy. The pressure exercised by the Americans was obvious and irresistible. However, things further deteriorated when, on 24 January, the government fell as a consequence of the division between Foreign Minister Stikker and his own party, the VVD, over the Dutch colony

---

[121] MinBuZa, 921.10 NATO inv. nr. 67, Brief Starkenborgh, 02-01-1951.
[122] Politisches Archiv des Auswärtigen Amts Bonn (PAAA Bonn), 230/00/53, Brieven DuMont, 01-25-1951 and 01-26-1951.

of New Guinea. Although government circles tried to deny it, it was clear that the chaotic defence policy also played a part in the fall of the cabinet. During the parliamentary debate preceding the overthrow of the government, Oud, the leader of the VVD, said that

The outgoing Drees cabinet carried on until 15 March, when a new government was formed. In the meantime, it was impossible to take such important decisions as raising the defence budget.

The US authorities were greatly disappointed with this delay and repeated that the Dutch were making a poor showing. On 31 January, as he reported on his tour through Europe during a meeting at the White House, General Eisenhower observed that every country except Holland seemed to be trying hard to build up its defence. He could not understand the attitude of the Dutch: 'All they seemed interested in was their Navy which did not make any sense, since the land defense was the only thing they ought to be worrying about.' Eisenhower needed a substantial Dutch army contribution - at least five divisions - to execute his strategic plans for the defence of Europe.

Comprehensive attention has been paid here to Eisenhower's visit and its immediate aftermath because they took place at a highly delicate political moment, and they give a perfect illustration of what was really at stake in the domestic defence debate during the early 1950s. The government was contemplating a fundamental change of policy, but doubts and hesitations continued to prevail before, during and immediately after SACEUR's stay in The Hague. The FRUS papers pay substantial attention to the Dutch situation in January 1951, presumably because the American administration considered the Netherlands a test case for what was possible in Europe, in terms of pressure and persuasion. Compared to other small NATO countries, the defence effort expected from the Netherlands was substantial, mainly because the government wished to protect the international position of the national Navy. As a war hero, Eisenhower had a very good reputation in the Netherlands, and it was felt that he was the obvious person to choose to convince the Dutch government of the necessity of compliance with American wishes.

2.2 The decision to raise the budget, and the ensuing problems

In the longer run, American admonitions proved effective. Since the Netherlands was greatly dependent on the US for economic and military support, it was dangerous to risk losing any of that nation's goodwill. On 1 February 1951, in an effort to convince US authorities of the government's sincere intentions, the Embassy in Washington drew up a report on the country's contribution to NATO, and mentioned that the outgoing government in The Hague considered,

a) Doubling the defence budget for 1951 to the amount of NLG 1,500 million ($ 394,7 million)[123]
b) Extending the training period to 24 months for all military forces
c) Using all available manpower, not only fresh recruits but also the greater part of the conscripts who had returned from the Dutch Indies
d) Cutting back on consumption, and thus on living standards, for the entire population, on an equitable basis.

Most of these ideas were Stikker's, who in his capacity of *informateur* was entrusted with the task of investigating the possibility of forming a new cabinet. Stikker's nomination for this position was telling: as an outspoken advocate of defence reforms, he was held to be the ideal person to pave the way for a new policy direction. If accepted, the plan would bring about a fundamental change in national defence policy. It was certainly not a programme on which any political party could expect to become very popular; it was calculated that, for instance, the purchasing power of wage earners would go down by 5%. The Labour party in particular, would run a heavy risk in the area of defending social security, if it accepted the programme.

---

[123] This amount was also mentioned in a special advisory report published in January by the Central Economic Committee, consisting of top civil servants, under the chairmanship of the influential Spierenburg. J.W.L. Brouwer, 'Om de beheersing van de defensieuitgaven', *Politieke Opstellen* CPG/KUN 10 (1990) p. 103.

At the same time, Dutch officials supplied the United States with background information on their defence organisation. On certain points this information deliberately distorted the existing situation, because The Hague wanted the US government to see the country from its best side. It was stated that:

a) All able-bodied men on reaching the age of nineteen were called up for military service. The Netherlands, with a population of over ten million [10,264 million in 1951, JvdH], annually selected 50,000 of the 80,000 men available for military service (20% were declared unfit on medical grounds, 8% were not examined due to holding ecclesiastical office, another 8% were exempted on legal grounds, and 2% because of deferment). Of the selected conscripts, 81% were incorporated into the army, 10% into the air force and 9% into the navy. The duration of service in peacetime as prescribed by law was 12 months for regular conscripts, 18-24 months for technical service in the army and 21 months for the navy.

b) No additional legislation was required for extending the conscription period from one to two years.

c) The defence share of the total budget over the previous years had been as follows:
   - 1948: 19.2% (including the task force in Indonesia; excluding Indonesia: 17%), 5.9% of Nat. Income
   - 1949: 23.8% (including Indonesia; excluding: 20%), 6.1% of N.I.
   - 1950: 27,3% (including Indonesia; excluding: 18%), 6.9% of N.I.
   - 1951: 23.0% (end of involvement in Indonesia), about 10% of N.I.

d) In 1950, the number of training camps had been increased by 100%. In the same year 1200 new instructors had been trained and another 1000 would be added in 1951.

e) Since 1947, the number of professional Air Force personnel had been increased by 700%. Airfields had been constructed or enlarged at the following rate: 6 in 1948, 17 in 1949, 22 in 1950.

f) All army corps were retrained in the use of US equipment.

g) At the defence ministers' conference held in Washington in October 1950, the target for the country's contribution to the Western European armed forces was set at three divisions to be ready by the end of 1951, and five divisions by the end of 1954. In addition to those three divisions, the required territorial troops (27 battalions) and national reserves (15,000 soldiers) would be ready for mobilisation by the end of 1951.

h) The hundred or so troops that had served in the Dutch Indies would be recalled to active service, to be trained for European warfare.[124]

It is doubtful whether the American authorities took this information seriously, because the figures presented were overly optimistic. For example, the formation of divisions was hampered as a result of deferment of the 1950-1 draft and a delay in the training of Indonesia repatriates.

On 15 March, when the new - second - Drees cabinet was formed, initially there seemed to be some continuity with the previous one: the composition of the coalition government was similar to the former Drees cabinet, consisting of KVP (Catholic party), PvdA (Labour party), CHU (Protestant party) and VVD (Liberal-conservative Party). Besides Drees, who was reinstated as Prime Minister, the influential Lieftinck returned as Minister of Finance, and Stikker as Minister of Foreign Affairs. A new face was Cornelis Staf[125] (CHU), who succeeded 's Jacob as Defence Minister. Although his war record was not irreproachable - as in the case of Hasselman - Staf was given the job because he was admired universally as an outstanding organiser, a quality that was needed to deal with the chaotic situation the army found itself in.

Notwithstanding such continuity and the return of many old faces, the new government acted rapidly. On 17 March, Prime Minister

---

[124] MinBZ, 921.10 NATO inv. nr. 67, Nota Slotemaker de Bruïne, 02-01-1951.

[125] C. Staf, Minister of Defence, 1951-1959.

Drees announced a programme which was to include an eighteen-month period of military service, a definite commitment to the creation of five divisions - by means of a special Indonesia veterans project - and, above all, the provision of an extra two billion guilders (4 x NLG 500 million) for defence over the next four years (1951-54). The new defence budget now totalled about NLG 1,500 million a year - as the embassy in Washington had announced on 1 February. The money was to be divided as follows:

Original budget		After the government declaration (in mlns of guilders)					
						Total	Total
	1951	1951	1952	1953	1954	1951-54	1945-50
Navy	325	320	325	325	325	1,295	1,400
Army	325	908	887	872	776	3,443	900
Air Force	150	203	292	317	278	1,090	300
	800	1,431	1,504	1,514	1,379	5,828	2,600

Source: MinBZ, DMA 01 inv. nr. 2 doos 1, Regeringsnota over defensiepolitiek, 02-01-1951

Although the figures were open to modifications in the ensuing four years, the tone was set; the Netherlands had finally committed itself. For the first time, the government had come with a multi-annual instead of an annual budget. On the one hand, this had negative consequences for the regulatory powers of the national parliament;[126] on the other hand, it increased the independence of the military in developing their programmes. The enormous increase in the army budget was particularly remarkable. A substantial part of the extra money was meant for building up the domestic defence industry, which was still in its infancy at that time. With the new defence programme the government had taken a drastic step, especially at a time of serious difficulties in its balance of payments

---

[126] Th.J.G. van der Hoogen, *De besluitvorming over de defensiebegroting. Systeem en verandering* (Leeuwarden 1987), p. 57.

caused by the steep rise in raw material prices after the start of the Korean War. The extra NLG 500 million a year was going to be financed by government loans (of NLG 100 million), a tax increase (NLG 250 million), and a retrenchment of public expenditure/investments (NLG 150 million), the latter being mainly at the expense of the country's house-building programme. It was clear that the state of full employment extant at the start of the new defence programme would come under serious threat. The social-democrat ministers Drees and Lieftinck had been forced to considerable concessions, sacrificing efficiency for a massive army development programme. The fact that Lieftinck finally took responsibility for this decision has been explained by the need for dollar aid (promised by Washington as a *quid pro quo* for the budget increase) to improve the country's fragile budgetary position. Lieftinck further anticipated that the army would be unable to commit the entire amount of allocated funds over the four-year period, and the resulting creation of a reservoir of non-depleted sums was expected to have a welcome, deflationary effect on the country' s finances.[127]

The new policy was perfectly in accordance with the demands General Eisenhower had made in January. On 21 March, Secretary of State Acheson commented on 'the very heartening action' the Dutch cabinet had undertaken.[128] It was thought that Holland would finally be able to meet the requirements set by NATO's Medium Term Defence Plan (MTDP). The new defence budgets of the NATO member countries were as follows:

---

[127] C.M. Megens, *American aid to NATO allies in the 1950s. The Dutch Case* (Groningen 1994) pp. 111-112. In later years, Lieftinck's assumptions turned out to have been right: in 1954, it was calculated that, on a total of NLG 6 billion, a reservoir of 1 billion had remained unspent. Brouwer, 'Om de doelmatigheid van de defensieuitgaven', p. 91; see also Appendix I.

[128] Ibid., Press statement by Acheson, 03-21-1951.

	1951	1951
	(originally)	(after Eisenhower's visit)
	(as percentage of GNP)	
Belg.	3.8	4.3
Lux.	NA	3.3
Den.	2.5	3.0
Fr.	9.7	9.7
It.	6.4	6.4
Neth.	*5.0*	*7.6*
Norw.	4.5	5.0
Port.	NA	2.5
Can.	6.3	8.8
U.K.	8.0	8.7
U.S.	NA	15.0

Source: FRUS 1951 Vol. 3 (1), Memorandum from Cabot to Acheson, 03-27-1951, 104.

By March 1951, and not sooner, the Netherlands became a faithful and reliable member of the Atlantic alliance: after a long period of qualms and hesitations, the government decided to comply with allied demands. The armed forces were finally allowed to execute their plans, and the long-awaited development of the domestic defence industry received serious impetus. The country's strategic problems were not yet solved, however: these were to remain until 1955, the year that Germany entered the North Atlantic pact. It was only then that the Netherlands was finally assured of an allied commitment to the defence of the entire territory.

Field-Marshal Montgomery, who visited the Netherlands early in April, said that he was happy with both the new army plans and the budget increase, but he worried about the lack of a professional core in the army divisions. He urged the military not to rely on conscripts and reserves but to augment the number of regular personnel, particularly for the three divisions of late 1951.[129]

---

[129] MinAZ, Raad MAK, Notulen 04-06-1951.

One of the first concrete results emanating from the new defence budget was the announcement of a development programme for the Air Force, which was set to become an independent service by 1953. This programme, somewhat less ambitious than the cabinet-approved plan of March 1949, was introduced in the *Raad MAK* by Major-General Aler, the chief of the air force staff. Aler stressed the distinction between air defence and tactical air forces: the latter - because of their direct link with land forces - were mobile, in contrast to the static air defence units. The Northern Tactical Air Force (TAF), including the Dutch tactical squadrons, was meant to give air support to the entire northern army on the ground, including Dutch army divisions. As a rule, tactical air squadrons amounted to three times the number of army divisions they supported. Aler indicated that the targeted number of five army divisions thus required a corresponding contribution of fifteen squadrons to TAF. This target proved difficult to achieve, however. The new plan estimated that by 1954, only 40% of the required TAF contribution would have been realised. As far as air defence was concerned, the plan described a commitment of 60% of what had been deemed necessary in the 1949 programme. The *Raad MAK* decided that the Netherlands should confine itself to only 40% of the resultant 60% of the required strength, especially because, during MTDP's first phase (up to 1954), the country could be a potential battleground - and in that event, air defence and tactical air forces would supplement one another.

It was eventually decided that the total Dutch contribution would be fixed at 374 aeroplanes by the year 1957, to be divided as follows:

9 squadrons of day-fighters
6 squadrons of night-fighters
6 squadrons of tactical fighters
1 transport squadron
2 reconnaissance squadrons.

This was no real improvement in comparison with the 320 planes mentioned in the original plan because these had been scheduled to be ready by 1955. Nevertheless, it was another sign that the Netherlands was no longer postponing concrete action.

Beyond these types of aircraft, the Air Force planned the formation of four A.O.P. (artillery observation plane) squadrons with 18 vehicles per squadron, i.e. 72 aircraft. It was expected that the tactical, transport, reconnaissance and A.O.P. squadrons could be realised through deliveries from MDAP.

A substantial amount of money was reserved and appropriated for the construction and extension of airfields, in line with Eisenhower's recommendations during his visit to The Hague. For some time, US authorities had even made the allocation of military assistance to Western Europe conditional on the availability of military base rights on the continent. The assumption was that in the first phase of the war, the transfer of ground forces from the other side of the Atlantic would present many difficulties, whereas US air force units could be launched at all times - and these units needed strategically located runways. The new government plan asked for the construction of thirteen airfields, most of which were already in operation, although mainly for civil purposes. Three of the military airfields were situated north/east of the Rhine-Yssel line (Eelde, Leeuwarden, Twente); of the ten airfields located west of the line, three were eminently suited for air defence tasks (Ypenburg, Valkenburg and Schiphol). The plan provided for two new airfields, Deelen and Woensdrecht. Geographical spreading was needed because Dutch airfields lacked camouflage, and the possibility of dispersal on and around the fields was extremely limited. It was thought that further decentralisation of the country's air defence would help to thwart hostile action.

The *Raad MAK* agreed to the revised air force plan on the condition that it respected the financial limits of the NLG 1.5 billion budget.[130]

On 21 April, during a *Raad* discussion on the army's personnel policy, Defence Minister Staf suggested utilising the annually

---

[130] Ibidem.

available manpower to the fullest extent, in line with Eisenhower's recommendations in January. It was estimated that from 1952, an annual force of 40,000 men - divided into three rather than two drafts - would complete military training (this concerned only the army). Starting from a term of conscription of twenty months (the official term at that time was still eighteen months), this would result in a permanent strength of about 53,000 men (as compared with 30,000 in July 1950). In Staf's view, substantial investments were needed for the construction of barracks and training camps because the majority of the conscripts would be trained on national territory; only 6,000 men were considered for training and stationing in Germany. Finance Minister Lieftinck wondered whether Staf's plan could be kept within the agreed budgetary limits, because the Defence Minister had also referred to an increase of 25% in the corps of regular officers and non-commissioned officers (in absolute terms, 500 officers and 3,000 NCOs). Lieftinck thought this too ambitious for a military organisation in peacetime; he also preferred having a short tenure of six years for regulars.[131]

The incorporation of Indonesia veterans in the Dutch army was accompanied by many problems. The original intention was to draft the repatriates into two divisions. At the end of April the so-called 'Crescendo-manoeuvre' was held in the province of Gelderland, an exercise meant to acquaint former Indonesia soldiers with the methods of mobile warfare along American lines using modern weaponry. However, the manoeuvres ended in total failure: the press reported that small groups of Indonesia reservists had 'detached themselves from their units, ranged the heath, molested men and women and committed burglary in farmhouses and villages'. Minister Staf was 'greatly disappointed' with this fiasco.[132] Former General Kruls's objections to the inclusion of Indonesia veterans in

---

[131] Ibid., Notulen 04-21-1951.

[132] PAAA Bonn, 230-00/53, Brief DuMont, 05-10-1951. This assessment was not shared by the *Sectie Militaire Geschiedenis*, which has written that the military manoeuvres in Gelderland were rather successful. *1 Divisie '7 December', 1946-1986*, Sectie Militaire Geschiedenis (ed.) Amsterdam 1986.

the national army now appeared to have had a substratum of truth. Home defence posed very different needs from counterinsurgency warfare in terms of organisation, equipment and training.

During the entire year of 1951, the US government urged the Western European countries to keep giving priority to rearmament over economic advancement, but in Europe this was not taken as binding. By June 1951, countries began to slow down armaments commitments they had entered into earlier that year. The actual course of fighting in the Korean War had an important impact on the efforts they made. In January the Chinese army had advanced far into South Korea, whereas in April the front-line coincided again with the 38th degree of latitude as if nothing had happened. Furthermore, post-Korea rearmament had caused a steep rise in the prices of imported raw materials with a corresponding slower rise in manufactured exports thus creating acute budgetary deficits in various NATO countries. Concomitant with the balance of payments crisis was a renewed increase in inflation that affected the prices of raw materials and foodstuffs. This induced the governments to a further reduction in investment and expenditure on civilian consumption, if only to finance rearmament. These economic repercussions created substantial domestic problems, for example in Great Britain, where the government had committed itself to extensive social welfare programmes, which were now threatened by arms expenditure. But the Netherlands, too, feared the adverse impact of defence spending on its social security and public housing system.

At the *Raad MAK* meeting of 8 June, Stikker pointed to political instability in France, West Germany and particularly Italy, where the outcome of recent elections were, in his view, a ground for pessimism, in that the communist PCI had again gained ground. During a conversation with Hoffman, US official and ECA[133] administrator, Stikker said that Western European rearmament had

---

[133] The European Co-operation Administration (ECA) aimed at providing policy guidance to secure a proper balance between economic recovery and the military assistance programme.

'practically come to a standstill, except for substantial British efforts'. Stikker felt that the United States considered international political dangers more acute than the European governments; in Washington, allowance was made for eventualities in 1952. According to Stikker, the 'level-headed' Frenchman Parodi - permanent under-secretary at the *Quai d'Orsay* - was of the same opinion.

Priorities diverged: the main problem for the United States was the immediate threat to collective security posed by the Soviet Union, whereas Western Europe's main problem was the immediate threat to the standard of living. Stikker analysed that the position of the Truman administration vis-à-vis Congress had become more difficult, also because of the declining prestige of Secretary of State Acheson. The Foreign Minister threatened that a negative outcome of deliberations in Congress on assistance to Western Europe would jeopardise Western European defence activities even more.[134]

On 11 June, during another visit to the Netherlands, Montgomery said that NATO strove for a state of maximum military preparedness by 1954. In the meantime, the year 1952 was 'critical', because German rearmament would then become visible (depending on progress made in the EDC negotiations), and the Soviet government would have to decide on whether or not to launch an attack against the West. For this reason, Montgomery advocated the build-up of standing divisions in Europe. The Netherlands was urged to call up one conscript division, one reserve division (for a period of one month), corps headquarters, and the accompanying tactical air forces by autumn 1952. Montgomery consoled Dutch army officials by saying that they were better off than their Belgian counterparts who were expected to supply three divisions in the same period of time. Montgomery needed the divisions ready for combined manoeuvres in the western zone of Germany, to be held in September 1952. To realise this, he urged the government to extend the term of conscription from eighteen to twenty months. Staf promised

---

[134] MinAZ, Raad MAK, Notulen 06-08-1951.

Montgomery his support, but only if the US managed a timely delivery of the required equipment.[135]

Indeed, on 23 June, in line with Montgomery's suggestions, Staf pressed the *Raad MAK* to call up drafts for a training period of twenty months. He said that a speed-up of the defence plan was possible because of good prospects of US equipment deliveries. Lieftinck and Drees regarded the announcement of the critical date of 1 September 1952 as an unwelcome means to deliver pressure by the allies to enforce the required speed-up, and they objected to Staf's rushed job. It was not the only time that they criticised the Defence Minister for being too eager to comply with international requirements. Staf, supported by Stikker, replied that considering the international situation, it certainly made sense to realise two combat-ready divisions by September 1952, rather than stick to the original defence plan whose implementation required many more years.[136]

Ten days later, the Cabinet decided to accede to Montgomery's demands by prolonging the term of service from eighteen to twenty months for all conscripts from 1951 onwards. Furthermore, one division of Indonesia veterans would be temporarily called back into active service, for participation in allied manoeuvres. This division, equipped with Canadian weapons, was declared available by July 1951. It was also decided to improve the quality of accommodation for troops stationed on national territory.

At Montgomery's request, the Dutch army participated in NATO's September manoeuvres with one active division and one reserve division, plus corps headquarters, corps troops[137] and four squadrons of tactical fighters. The government proudly told US authorities that in September 1952, due to a programmed acceleration, the Dutch army would reach a state of readiness that had been previously targeted for the summer of 1953. At the same time, the US

---

[135] ARA, MR, Bijlagen 469, Nota De Savornin Lohman, 06-11-1951.

[136] MinAZ, Raad MAK, Notulen 06-23-1951.

[137] An army corps associates army units at a higher level. Army corps troops reinforce infantry divisions with additional forces like artillery units and tank battalions.

government was given to understand that the gain of almost a year could be realised only through a substantial increase in US end-item deliveries.[138]

The Hague's continuous begging for support obviously inspired irritation in the United States. Disagreement on this score was a vicious circle: the Netherlands waited for US assistance to build up the army, while the US made such assistance conditional on Dutch willingness to make additional efforts, both financially and in terms of manpower. Several times they urged the Dutch government to overstep the NLG 1,500 million ceiling and look for additional funds (about NLG 500 million a year) to improve the country's defence situation. As for manpower, General Gruenther condemned the poor strength of army corps troops in the Netherlands, and also felt that public opinion should be better informed of national and allied defence plans.

At that time, Hasselman, army chief of staff, announced an increase in the number of regular officers from 2,300 to 3,000[139], as a result of the return of KNIL officers from Indonesia.

Meanwhile, military consultations within the Benelux continued to take place, though the staff committee discussions were generally dull and unproductive. In June 1951, Staf proposed to breathe new life into the secret military agreement of 1948 (see 1.1), particularly for the benefit of exchanging military trainees. The fact that this initiative soon fell flat was another sign that the staff committee was less influential than some had hoped for.

One of the few interesting notes presented by the staff committee concerned a joint Belgian-Dutch analysis of Soviet strategy and of hostile paratroopers and fifth column elements in the two countries. It was expected that in the event of an attack on the northern ring of the Rhine defence, the Soviets would combine a concentric advance of ground troops with the launching of airborne troops behind the Rhine-Yssel defence. It was estimated that the Soviet Union had at

---

[138] MinBZ, DMA inv. nr. 27, Addendum to the Netherlands Aide-Memoir dated 18 June 1951, 07-07-1951.
[139] MinDef, archief Legerraad (zeer geheim), Notulen 07-14-1951.

most ten airborne divisions (at about 7,000 men each) at its disposal; their usability was presumed to be limited because of the proportionately low number of available transport planes in the Soviet Union - estimated at only 1,000 to 1,200. The Russian transfer capacity was therefore rated at just two airborne divisions in one lift. The Dutch military thought it essential to strengthen the Yssel defence to prevent Soviet ground troops from meeting and supporting their airborne colleagues.

As far as fifth column activity was concerned, the staff committee estimated the number of militant communists in the Netherlands at 10,000. Revolutionary elements were for the greater part situated in Amsterdam and its environs, and in Twente[140]. It was assumed that the communists still possessed a considerable stockpile of weapons originating from the occupation period. Although their organisation was not considered subversive, 10,000 militant communists were supposed to be capable of committing a great deal of sabotage. [141]

As far as the Soviet threat was concerned, The Hague obviously thought in terms of a conventional attack on national territory. The possibility of a nuclear strike was excluded because, in the government's view, there were no military targets in the country that could provoke the Soviet Union to use the atomic bomb.[142] This perception soon changed when the government started to become aware of the vulnerability of the port of Rotterdam to hostile aggression (see 2.4 and 2.5).

At the North Atlantic council meeting in Rome, in November, considerable attention was paid to Soviet strategic intentions. General Gruenther analysed military capabilities on both sides of the Iron Curtain, saying that the West was still unable to counter the

---

[140] The region of Twente in the province of Overijssel was a communist stronghold because of the presence of a large amount of low-paid workers in the textile industry.

[141] Ibid., Belg./Ned. Militaire samenwerking, Benelux Stafcommissie doosnr. 2, uit: bundel correspondentie 1951, Ontwerp samengestelde Belgisch-Ned. analyse betreffende het optreden van vijandelijke parachutisten en vijfde colonne, 06-19-1951.

[142] PAAA Bonn, 230-00/53, Brief Du Mont, 07-10-1951.

enormous presence of Soviet conventional forces, and that in the short run the maximum achievable aim was to inflict losses on hostile communication lines in the hinterland. In the longer run, the General expected a substantial amelioration of the western position. Stikker was more pessimistic: his interpretation of the term *pax sovietica* was that the Soviets regarded politics as war by other means and that their 'peace campaign', particularly aiming at the reunification of Germany, was a 'real act of war in the Soviet sense of the word'.[143] He assumed that the Soviet army had the capacity to fight a large-scale war in different areas at the same time. On the other hand, it was Acheson who illustrated Soviet tactics by saying: 'Why cut a man's throat if you can poison his soup?'[144], referring to the strong position of communist parties in certain Western European countries.

Concerning allied strategy, the Dutch feared that the *French* military preferred setting up a rampart consisting of France and North Africa, from where the West would be defended. Dutch army authorities viewed the French doctrine as potentially deleterious to their national security, and in 1952 it was discovered that there was an element of truth in this (see 2.4).

The government was also highly uncertain about *British* strategic conceptions. The assumption was that in terms of air defence the British had a special interest in moving their continental airbases further east because of the advantage in intercepting hostile aircraft far away from their home country. Concerning their army however, The Hague feared that in a war situation British troops on the continent would beat a hasty retreat back home, partly over Dutch territory. Although British soldiers were supposed to defend a crucial sector of the northern Rhine front, The Hague seriously doubted British willingness to fight to the end. In that respect, Paris and The Hague found themselves following the same line of thinking.

---

[143] FRUS 1951 Vol. 3 (1), Telegram US delegation at the seventh session of the North Atlantic council, 09-17-1951, p. 665. Stikker referred here to the Stalin-notes of March and April 1952, which aimed at reunifying Germany on a neutralist basis.
[144] MinAZ, Raad MAK, Notulen 12-01-1951.

According to Dutch assessments, the *German* military wished to move their land defence in an easterly direction, as far as the river Elbe. From later research we know that this was indeed true.[145] German strategists thought in terms of an offensive defence with rapid, relatively small and highly mobile armoured divisions. In case of a retreat, they would attempt to attack the enemy in the flank in order to curb or even cut off the hostile advance. From a German strategic standpoint, the enemy would attack from the east westward, with large concentrations of men and equipment, and the offensive would be directed towards the geographically most suitable and historically most utilised areas, north and north-east of France. The Germans felt that the West should try to hold the flanks as long as possible, therefore, key positions needed to be retained north of the North German lowlands and north of the Alps. In the Netherlands it was thought that the German strategy served Dutch interests most, more than French or British doctrines, but that such a strategy was only realisable with a real German military contribution, and a declared allied commitment to forward strategy.[146]

Dutch military doctrine seemed similar to the German, but it differed in one important respect: the Dutch military preferred to concentrate the allied force in the centre and to have mobile parts on the flanks, as far to the east as possible.[147] Germany, of course, feared that focusing on the centre would be devastating for its own country and population, and therefore emphasised the flank defence.

The government kept pressing for a direct German involvement in NATO on a non-discriminatory basis. In September 1951, the ambassador to Washington, De Beus, said:

---

[145] W. Meier-Dörnberg, 'Politische and militärische Faktoren bei der Planung des deutschen Verteidigungsbeitrages im Rahmen der EVG'. In: Militärgeschichtliches Forschungsamt (ed.), *Die EVG. Stand und Probleme der Forschung* (Boppard am Rhein 1985) pp. 287-288.

[146] ARA, MR, Bijlagen 470, Nota Min.Buza, 08-20-1951, pp. 6-7.

[147] ARA, MR, Verslag over de studieconferentie voor het Europese leger, 08-13-1951.

The Dutch have no deep love for the Germans, but consider that there is no choice in the matter of German rearmament. Since the Germans must rearm, they must be given a sense of equality in their participation, and the occupying powers should go as far as possible in dropping controls in order to enlist German co-operation.

On the issue of a military arrangement with Germany, De Beus said:

The Federal Republic should be admitted to NATO in the not too distant future; it would then have a security guarantee and would be prevented from making any agreement contrary to the North Atlantic treaty. (...) At present, Germany is protected by the provision in the treaty which declares an attack on the occupation forces to be an attack on the signatory powers, and by the statement of the Foreign Ministers, made in September 1950, that an attack on the Federal Republic would be treated as an attack on the three occupying powers. These safeguards would be formalised by membership in NATO.[148]

However, at least in the short term, French support for these ideas was not to be expected.

2.3 The McNarney plan

During the second half of 1951 the tone in US-Dutch relations changed radically. Compared to the heated disputes of late 1950/early 1951, Washington moderated its criticism after the fixing of the defence ceiling in March 1951. From then onwards, discussion centred on military assistance deliveries, the requirement of end-items and the composition of troop lists, but 'never again would the Netherlands be pilloried in public as it had been in January 1951'.[149]

This is not to say that bilateral problems had suddenly vanished. Perhaps the most contentious issue between Washington and The Hague concerned the build-up of combat-ready divisions. Early readiness was deemed necessary to facilitate a strong defence east of

---

[148] FRUS 1951 Vol. 3 (2), Memorandum of Conversation, Contractual arrangements with Germany, 09-11-1951, pp. 1219 and 1221.
[149] Megens, *American aid to NATO allies*, p. 115.

the river Rhine. For that matter, the US proposed a serious adaptation of the military obligations embodied in NATO document DC 28 (dating from October 1950), which stipulated that on D-day, that is the first day of the war, total Western European army strength should amount to 49 1/3 divisions; on D-day +30, that is, after a lapse of thirty days from the start of the war, the required total strength was to amount to 78 1/3 divisions; and on D-day +90, 95 1/3 divisions needed to join. According to DC 28, the total Dutch contribution was to consist of 5 divisions, by 1 July 1954. One of these divisions was scheduled to be under arms at D-day - a so-called combat-ready division - and another would be ready within three days, so that this division was also considered as available at D-day. The other three divisions were basically reserve divisions, which could be mobilised only after a long period.

For Washington, the DC 28 targets were unsatisfactory because they failed to provide military readiness at an early stage. What the Americans wanted from the Netherlands, and the other countries, was to prioritise the change from reserve divisions to combat-ready ones, to improve the chances of implementing a forward strategy. Although in principle The Hague strongly favoured this idea, it was reluctant to face the implied necessity of reforming its traditional army development plans.[150] For the rest of 1951 and the first half of 1952, this issue was to lead to serious bilateral friction.

Also, the money problem was still not entirely solved. In October 1951, during hearings on the Mutual Security programme for the year 1952 in the US House of Representatives, General Olmsted[151] gave an account of the state of Dutch defence. Olmsted started by saying that 'morale in the Netherlands had been building up notably and that the Dutch were pretty well on schedule' as far as the manning and training of forces for NATO was concerned. Manpower on active duty in Europe (calculated at 9.7 per thousand of population) was above pre-war figures for all armed forces, including

---

[150] MinBZ, DMA 01 inv. nr. 2 doos 1, Nota Van der Esch, 09-08-1951.

[151] G.H. Olmsted, head of the Office of Military Assistance at the Ministry of Defence in Washington.

troops and naval units in Indonesia. The General was less satisfied with the country's financial efforts, and urged an increase in the defence budget to $525 million (around NLG 2 billion). Olmsted said that there had been recent indications that the Netherlands would meet commitments, 'but it could and should support greater forces than these commitments now represent'. He added that Dutch army strength on 1 June 1951 represented the equivalent of two regimental combat teams, which was only two-thirds of a division.[152] Apparently, he had no high expectations of the infantry division consisting of Indonesia repatriates, declared available in July 1951.

Foreign Minister Stikker was vexed regarding the $525 million sum Olmsted had mentioned during the hearings in Congress. In a letter to US Under-Secretary Foster, Stikker wrote that this amount did not correspond to what his government had decided to spend annually (viz. NLG 1.5 billion), and he thought it regrettable that such figures were circulating without the slightest consultation with the Dutch government. He worried that the work done by NATO's Temporary Council Committee (TCC)[153] would be unduly influenced by Olmsted's public statement. It was the TCC's task to reconcile the requirements of collective security with the political and economic capabilities of the member countries.[154]

On 5 November, Hirschfeld, the government commissioner,[155] headed a delegation that discussed the problems related to another increase in the defence budget during a meeting with US General McNarney at TCC's executive bureau in Paris.[156] As far as military aspects were concerned, McNarney sharply criticised the Dutch

---

[152] MinBuZa, DMA 01 inv. nr. 2 doos 1, Hearings before a subcommittee of the Committee on appropriations - House of Representatives - 82nd Congress - First session on Mutual Security Program - Appropriation for 1952, 10-16-1951.

[153] Ibid., Brief Stikker aan Foster, 10-18-1951.

[154] TCC was founded at the Ottawa meeting of the North Atlantic Council in September 1951. The 'Three Wise Men' Plowden, Harriman and Monnet functioned as its executive board.

[155] In charge of the distribution of economic and military aid in the Netherlands.

[156] J.T. McNarney, head of a TCC working group dealing with the military-organisational aspects of the European defence efforts.

system of army organisation, and particularly the arrears in the recruitment of regular servicemen. Hirschfeld replied that the Netherlands had recently extended the number of regular officers from 2,300 to 3,000, which brought the total number of regular personnel up to 9,000 men, but in McNarney's view this was not enough; he asked for 20,000 professional soldiers. What the American general wanted from the Netherlands was the creation of three D-day divisions at 75 percent combat-ready strength, instead of one division at 100 percent strength. The remaining 25 percent was to be made up of reservists. Likewise, the active core of the other two divisions needed to be expanded.

In more detail, the McNarney plan entailed:

a) Building up corps troops and divisions simultaneously.

b) Changing the system of drafting recruits, in line with the so-called 'J-system' (filler system): every two months 1/6 of the annual draft was to be called up, instead of 1/3 every four months.

c) Creating 'divisional slice' - the manpower needed to support effective fighting divisions - at full strength (with 'slice', a division comprised 36,000 men instead of 18,000).

d) Increasing effectiveness by means of a permanent presence of the core (50-75%) of divisions.

This system had two advantages: firstly, in accordance with American preferences, more units could be mobilised at short notice, and secondly, the first active division would be ready by 1952 instead of 1954.[157] To underline the need for all this, McNarney threatened to limit the delivery of US equipment to only those units that were, according to American standards, well trained and organised.[158]

For the Netherlands, this seemed to be an impossible task. In the *Legerraad* (army council), Staf said that the Netherlands had only

---

[157] J.W. Honig, *Defense Policy in the North Atlantic Alliance: the case of the Netherlands* (Westport 1993) p. 34.

[158] Ibid., Code telegram Hirschfeld, 11-06-1951; idem, Verslag van de bespreking op het 'executive bureau' van de TCC, 11-08-1951.

one division that fully met McNarney's D-day requirements. Initially, the Defence Minister had hoped that the Dutch D + 3 division would be considered a ready division (in line with the criteria of DC 28), but McNarney had classified this division as only D + 15. The *Raad MAK* worried that McNarney advocated a system of army formation substantially different from the original 5-division plan. Staf thought it essential to adhere to the original plan, even if part of the five divisions was to remain excluded from material support. He said it was impossible to realise McNarney's proposal within the budget limit of NLG 1.5 billion, and pointed out that the Netherlands was unable to train 20,000 regulars - as McNarney had suggested - because of the shortage of camps and terrain. In comparison with Belgium, the Netherlands was at a disadvantage because the Belgian army, unlike the Dutch, utilised bases in Germany. Lieftinck said there was also a technical objection to increasing the number of active troops, namely differences in salary. Belgian soldiers earned 16 (Belgian) francs per day, compared to the equivalent of 10 (Belgian) francs for Dutch soldiers. Unattractive wage levels in the Netherlands hampered the enlistment of new recruits.

Hirschfeld tried to see the positive aspects of the TCC recommendations, explaining that according to McNarney's provisional calculations the implementation of MTDP required a total expenditure of $ 200 billion (covering the whole of Western Europe), including American aid to the European NATO countries. At the time there was a shortfall of $ 8 billion, accounting for just 4% of total expenditure. Based on these calculations, Hirschfeld thought it possible for the Netherlands to stick to the budget ceiling of NLG 1.5 billion. Furthermore, Hirschfeld pointed to organisational problems within NATO, particularly duplication in the activities of the Defence Production Board[159]. Rather than multilateral defence production, Hirschfeld spoke out in favour of bilateral consultations with the United States, and made a plea for

---

[159] The DPB sought to stimulate standardisation and co-operation in defence production.

upgrading the position of Eisenhower's headquarters.[160] He obviously hoped that SACEUR would be less insistent on reforming the domestic army organisation than McNarney and the TCC, and more willing to resume the delivery of US assistance.

This appeared to be a vain hope. In December 1951, in its final report, the TCC told the European allies exactly how and by what amount to increase their defence efforts. The report contained a financial and a military section, the latter based on the McNarney report. For the Netherlands, the part on finance was less exigent than General Olmsted had hinted at in October. The TCC recommendations implied an 18% increase in expenditure (NLG 1.8 billion for 1952), which was modest in comparison with the requirements for Belgium (36 percent). The government felt it was possible to reach this target by the utilisation of so-called 'counterpart funds' (the counter-value in guilders of Marshall aid received from the United States) for military purposes. Minister of Economic Affairs Van den Brink welcomed the allocation of new funds for military purposes, pointing to a contraction of activity in the civil sector, which had occurred faster than expected. At the time, the country's unemployment figure was 85,000, but Van den Brink expected this to increase over the next few years if no further action were taken. Drees and Lieftinck were more reluctant to accept another budgetary increase, but they also realised that the final outcome of the TCC's advice could have been much worse for the Netherlands. Moreover, since the country's balance of payments position had undergone a substantial improvement in the second half of 1951, it was clear that the TCC was not prepared to make special allowances for the Dutch situation.[161]

The McNarney section of the TCC report was more controversial because it reiterated the importance of increasing regular personnel and improving training facilities and organisation. Staf thought it impossible to realise the McNarney plan within the projected period because it called for a considerably higher number of regulars than

---

[160] MinAZ, Raad MAK, Notulen 12-01-1951.
[161] Ibidem.

was provided for in the original Dutch plans.[162] Apart from a lack of drill-grounds, barracks, instructors and equipment, the main objection put forward to the McNarney plan concerned the complex alternation of military units within the regimental combat team, the so-called 'filler system'.[163]

In reality, Staf's position was more flexible than would appear from the above statements, probably due to international pressure. Early in January 1952, during another *Raad MAK* discussion on the TCC report, the defence minister remarked that, notwithstanding all objections, the government's reply to McNarney should be 'constructive'. He added that by September 1952 - deemed the crucial period - two divisions needed to be under arms, one of which consisted of former Indonesia soldiers who would then be called up for retraining. Staf now shared McNarney's criticism of the weakness of corps troops in the Netherlands. The build-up of these troops should, in his view, have priority, and he felt that this was even more important than the formation of a fifth division. Staf suggested adjusting the size of the army to four divisions, in order to meet the problem of the lack of war-stores.

Drees reproached Staf for being too compliant with international demands, and objected to what he called an 'excessive increase' in regular personnel. He thought it regrettable that the required remodelling of the army would result in a decrease in the number of reservists. The McNarney report had mentioned a term of conscription of 24 months, but Drees doubted whether another extension of the service period would help to boost the morale and skills of the troops. Staf replied that the figure of 24 months had not featured in the Dutch paragraph in the McNarney report, so he presumed it would not apply to the Netherlands. He expected that a definite decision on the term of conscription would have to be taken within the framework of the European Defence Community - under discussion then in Paris. In conclusion, as far as regular personnel

---

[162] Ibidem.
[163] MinBuZa, DMA 31 inv. nr. 33 doos 6, Verslag Everts over besprekingen met Kolonel van Dun, 02-14-1952.

was concerned, Staf announced an increase of 25%, which was considerably less than McNarney had asked for. Staf also said that he would strive for a short term of enlistment of six years - as Lieftinck had proposed in April 1951.[164] This was also in line with Drees's preferences, who rejected the structural formation of a military 'caste' in Dutch society.

However, as before, external developments forced the government to adapt its position. In February 1952, the North Atlantic Council, assembled in Lisbon, passed a resolution providing for a military force of no fewer than 96 divisions, to be ready by 1954. Although this target soon appeared unattainable, the United States was pleased to see that the countries of Western Europe had bound themselves to concrete figures, so that they could no longer avoid their responsibilities. The Lisbon goals were also expected to have a positive influence on the outcome of the Congressional debates on military assistance.

In the Netherlands, the *Algemene Verdedigingsraad* (AVR, general defence council), which replaced the *Raad MAK* in May 1952,[165] announced that as a result of the approval of the McNarney report and the subsequent decisions in Lisbon, a change in the original army plan was called for. In line with the McNarney report, the AVR concluded that the Netherlands should strive for two or three immediately ready divisions at 70% strength (the remaining 30% would be ready for mobilisation within four days), instead of one ready division up to full strength. Simultaneously, the build-up of the other divisions needed to be continued. The AVR felt that the financial implications were acceptable, though it was feared that the shortage of training facilities would become untenable with the

---

[164] MinAZ, Raad MAK, Notulen 01-08-1952.

[165] The AVR was established in order to broaden the field of activity of the former *Raad MAK*. Apart from problems with a specific military character, the AVR occupied itself with civil defence and defence preparation in general. In practice, however, the AVR appeared to be much less powerful and influential than the *Raad MAK*. Most of the important military problems were dealt with by cabinet, and no longer by the sub-council. It seemed as if from then on the government preferred to exclude the military from the decision-making process.

influx of an extra 6,000 men a year for military training.[166] During the same meeting a note was circulated concerning the build-up of a professional cadre within the army and air force. The government expected that by the end of 1954, 20% of that cadre would consist of regulars. As far as finances were concerned, the note stated that as a result of increasing expenditure on social security, the Netherlands had almost reached the stage where regular personnel was becoming less costly than conscripts and reserve personnel. The number of regulars had increased substantially in the preceding years, as the following figures show:

Regular personnel army			
	Present 1/1/50	1/3/52	Increase in %
Officers	1,468	2,650	80
Non-commissioned officers	3,907	8,690	123
Corporals and ratings	1,211	4,850	300
Regular personnel air force			
	Present 1/1/50	1/3/52	Increase in %
Officers	225	640	190
Non-commissioned officers	298	2,140	614
Corporals and soldiers	243	3,300	1,223

Source: MinBuZa, DMA, AVR, Notulen 05-30-1952

In June 1952, after long and heated discussions, the Netherlands assented by and large to the terms of the McNarney plan. Further resistance was thought to be counterproductive. It was also realised that McNarney's 'J-system' (filler system) would, if necessary, be

---

[166] MinBuZa, DMA, AVR, Notulen 05-30-1952.

transferred to the framework of the EDC (the EDC treaty had just been signed on 27 May 1952).[167]

Once again, the government had, after initial opposition, fallen in with American desires. In return, Washington promised a speeding up of deliveries of economic and military aid to the Netherlands.

2.4 Opposition to the French fortress strategy

In June 1952 the General Staff was informed of NATO's priority scheme for combat units entailing the following elements:

a) First priority: units charged with countering a first assault by the Soviet Union, whether over water or land or through the air

b) Second priority: units meant for the immediate reinforcement of the first priority units, and units for the remainder of tasks to accomplish NATO objectives

c) Third priority: other NATO forces not covered by the above priorities.

The priority scheme was used as a guideline for the distribution of military aid among the NATO countries. Dutch objections to this priority system were twofold. First, as the General Staff argued, the troops that were lined up on D (start of the war) +15 and D +30 (for example, the two Dutch reserve divisions) should have a higher priority than the units which on D +15 and D +30 were ready for shipment to the theatre of operations (for example American divisions in the United States and French divisions in North Africa). According to the GS, the former units should be given first priority status instead of second. Second, air force authorities urged first priority for ground troops (home defence forces) charged with defending airfields. Likewise, the Navy desired first priority status for aircraft used for the protection of harbours against mines and submarines. At that stage, the ground troops and planes were still considered only of second priority, but the GS demanded a higher

---

[167] MinDef, archief Legerraad (zeer geheim), Notulen 06-04-1952.

status for securing deliveries of American equipment.[168] In reality, US authorities were not terribly impressed by Dutch objections to the priority scheme.

At the AVR meeting of 30 May, Minister Staf remarked that General Eisenhower took an optimistic view of the Dutch inundation plans, implying the flooding of land east of the river Yssel in the event of a Soviet attack on Western Europe. The implementation hereof (started in 1952 under strict secrecy) would make an Yssel defence much more realistic. Lieutenant-General Hasselman listed the adverse consequences of inundation: removal of the civilian population from inundated areas, problems in the supply of water to big cities and of cooling-water to industries in the west of the country, and unnavigable waterways in north-south direction. In view of these consequences, Hasselman warned that inundation plans should be executed only under the direst possible contingency because, once started, it was technically impossible to undo or reverse the flooding. NATO's supreme headquarters (SHAPE) had proposed to start inundations as soon as the Soviets crossed the demarcation line in Germany, but as long as difficulties were confined to West Berlin, there was still space for diplomatic consultation. Staf said that SHAPE had responded enthusiastically to the Dutch inundation plan, and added that in the event of war SHAPE wanted to hold Holland west of the Yssel as a firm base.[169]

In the course of 1952 the Dutch government started to doubt the sincerity of these intentions. In April, at his installation as Supreme Commander of Europe, General Ridgway said that under the prevailing circumstances he would prefer to withdraw allied forces to a bridgehead - probably the river Rhine - and to launch a counterattack from that point, rather than to maintain, at any price, certain strategically exposed parts of Western Europe.[170] Suspicions increased when in the summer of 1952, NATO's Central Command

---

[168] MinBuZa, DMA 31 inv. nr. 33 doos 6, Aantekening voor Everts betreffende NATO-prioriteiten systeem voor combat units, 06-12-1952.

[169] Ibid., DMA, AVR, Notulen 05-30-1952.

[170] ARA, MR, Bijlagen 498, Nota Staf, 02-08-1954.

Europe - including the Benelux, French and British forces - was placed under the supervision of a French commander, General Juin. The government was far from pleased with Juin's appointment, fearing that the French General would seek to loosen the link between EDC and NATO, so that the latter's grip on EDC affairs would become less secure. But above all, the government surmised that in the event of Soviet aggression, Juin would concentrate on the defence of French territory, at the cost of the Netherlands.[171]

In August 1952 the government was startled by an article in the *New York Times* - written by the influential journalist Drew Middleton - on French views regarding European defence. Middleton wrote that

> French defensive concepts include a series of counter-punch battles in Germany east of the Rhine preparatory to a prolonged battle on the river line, which, in the north, would follow the line of the Rhine up to the line of the Waal in the Netherlands. This means the surrender of most of the northern Netherlands, including most of the industrialized section of the country, and of north-western Germany to the aggressor.

Middleton added that 'French planners were not interested in Britain's strategic position or the importance of the Low Countries in protecting that position'. He concluded that in the event of hostile actions, defence of the Netherlands within an allied framework was 'a questionable case'.[172]

Dutch authorities vehemently protested against the idea of creating a 'French fortress', proclaiming that they had not joined NATO and built up their forces to surrender the nation at first attack. The General Staff complained that French strategists underestimated the importance of the Ruhr and the Low Countries to the fighting strength of Western Europe. Dutch generals preferred a plan developed by their German colleague Hans Speidel, who claimed that the main battle should be fought east of the Rhine, instead of

---

[171] MinDef, EDG-archief doos 55 codetelegrammen EDG, Code telegram Van Roijen, 03-05-1953.

[172] MinBuZa, 921.13 NATO inv. nr. 71 doos 589, Artikel New York Times, 08-17-1952.

behind this river. Speidel also proposed the creation of a defence belt formed by Denmark, North-West Germany and the Netherlands, the latter being linked with Denmark by means of the Dutch inundation system. Once again, the General Staff made a plea for rearming West Germany at the earliest possible moment, and sketched a future where German troops, along with those of the Benelux and Scandinavian countries, would take up positions along the Elbe. French and British troops could then be prised out of their positions to the rear and sent forward to join in the immediate defence. These ideas remained wishful thinking, however, as long as the French government opposed German rearmament within NATO, and as long as the EDC treaty was not ratified. The Hague feared that the French fortress concept would be acceptable to Britain, the US and to NATO's General Ridgway. They suspected that the United States 'would not shed a tear if north-western Europe was trampled under the feet of the Russian hordes'. Minister Staf told SACEUR Ridgway that the Netherlands had joined NATO to repel foreign troops, not to be first overrun and liberated at a later stage. It was Staf's conviction that his country deserved allied guarantees for its defence, particularly after the enormous rise in the defence budget in March 1951. In parliament, the question arose whether Dutch citizens would continue to pay high taxes if they were not given the slightest security protection in return. Staf tried to reassure MPs, arguing that the country's considerable defence effort could not be separated from an allied commitment in the event of an invasion,[173] but he failed to succeed in allaying prevailing doubts in the country.

It was not until 19 September that Staf explained in the AVR what had actually happened during the preceding month. This was precipitated by the formation of a new cabinet following the national elections in June 1952. On 1 September, the third Drees cabinet was inaugurated, consisting of the PvdA, KVP, CHU and ARP (the latter

---

[173] Ibid., Artikel Chicago Daily Tribune, 08-26-1952; J. Barents, 'De verdedigbaarheid van Nederland', *Socialisme en Democratie* (November 1952).

party replacing the VVD in the new coalition).[174] Staf said that in the summer of 1952 NATO had drafted the ALFCE (Allied Forces Central Europe) Emergency Defence Plan, which underlined the need to maintain two firm bases, Holland and the Ardennes. Although SHAPE had accepted the original version of EDP, in August it was discovered that General Juin had arbitrarily introduced changes to the plan. In his version, only the Ardennes was to be defended as a firm base, while 'the passage through the Netherlands would be thwarted by inundations and demolitions'. The Hague wondered whether defence on the Yssel was still a serious option, given the fact that in Juin's strategic deliberations the Yssel was hardly mentioned at all. Staf remarked that the French general thought instead of a defence along the large rivers running East-West (Rhine and Waal; see Middleton's statement above). He added that these presumptions were confirmed by the way in which the commander of the northern army group, Harding, wished to line up the Dutch troops placed under his command. On several occasions - during talks with the highest NATO authorities - Staf and Hasselman raised their objections, emphasising that Yssel defence should be respected and the heart of the country should be kept as a firm bridgehead. They pointed out that in the event of a hostile breakthrough south of the large rivers, it would be of great advantage:

a) To utilise the country's airbases from which the enemy's communication lines could be harassed.

b) To refuse the enemy the use of the airbases, since the latter were eminently suitable for launching air raids and attacks with guided missiles (whether or not equipped with atomic warheads) against strategic airbases on the British islands.

c) To refuse the enemy the use of the Dutch coasts with their numerous harbours and coves which were perfectly suited for

---

[174] In the new coalition, Drees and Staf remained in office, while Beyen and Van de Kieft had taken the place of respectively Stikker and Lieftinck.

submarine bases. Capturing those bases would enable the enemy to exploit its superior submarine power.

In a letter to General Ridgway, Staf emphasised the importance of Rotterdam as a supply port. This was contrary to ALFCE, which had stated that the port of Rotterdam had little military use because of the enemy's superior air power in the region, the lack of accessibility of the port due to the presence of sea-mines, and the difficulty of defending the port and its approaches. At allied staff talks, national authorities exhausted themselves emphasising the necessity of maintaining Rotterdam as a supply port. They feared that without Rotterdam, the Yssel front would be sacrificed, and added that in the event of war, supply from southern ports (Zeebrugge in Belgium and French ports along the Channel) would be hard to realise. In their view, these ports should be considered additions to rather than substitutes for Rotterdam. During allied discussions, The Hague insisted that priorities be shifted in such a way that Rotterdam, and also Antwerp, would retain their function as supply ports.

In his reply, General Ridgway made no reference to the status of Rotterdam, but he urged the development of an alternative line of communication by land to the Channel ports. Concerning existing NATO plans for the defence of Dutch territory, Ridgway was much more reassuring:

a) I hasten to reassure you at once that I have no intention whatever of allowing Netherlands territory west of the Yssel to be overrun.

b) I am firmly determined (and so is Marshal Juin) under the EDP to defend the Rhine-Yssel line to the last. I do not countenance any thought of failure to this strategy and therefore no planning for withdrawal into national redoubts is possible.

c) Adequate deployment of Netherlands forces to cover the inundation and demolitions on the Yssel line will be planned as first priority in order that the major portion of Netherlands territory shall be secured. When this has been achieved, plans must be made to deploy a portion of the Netherlands forces for the defence of the Rhine in the Nijmegen area. This is as important to the Netherlands as it is for the defence of Western Europe as a whole.

In the conclusion to his letter, Ridgway urged the need for reflecting these views explicitly in all Emergency Defence Plans.[175]

On 11 September, in a letter to Drees, General Juin explained that EDP's objectives had been substantially changed in that the plan had been largely adapted to Dutch wishes. Drees's spokesman Fock was happy to see that the original plan had undergone 'considerable improvements', but he added that the need to introduce such improvements was cast-iron proof that the plans up to then had been unacceptable, 'notwithstanding the optimistic views of Minister Staf' - said in response to questions in parliament. Nevertheless, in Fock's view, following the reassuring report, 'the hatchet could be buried'. Staf said that the letters of Ridgway and Juin made clear that Dutch troops would be used for the defence of the Yssel, and added that for the moment there could be talk only of delaying actions east of the Rhine-Yssel line. Only the availability of German troops could put a different complexion on this problem, and Staf was pleased to see that NATO had begun to consider a defence on the river Weser in Germany.[176] That was at least a start, a forward defence on the Elbe being the ultimate objective.

Notwithstanding the letters of Juin and Ridgway, the Dutch continued to be concerned about NATO's operational plans. In September 1952, at the so-called 'ambassadors' conference' (an annual meeting of Dutch ambassadors at the Foreign Ministry in The Hague), reference was made to the existence of two operational plans: a short-term Emergency plan, which was mainly an attempt to consider what should and could be done in wartime with curtailed financial outlay; and a plan which would come into operation after

---

[175] In his memoirs Ridgway made his promises subject to one proviso: 'that we were not going to throw away any of our troops in a hopeless last-stand defense of a non-defensable position. Our resources in manpower were too meagre for that'. Quoted from: J.W.M. Schulten, 'Die militärische Integration aus der Sicht der Niederlande', in: MGFA (ed.), *Militärgeschichte seit 1945. Die westliche Sicherheitsgemeinschaft, 1948-1950* (Boppard am Rhein 1988) p. 92.

[176] MinBuZa, DMA, AVR, Notulen 09-19-1952.

the NATO countries had reached the peak of their military preparedness (estimated at late 1954). The Dutch complained that they did not have adequate information about their contents, and emphasised that a thorough knowledge of the plans was important not only for the morale of the troops but also for the planning of infrastructure works. It was hoped that NATO would develop into a solid community capable of giving guidance to the 'European organisation' - by which was meant the EDC.[177]

2.5 The build-up of Dutch defence, 1952-1954

In paragraph 2.3 we have seen that in February 1952 the Dutch government had agreed to the ambitious targets set at the NATO Council meeting in Lisbon, providing for a total of 96 divisions and 9,000 aircraft. However, these goals soon proved to be too optimistic and they were adjusted to 70 divisions and 7,000 aircraft. This was caused, amongst other things, by the implications of the McNarney proposals (see 2.3), which emphasised the build-up of corps troops and combat-ready units rather than reserve units, because quality and direct usability were deemed more important than additional numbers. In line with this, the third Drees cabinet - installed in the summer of 1952 - announced a new army reconstruction plan, ('plan 1952'), which abandoned the original commitments as agreed on in October 1950 in Washington (five divisions) and in December 1950 in Brussels (three divisions in corps organisation and two independent divisions). The new army reconstruction plan provided for three 'strong' divisions (including artillery units and tank battalions) in the place of five 'weak' ones. The build-up of the three divisions would occur in line with the filler system, meaning that every two months (instead of every four months) parts of the annual levy would be called up. These conscripts would receive initial training of four months (instead of eight months) and subsequently, a

---

[177] Ministerie van Financiën (MinFin), 1262/1 II Integratie algemeen; Documentatie juli 1952-september 1954, Resumé van de Ambassadeursconferentie van 3-5 sept. 1952

follow-up training programme within a divisional framework. This system made it impossible to demobilise an entire unit at once and to replace it with a new unit without any experience. Within the smallest units, servicemen would take turns individually (per soldier, instead of per regimental combat team) every sixteen months. Emphasis was laid on effective but expensive active troops, as opposed to the less effective and less costly units in the old system. The main objections to the old system were that, in some ranks, experience with war organisation was lacking, and that at the outbreak of war a third of the division would have practically no combat value.[178]

In the AVR, Staf said that the army reconstruction plan was cost-effective, and he hoped it would stimulate the delivery of weapons and equipment from abroad. Drees once again doubted the usefulness of immediately ready troops, indicating that reserve troops could also be put rapidly on a war footing. Staf replied that the combat-ready forces formed only one-fifth of total strength; reserve troops continued to be of utmost importance, also in the new configuration.[179]

It was not the first time that Staf and Drees held different views on the country's defence organisation. Drees suspected his Defence Minister of being too inclined to respect NATO obligations whereas, in his view, it was impossible to assess these obligations in an objective manner. He also felt that Staf sometimes deliberately exaggerated the pressure exerted by the US and NATO, and the acuteness of international tensions to gain support for his policy. Criticising the Defence Minister, Drees pointed to three factors to illustrate the difficulties surrounding domestic defence: continuing uncertainty and delays on the score of a German military contribution, the start of a long period of economic prosperity which increased the attractiveness of a civilian career, with its employment opportunities and high wages, at the expense of a military career, and

---

[178] MinBuZa, DMA31 inv. nr. 33 doos 6, Aantekening Everts voor Hirschfeld, 09-18-1952.
[179] Ibid., DMA, AVR, Notulen 10-10-1952.

the irregular supply of American aid. From 1953, the Prime Minister started using two other arguments as well: the 'smile' policy of the Kremlin (following Stalin's death) and the adoption of atomic weapons as part of a new NATO strategy (the so-called 'New Look'), both of which at least temporarily reduced the necessity of implementing a military crash programme. We will come back to these developments further on in this sub-chapter.

This did not imply that Drees was completely unperturbed by possible threats to national security. In October 1952, he supported the creation of the national *commissie voor algemene verdedigingsvoorbereiding* (committee for general defence preparation), charged with the preparation and co-ordination of national security including civil defence. The annual budget for civil defence was increased from NLG 80 million to NLG 105 million.[180]

In the course of 1952, the co-operation between the Dutch and Belgian General Staff seemed increasingly futile. Staf and the newly-appointed Minister for Foreign Affairs Beyen[181] (Stikker's successor) quarrelled about the question of whether or not the Belgian-Dutch military agreement of May 1948 should continue to be classified as secret. Beyen suggested getting rid of its secret classification, but Staf wished to maintain the existing situation, at least until the moment of ratification of the EDC treaty.[182] At the time, most military discussions were influenced by uncertainty about the fate of EDC. The initiatives taken in the Belgian-Dutch armament committee were more successful, providing, for example, for a joint venture between Fokker (Amsterdam) and the Fabrique Nationale (Liège) in the production of interceptors for the air forces of both countries.[183]

---

[180] Ibidem.
[181] J.W. Beyen, Minister of Foreign Affairs, 1952-1956.
[182] MinDef, Correspondentie Benelux Stafcommissie 1/1/52-31/10/56 doos 3, Nota MinBuZa kenmerk DEU/BE aan Staf, 09-20-1952; idem, Brief aan MinBuZa afgedaan VCS no. 7683c, 11-10-1952.
[183] MinBZ, DMA, AVR, Notulen 09-19-1952.

Belgian authorities were not pleased with the new Dutch army plan projecting three fully equipped divisions, because they preferred the Netherlands to stick to building up five divisions, instead of reducing the effort. Drees shared the Belgian view and, during a *Ministerraad* meeting in November, he re-emphasised his opposition to the army plan, preferring small divisions of 13,000 men - the projected size of EDC divisions - to complete divisions including corps troops.[184] Drees continued to be concerned about the considerable increase in regular personnel.

By October 1952 the figures for regular personnel, personnel in various stages of training and fresh recruits were as follows:

Navy	22,000	(20,000, July 1950)
Army	75,000	(30,000, July 1950)
Air Force	17,000	(9,000, July 1950)
	114,000	(59,000, July 1950)

Source: MinBuZa, 921.10 NATO inv. nr. 67, Brief Kiès (hoofd legervoorlichtingsdienst), 02-23-1953.

These figures reflected an overall doubling of manpower over a period of two years. The final aim was the mobilisation of between 250,000 and 300,000 men. The defence budget share of the total budget for 1953 amounted to 28.6% (1951: 25%) and 7.53% of N.I.[185]

In the meantime, the government worried about continuous delays in the supply of American equipment. This was caused by formal and bureaucratic impediments on the part of the US: early in 1953 American authorities were still calculating on the basis of the old

---

[184] ARA, MR, NATO, 11-24-1952.
[185] MinBuZa, 921.10 NATO inv. nr. 67, Cijfers Hanson Baldwin (New York Times), 03-16-1953.

(pre-McNarney) Dutch army plan, both for the programming of new assistance and for the delivery of existing aid. As a consequence, much superfluous work was done, and the supply of materials to certain units lagged behind schedule.[186] Another complication was that American aid was allocated on an annual basis, whereas from March 1951 the Dutch government prepared the national defence budgets on a multi-annual basis. In addition, US authorities pointed to the substantial volume of military stores in the pipeline, referring to equipment which was in production or already on the way, and which would certainly arrive in Holland, although later than originally planned.[187] Apart from bureaucracy and organisation, a more substantial factor concerned the use of the stock on hand by US forces in Korea and elsewhere. The fundamental difficulty was that the available equipment was needed simultaneously for foreign aid and for own operations by the US military, and in most cases the latter was given priority. As a result, The Hague concluded that Washington gave only low priority to MDAP and aid to their European partners. By early 1953, the programme was running at least eighteen months behind schedule.

In February 1953, the government drafted a memorandum to express its concern about the programming and untimely delivery of end-items meant for:

a) Units whose build-up required urgency, especially those supporting the army corps.

b) Territorial troops with their practical value as line-of-communication troops; these troops were in urgent need of anti-aircraft artillery.

c) The 44th regimental combat team (parts of 1949 draft II) and the two regiments consisting of former Indonesia soldiers.

---

[186] Ibid., DMA 13 inv. nr. 16 doos 2, Memorandum Everts betreffende Militaire vraagstukken i.v.m. gesprek met Dulles en Stassen, 02-04-1953.
[187] Ibid., Nota Amerikaanse ambassade, 06-30-1953.

d) Reserve units, which, after the outbreak of hostilities, would soon be involved in fighting.[188]

The Dutch authorities were particularly annoyed that their territorial troops and reserve units were excluded from MDAP aid in the form of anti-aircraft artillery. The Hague's emphasis on territorial troops stemmed from a World War II trauma: in May 1940 German parachute troops landed behind Dutch lines and pried open 'Fortress Holland'. To avoid a repetition of that defeat, the General Staff sought to develop at least four territorial divisions and large numbers of anti-aircraft batteries.[189]

In June, US authorities made known that the supply of materials for territorial troops would be placed under the command of SACEUR, implying that the troops were now considered to be in direct support of NATO forces. However, the actual impact of this American response soon turned out to be illusory. In the end, only a few battalions - comprising a total of 23,000 territorial soldiers - were equipped with anti-aircraft artillery of American origin.[190] In Washington's eyes, Dutch territorial troops were overly sizeable and not reliable in a combat situation. Despite this, The Hague kept pressing for a more positive assessment of the domestic forces. According to Megens, it constituted one of the two occasions, together with the Navy issue, in which the government refrained from sacrificing its position vis-à-vis American opposition.[191]

After the turbulent discussions over the status of the port of Rotterdam in allied strategic plans (see 2.4) in August and September 1952, Dutch worries about provisioning in wartime still ran high. In April 1953, Drees remarked that in the event of war, protection of supply lines to the Netherlands was of crucial importance, and he wondered how these lines could actually be kept open, taking into account Rotterdam's delicate position. Vice-Admiral De Booy, chief

---

[188] MinDef, archief Kabinet Minister Stasvo (inv. 66) dossier 1953, Memorandum BuZa aan de US, 02-13-1953.
[189] Honig, *Defense Policy*, p. 32.
[190] Megens, *American aid to NATO allies*, p. 140.
[191] Ibid., 301.

of navy staff, commented that ALFCE was still sceptical of the port's strategic importance, given that (a) the enemy's airfields were a short distance from Rotterdam, so that hostile bombers could be escorted by jet fighters (Channel ports like Le Havre were further away and thus less exposed), and (b) the shoal of the southern part of the North Sea made the port vulnerable to mine laying. According to Staf, the French military were inclined to favour Le Havre above other ports, and the position of Rotterdam would remain insecure until after the arrival of adequate supplies of anti-aircraft artillery (expected in 1955 or 1956). Staf also urged that more minesweepers should become available for cleaning the North Sea of dangerous objects. He finally pointed out the inherent link between 'Rotterdam' and the delivery of MDAP aid. Because of the low priority given by ALFCE to Rotterdam, MDAP and infrastructure support continued to be focussed on ports in northern France. Staf consequently feared that his government's request for anti-aircraft guns and shallow-draught minesweepers would fail to receive the 'condign support' from allied military quarters. Although even Drees doubted whether Rotterdam was defensible against the technologically far-advanced V-weapons, he was nonetheless convinced that the protection of Rotterdam and Antwerp should be given first priority in international military planning.[192] To attract attention abroad, the government emphasised the strategic importance of the Netherlands to the defence of the British Isles.[193]

At the North Atlantic Council meeting in April 1953, the Foreign Ministers formally recognised and sanctioned the relaxation of NATO's defence effort. Maintenance of forces in peacetime proved to be difficult for Western democracies. In most countries, the working conditions for the military were far from attractive, and pay levels were traditionally low. In times of economic expansion, with employment opportunities plentiful and incomes rising, military service, whether conscripted or professional, ran an increasingly poor

---

[192] MinBuZa, DMA, AVR, Notulen 04-17-1953.
[193] Ibid., DMA 13 inv. nr. 16 doos 2, Rapport DGEM/DMA betreffende Militaire Hulpverlening, 07-10-1953.

second to the attractions of civilian life. In the Netherlands, the army faced an appalling shortage of technicians because of attractive and better-paid job opportunities in the civilian sector.

In the meantime, the government kept complaining about delays in MDAP deliveries, arguing that at the start of the defence effort, Holland had been the only country that had proceeded to an active reduction in consumption (through a tax increase of NLG 250 million). Moreover, after the announcement of the defence programme, government spending on housing construction and on the maintenance of dykes, roads and bridges had been cut. The Hague became even more irritated when it was informed of a programmed 50 percent cut in MDAP deliveries for 1954. Staf lamented that the decrease in American end-item aid had to be regarded as a 'punishment for the government's faithful co-operation'.

Early in July, Congress was considering the termination of all military support for Europe within a few years. Drees feared that if this happened, defence of the West would be seriously weakened because of the high costs of maintenance of equipment already received.[194] Soon afterwards, the Congressional debates on the future of military aid became more and more intertwined with the discussion on the realisation of the European Defence Community. Washington threatened to punish those countries, which refused to ratify the EDC treaty (see Chapter 3).

On the other hand, Drees grasped the aid problem as a useful excuse for cutting the defence budget after the termination of the build-up programme, scheduled for the end of 1954. Apart from financial considerations, he was favourably disposed towards changing international circumstances following the death of Stalin (in March 1953), anticommunist rioting in East Berlin (in June), and the fall of the powerful Soviet secret police chief Beria (also in June). The concomitant 'smile policy' of the Kremlin did not fail to impress the Prime Minister, whose altered perception of Soviet

[194] ARA, MR, Amerikaanse hulpverlening aan Nederland, 07-06-1953; idem, De Nederlandse defensie en de NATO, 07-13-1953.

intentions was shared by the greater part of the public. In 1948, 71% of those polled still expected another world war within their lifetime, but in 1953 this had fallen to 31%. In both cases, the fear of war was clearly a fear of the Soviet Union.[195]

Defence Minister Staf - whether or not for tactical reasons - was much more pessimistic about changes in east-west relations, and he objected to reducing defence expenditure in the near future. High budgets were still a necessity due to the high prices to be paid for raw materials, the required modernisation of jet fighters destined for air defence, improvements in social circumstances and increasing salaries, the implementation of large infrastructure works, the revised system of army formation resulting from the McNarney plan, et cetera. Staf expected that by the end of 1954, Holland would have met only 80% of its military requirements, and that consequently, a spending cut was out of the question. He felt that if the Dutch refused to continue developing their forces, they would be unable to fulfil their 'bridgehead function', at least as long as Germany was not rearmed. For the period 1955-57, Staf asked for NLG 4,300 million (about NLG 1,430 million per year), but this went contrary to Drees's intentions that after 1954 (with the barracks under construction, the acquisitions made and the stocks replenished) the defence ceiling could be lowered from NLG 1,500 million to NLG 1,000 million per year.

In the end, Staf's views carried the day. The budget was fixed at NLG 1,350 million a year for the period 1955-57 (this was NLG 80 million less than Staf had asked for but substantially more than Drees wanted to spend), so that total defence expenditure, including revenues emanating from counter-value funds (about NLG 200 million), was to remain within the limit of NLG 5 billion.[196]

---

[195] J.G. Siccama, 'The Netherlands Depillarized: Security Policy in a New Domestic Context', in: G. Flynn (ed.), *NATO's Northern Allies. The national security policies of Belgium, Denmark, the Netherlands and Norway* (New Jersey 1985) p. 119.

[196] ARA, MR, Financiering opbouw defensie na 1954, 09-21-1953; idem, Bijlagen 493, Nota Staf op 5/9, 09-21-1953.

At that time, plans for the build-up of the army were changed continuously and as a result, it was sometimes not possible to see the wood for the trees. Late in 1953, the government announced the creation of a big army corps of five divisions, and in addition to this, one regimental combat team to be ready by the end of 1956. This was said to be in full accordance with the requirements of SHAPE. How would the five divisions be drawn up in the event of war?

It was determined that one of the reserve divisions would be stationed on the river Rhine (between Nijmegen and Rees), while the other three reserve divisions would occupy the Yssel line. One infantry regiment of the combat-ready division was to defend the dykes between Arnhem and Nijmegen; another infantry regiment of the same division would be sent ahead to the Dortmund-Eems canal to delay the enemy's advance; the remaining part of the ready division would be held in reserve on the Veluwe. After completing their tasks, the two infantry regiments mentioned above would also return to the Veluwe as reserve units, so that the army corps would then consist of one complete division. The decision to use three divisions for the occupation of the long Yssel-front was deemed justifiable because of the possibility of inundating areas east of this river. In the meantime, the territorial troops would be available as a general reserve in the centre of the country, to be used either in the hinterland or on the Yssel.[197]

In mid-December, during a discussion in Paris on the perceived strength of the Soviet Union, the foreign ministers of the NATO countries expected that the danger of a Soviet invasion had become less imminent, mainly because of agricultural problems in the Soviet Union caused by crop failures. On the other hand, the existing shortage of D-day divisions in Western Europe caused concern, and Van Tuyll, the secretary general of the Ministry for Foreign Affairs, stated that the military threat should still be taken seriously.

In January 1954, the country's strategic difficulties were brought up again, this time in a reply by the Department of Foreign Affairs to

---

[197] Ibid., DMA 340 inv. nr. 38 doos 6, Nota Staf over defensiepolitiek, 05-1954.

the defence note drafted by Minister Staf in 1953/54. The Department of Foreign Affairs argued that there should be a distinction made between the period before the availability of German divisions - expected by 1956 - and the period after. Before 1956 NATO forces would be unable to perform more than a delaying action against a Russian attack, because the Yssel line was likely to be outflanked from the south. Once again, Foreign Affairs posed the crucial question: whether NATO authorities considered Netherlands territory vital for allied defence or only as a bridgehead for operations in other NATO countries. The defence note had failed to clarify whether protection of the Netherlands was only wishful thinking, or a deliberate NATO decision. In the opinion of the Department of Foreign Affairs, surrender of the Rhine-Yssel automatically implied the abandonment of the entirety of Dutch territory.[198]

In February, in a sequel to his defence note, Staf wrote that even after the deployment of German divisions, a forward strategy would be hard to effect. Instead of relying on conventional reinforcements, he hoped that the inclusion of nuclear arms in military planning would enable NATO to move the potential battlefield eastwards, because the 'new weapons' were expected to boost the defensive power of the combat-ready units. Staf said that in the event of a war, NATO considered using tactical nuclear weapons to stop a hostile attack - as was announced in NSC-162/2 (October 1953). In the meantime, the Rhine-Yssel line would retain its importance as a rallying-point for the reserve divisions required to support the ready units.[199]

The possible use of tactical nuclear weapons, to which Staf alluded in his defence note, sprang from a remarkable turnaround in American military-strategic thinking. This change had its roots in the Korean War: in 1951, the American Congress had begun to show a lack of patience with a deadlocked conventional war in Northeast Asia. Secretary of Defence Lovett realised that the public consensus

---

[198] Ibid., Commentaar MinBuZa op defensienota, 01-1954.
[199] ARA, MR, Bijlagen 498, Nota Staf, 02-08-1954.

behind defence spending was rapidly eroding. In the period 1951-52, Lovett presided over a process that designed a military force which would be smaller in its ground component and would rely much more on the strategic nuclear deterrent of the Strategic Air Command. These forces and the basic military doctrine for their use would be passed on to Eisenhower's new Republican administration, inaugurated early in 1953. Eisenhower baptised the changed approach the 'New Look', referring to its strategy of massive retaliation. The New Look rejected the premise of NSC-68 that the United States could spend 20% of its GNP on arms, it rejected deficit financing, and it maintained that enough of NSC-68 had been implemented to provide security for the United States and to support a policy of containment.

During a visit to Eisenhower in February 1954, Staf expressed his concern about certain aspects of the New Look policy, saying that he feared a fundamental shift in American attention from Europe to Asia (Indo-China) and to the United States itself. Looking at the US policy establishment, he suspected that the advocates of a peripheral strategy, relying primarily on air and naval power, had overruled supporters of a forward strategy. Eisenhower replied that the New Look indeed laid more emphasis on the strategic air force in the United States, at the cost of the prominent position of the army, but that there was no need to worry about the American commitment to Europe. As far as the US presence in Europe was concerned, he hoped that in the long run he would be able to reduce the number of American soldiers stationed there, but certainly not at that time. Moreover, he tried to make clear that the New Look would increase rather than decrease the chances of implementing a forward strategy.

Eisenhower, in his new position, was pleased with the Dutch government's decision to build up five divisions within one big army corps, and he promised his support for the execution of the 5-division programme. Furthermore, Eisenhower agreed to the stationing of a squadron of American fighter planes in Soesterberg - in the province of Utrecht - and to the training of Dutch air force pilots in the United States. Concerning the maintenance of equipment, the US government confirmed that as long as the threat of war existed, American aid would be continued. The formation of the fourth and fifth division would cost about NLG 1 billion, of which only NLG 185 million would be chargeable to the national budget. The Americans promised to cover the deficit in materials, needed for the implementation of the defence plan (at NLG 815 million).[200] Staf was completely satisfied with the results set down in Washington, but he remained pessimistic about retaining adequate strength in the event of a sudden termination of American support.

In spite of Eisenhower's reassurances, the effect of America's New Look was to discourage rather than encourage the development of the Dutch national army. For if the richest and most powerful ally felt compelled to rely more upon nuclear deterrence and less upon ground resistance for reasons of retrenchment, why should its less affluent partner continue to sacrifice its economic advancement for the construction of a large ground force? Another problem concerned the military practicability of the New Look policy. How could the nuclear bomb be used in a conflict situation? Very little thought had been paid at the time to the likelihood of escalation. Nor had much thought been given to the capability of the other side to produce nuclear weapons as well.

In the meantime, the build-up of the national air force had been pulled off quietly. As compared with the army and navy, the air force had hardly been involved in the struggle in Indonesia, and more time could therefore be spent on developing and modernising this service. At the end of the war, a basis for this sort of development was still lacking, but in the early fifties, the air force started a build-up programme (see 2.2) that led in 1953 to its recognition as an independent service beside the army and navy. From the beginning, it was clear that the air force was going to function within an allied

---

[200] MinBuZa, DMA 31 inv. nr. 33 doos 6, Code telegram Van Royen, 02-18-1954; DMA 312 inv. nr. 34 doos 6, Uittreksel van Notulen van de MR, 03-08-1954; ARA, MR, Bijlagen 499, Brief Kyes aan Staf, 03-02-1954.

framework, and that Belgium and the Netherlands formed one strategic area for air defence.[201]

In April 1954, the French government relieved General Juin of his military command in France, after he had openly declared his opposition to the ratification of the EDC treaty. Although The Hague secretly sympathised with Juin's aversion to the EDC, Dutch authorities nevertheless felt that the French general should now also resign from NATO, still considering him a representative of the 'French fortress' doctrine (see 2.4). However, once Gruenther had taken his side, Juin eventually decided to stay in office.[202]

At a meeting of the foreign ministers in Paris in April, the appraisal of Soviet strength was as follows:

> From 1947 to the present time, the numerical strength (175 divisions) of Soviet ground forces has remained fairly constant. Nonetheless, significant changes have been made in favor of increased mechanization with sturdy and efficient modern equipment; they also now have organic tanks and additional artillery. Thus, the mobility and firepower of all Soviet divisions has been increased through the introduction of improved weapons and equipment.

It was further estimated that the USSR, East Germany and the East European satellites had over six million men under arms, the larger part - 4.5 million - being foot soldiers. The number of 'satellite divisions' had almost doubled since 1947, bringing their total to about 80 divisions. Another assumption was that the USSR had deployed a ready-made spearhead - consisting of 22 divisions in eastern Germany - for a rapid advance into Western Europe.[203]

With these figures in hand, NATO did not desist from putting pressure on the Netherlands to increase the number of combat-ready divisions, arguing that the Dutch share of one active division contrasted unfavourably with the Belgian contribution of three D-day divisions. General Gruenther urged The Hague to provide a second

---

[201] Ibid., DMA 340 inv. nr. 38 doos 6, Nota inzake het defensiebeleid, 04-07-1954.
[202] ARA, MR, Ontslag van Generaal Juin, 04-05-1954.
[203] Ibid., Bijlagen 501, Nota Beyen (DWS), 04-29-1954.

D-day division, but the government refused to comply, arguing instead that it was considering a decrease in the term of conscription from 20 to 18 months - following the termination of the 'old' army plan in October 1954. The government also contemplated a reduction from 24 to 21 months for cadre and specialist functions. The aim was to trim the combat-ready strength of the army from 110,000 to 90,000 men.[204] Clearly, the American 'New Look' policy was having an impact on Dutch defence planning.

In July, the government decided to put these plans into practice. This time, the Drees faction bested the Staf faction. The Prime Minister pointed out that at the EDC negotiations, agreement was reached on a unitary term of conscription of eighteen months, which was already policy in France and Belgium, while the terms in Scandinavia and Italy were even shorter. Accordingly, Drees said that there was no reason for the Netherlands to stick to a longer conscription period. Another consideration was the need to provide some relief for the country's labour market, in view of the fact that full employment had been achieved. Finally, Drees remarked that the increase in the budget from NLG 1 billion to NLG 1.5 billion (decided in March 1951) had never been regarded as a permanent measure, but rather as a device to span the four-year crisis period of 1951-54.[205]

The decision to reduce national service was condemned in the United States, where the term of conscription was fixed at twenty-four months. The result was a long series of US-Dutch disagreements about the drafting of troop lists, entailing an enumeration of the units to be developed in the following years. For the rest of the 1954, the army remained in suspense about the delivery of US equipment, especially when in September, Congress decided to cut support funds for Europe again. This decision was deeply regretted in the

---

[204] ARA, MR, Duur eerste militaire oefening, 06-08-1954; MinBuZa, DMA 31 inv. nr. 33 doos 6, Telexbericht van DGEM n.a.v. nota minister van defensie, 06-16-1954. For a survey of the size of the Dutch army in the period 1949-1954, see Appendix II.
[205] MinBuZa, DMA, AVR, Notulen 07-29-1954.

Netherlands, where the *Ministerraad* threw doubt upon the maintenance of an army corps of five divisions, following the definite termination of American assistance.

In later years, it turned out that these doubts had been somewhat exaggerated because American military aid, though drastically cut, was to continue until 1961. In that year, Minister of Defence Visser decided to increase the defence budget by an annual amount of about NLG 420 million for the period 1961-63 (see Appendix IV). It was clear that military aid exerted permanent pressure on the defence budget, as was the case in the fifties, and again in the early sixties, after American assistance had dried up. [206]

In 1960, the Dutch army transformed from a five-division force[207] that relied heavily on its capacity for mobilisation - in spite of the implementation of the McNarney plan - to a three-division force consisting of two combat-ready divisions and one mobilisation-ready division. This process involved a reduction in manpower, especially in the number of conscripts, and required the acquisition of new material to improve the army's mobility.

In the meantime, in May 1955, West Germany entered NATO, Italy and West Germany acceded to the Brussels pact, and the Western Union of 1948 was thereby transformed into the West European Union. The United States and the United Kingdom made historic pledges to keep their troops on the European continent. The Dutch government and parliament welcomed these developments. Even the Social Democrats, once the centre of a pacifist tradition, now attempted to persuade their German colleagues - who at that time still followed a policy of neutrality, or at least one against rearmament - of the need for a West German military contribution against the Soviet military threat.[208]

---

[206] C.M. Megens, 'Militaire hulpverlening in de jaren vijftig - de Amerikaanse hulp aan Nederland', in: *Internationale Spectator* 36 (1982) 8, p. 466.

[207] Although the number of five divisions was in practice never really attained, see also Schulten, 'Die militärische Integration', p. 100.

[208] Siccama, 'The Netherlands Depillarized', p. 123.

One of the main goals of Dutch foreign policy - German rearmament within NATO - had finally been achieved, and as a result, the strategic position of the Netherlands improved substantially, in that a forward defence had now become feasible. Also, the country's northern and eastern provinces were henceforth assured of protection. Moreover, the re-establishment of a German army helped to relieve the Dutch defence burden, both in terms of money and personnel.

Conclusions

In March 1951, with the government's decision to increase the defence budget to unprecedented levels, the Netherlands became a loyal participant in Western defence and a faithful member of the North Atlantic treaty organisation. After two years of hesitation and qualms, the government gave in to international pressure to make a serious start on the building up of a well-equipped army corps.

The decision to fix the defence budget at NLG 1,500 million per year, for a period of four years (1951-1954), obviously had been a very difficult one to take, as it entailed a serious cut in both private consumption and public investment, most notably affecting the government's social housing programme. For the social-democrat section of the government coalition, this was particularly hard to swallow, and hence it was not surprising that the PvdA ministers Drees and Lieftinck emerged as the main proponents in the campaign against the budget increase. Eventually, the Atlantic-oriented Foreign Minister Stikker succeeded in convincing the government of the need to proceed to action, and bringing the Netherlands into compliance with international requirements. How difficult this was, is further illustrated by a sequence of radical developments in national politics during January 1951: the influential visit of SACEUR Eisenhower, the dismissal of General Kruls and the resignation of the government. US suspicions that especially the latter event would bring about a further delay to much-needed defence reform soon proved wrong; within two months a new government was installed, which immediately announced a detailed and ambitious military programme on a multi-annual basis.

The generous budget increase and the promise to build up a five-division army corps contributed to a rapid normalisation of US-Dutch relations. Washington was pleased to see that the Dutch government had finally committed itself, and, after having been ridiculed and criticised for more than two years, the Dutch army was from now on presented as a rather efficient organisation with disciplined and dedicated personnel. The bilateral co-operation was strengthened by two other factors: the appointment of Cornelis Staf as the new Defence Minister, who soon proved successful in winning US confidence after the difficult experiences with his predecessors Schokking and 's Jacob, and The Hague's decision in the autumn of 1951 to become a full participant in the EDC negotiations in Paris, a step warmly welcomed in Washington (see chapter 3).

This does not imply that from March 1951 on US-Dutch relations were free from any form of discord and irritation. Even after the budgetary decision, the Americans put pressure on the government to do more in terms of expenditure and manpower. They urged the use of counterpart funds as an additional instrument for military spending and they also wanted the Dutch army to concentrate on training active combat-ready forces instead of reserve units which could be operational only after several weeks. The Hague sometimes did not conceal its irritation about the direct nature of US interference in internal defence affairs, and attempted to stick to the promises made in March 1951, rather than switch to new programmes and targets. It also emphasised the need for regular and generous deliveries of US military assistance to combat financial problems and mitigate the strain of rearmament. There was a certain ambiguity in the Dutch approach to this problem. Despite continuous complaints about delays in the delivery of American equipment, it was also clear that the latter had a lasting impact on the development of the Dutch army, during the 1950s and later. Also, the build-up of the air force would have been impossible without the supply of aircraft and parts from the other side of the Atlantic Ocean[209]. During the period 1949-1961, the Netherlands obtained US military assistance to the value of $1.188 billion, which was only a little less than the vaunted economic assistance (Marshall aid) received over the same period. Apart from the army (receiving tanks, trucks, engineering equipment and artillery) and air force (jet fighters), the fledgling defence industry benefited substantially from the supplies and funds - partly in the form of offshore orders - coming from the US.

The military crash programme announced in March 1951 was so ambitious that during the first four-year period it proved impossible to commit all the funds allocated for military development. This was more a problem for NATO and the US, who urged the complete use of available money, than for Finance Minister Lieftinck, who deep in his heart welcomed the deflationary effects of non-utilised funds. For the subsequent four-year period (1955-58), defence ceilings were reduced from NLG 1,500 million to NLG 1,350 million per year. The international fear of an imminent military attack from the East waned somewhat and, more importantly, the American retrenchment policy resulting from the 'New Look' discouraged rather than encouraged the Netherlands to maintain high defence budgets.

In chapter 1, we observed that during 1948-50, the Netherlands refused to increase defence expenditure, as long as the allies were not prepared to commit themselves to a direct defence of Dutch territory. In that respect, the budget increase of March 1951 was a considerable concession on the part of the Dutch government, because at that moment there was no incontrovertible evidence that the entire country was going to be protected in the event of hostile action. The intention proclaimed at NATO's September 1950 meeting to move the allied defence line eastwards into Germany had still not been converted into a firm guarantee. The government was particularly annoyed with French strategic plans for a defence build-up south of the river Rhine, without taking into account the northern

---

[209] Megens, *American aid to NATO allies*, 198.

part of allied territory. The American New Look policy of 1953 also caused concern because of the inherent danger of a future withdrawal of US conventional forces from the continent. It thus appeared that the New Look had both a positive (see above) and a negative side for the Dutch government. Only a German conventional contribution to the defence of Western Europe was expected to provide the desired buffer, and the government had to wait until 1955 before this could finally be effected, with Germany's entry into NATO. The reasons why this took so long will be dealt with in Part II of this work, which shall illuminate the Dutch reception of the French plan for creating a European Defence Community (EDC), an initiative aimed at making German rearmament palatable to France. The above two chapters serve as a general background to make The Hague's stance towards European defence and security understandable.

PART II

The Netherlands and the European Defence Community, 1950-1954

CHAPTER 3

The politics of the European Defence Community

Introduction

From 1950 until 1954, developments within the framework of NATO were strongly influenced by the passionate debate on the creation of a supranational European defence organisation.

The Pleven plan, envisaging such an organisation, was the French answer to the proposal for German rearmament, put forward by the United States after the start of the Korean War in June 1950. Without the contribution of German soldiers, it was deemed impossible credibly to execute NATO's 'forward strategy', a defence as far to the east in Europe as possible. This kind of strategy was advocated in September 1950 by both US Secretary of State Acheson and Dutch Foreign Minister Stikker. It was argued in chapter one that Stikker welcomed German rearmament for military-strategic as well as financial reasons. After the Atlantic Council meeting in September, the problem in question became *how* German army units could be integrated into Western defence. The Dutch government preferred an Atlantic solution to this problem, advocating Germany's entry into NATO, but in October the French government, fearing the remobilization of a German national army, instead proposed the build-up of an integrated European army. The Pleven plan roused considerable suspicion in the Netherlands. Although it was clear from the beginning that the European army - later designated European Defence Community, EDC - would fall under NATO's operational guidance, The Hague wondered to what extent the United States would remain interested in safeguarding European security *after* EDC's realisation, and what it would mean for the stationing of GIs on the European continent. Moreover, should the Atlantic option be rejected, the Dutch army expected further delay in German rearmament and 'forward defence'. For a period of four years, the French proposal remained at the centre of European (and American) interest.

In this and the following chapters, Dutch attitudes towards the EDC will be considered from three different angles: political, military and financial-economic.

The present chapter deals with policy-making and policy implementation by the *Ministerraad* (cabinet) and the Ministry of Foreign Affairs. Initially, both were hostile to the idea of creating an integrated European army. Later, after the signing of the EDC treaty in May 1952, the Netherlands became the first of the six participating countries to ratify the treaty.[210] The reasons for this curious U-turn will be dealt with in this chapter.

Although the General Staff generally shared the views held by the government and the Ministry of Foreign Affairs, the relationship between civil and military authorities in the matter of EDC was far from smooth. Chapter 4 shall attempt to survey the anti-EDC arguments by military authorities in the Netherlands, and these arguments' reception in the civil circuit.

Dutch industrialists were more divided on the issue, as will be shown in chapter 5, which focuses on the preferences and objections of the Ministry of Economic Affairs and the business community in general.

3.1 The announcement of the Pleven plan, and the Dutch objections to it

After the start of the Korean War in June 1950, Washington openly advocated the need for rearming Germany. Secretary of State

---

[210] A.E. Kersten, 'Niederländische Regierung, Bewaffnung Westdeutschlands und EVG'. In: Militärgeschichtliches Forschungsamt (MGFA) (ed.), *Die Europäische Verteidigungsmeinschaft. Stand und Probleme der Forschung* (Boppard am Rhein 1985) pp. 191-219. This article offers a comprehensive analysis of Dutch EDC policy before the signing of the Treaty.

Acheson announced a 'package deal', containing the following elements:

a) An integrated NATO command under an American commander
b) An increase in American troop presence in Europe
c) The extension of military aid to the West European partners
d) An increase in the military expenditure of the West European NATO countries
e) A limited German contribution to NATO, at the size of 12 divisions, under German command.

Western European obligations (d and e) were meant as a *quid pro quo* for additional US efforts evolving out of the first three points. In September, at the North Atlantic Council meeting in New York, Acheson's package deal was accepted in principle by all NATO member countries, except France. Foreign Minister Schuman objected to what he saw as an unverifiable revival of the German national army. At that time, the French army had many non-European commitments, mainly in Indo-China, and the fear was that, in the event of German rearmament, Germany would soon have the largest army in NATO, consigning France to an inferior position. France had previously hoped to solve the German problem through economic measures, and the Schuman plan aimed at integrating heavy industry in the Ruhr in a supranational framework. However, given the results of the New York Council meeting, and given US determination on this score, a non-political approach to the problem was no longer realistic. Unlike France, the Dutch government had no hesitation whatsoever in supporting Acheson's scheme.

At the end of September, as the discussion on German rearmament developed, the French government found itself in an awkward predicament, partly as a result of internal divisions. One section opposed any form of German remilitarization, while another was prepared to discuss the deployment of German military units within the framework of an integrated European army. The latter advocated a supranational European organisation - including West Germany - to create a formal basis for French control and German dependence.

The aim was to integrate small German army contingents into multinational European divisions operating under non-German commanders. The pro-European section, headed by Prime Minister Pleven and Foreign Minister Schuman, speculated that such a construction would also have a positive impact on the acceptance of the European Coal and Steel treaty (Paris treaty), which had then not yet been signed.

In developing European policy, the French government found itself handicapped by dependence on the United States for continuance of the colonial struggle in Indo-China. The Indochina war constituted an immense drain on the national economy and finances, hence foreign support was desperately needed. Between January 1950 and 7 May 1954, the day of the defeat of the French army at Dien Bien Phu, US assistance to the French war effort in East Asia amounted to about $ 2.6 billion, which equalled almost 70% of total expenditure on the war. The result was that, just at the time of the controversial debate on West German rearmament, French foreign policy consisted of two incompatible elements: the waging of a colonial war with American money and domestic resistance against the US-favoured rearmament of Germany. It was clear that sooner or later Washington would use its diplomatic leverage to put France under pressure. Early in October, France found itself in an isolated and vulnerable position. Isolated, because in New York all the NATO partners had spoken out in favour of German rearmament, and vulnerable, because American military aid was indispensable and the presence of US troops in Europe and particularly in West Germany was needed as a counterbalance to the rearmament of the Federal Republic, which was, in the long run, considered inevitable, even in France.

Aware of these dangers, the French government realised the importance of making the first move. At the meeting of the French National Assembly on 24 October 1950, Prime Minister Pleven proposed the creation - for the common defence of Europe - of a European army, which would include some German contingents 'under the control of the political institutions of a united Europe'. This proposal, Pleven argued, sprang directly from a resolution of the

11 August Assembly of the Council of Europe in Strasbourg, which had called for

> The immediate creation of a unified European army, under the authority of a European minister of defence, subject to proper European democratic control and acting in full co-operation with the United States and Canada.

The Pleven plan in fact meant a supranational solution to the problem of a West German defence contribution. For the French, the integrative approach - on the lines of the Schuman plan - seemed the only way to ensure effective control over the re-establishment of a national German army. Warner has written that the French 'hoped to spin a cocoon of supranational restraints around West Germany from which it could never escape'.[211] Apparently, within the French cabinet the pro-European section had managed to persuade hard-liners such as Defence Minister Jules Moch, who had previously emerged as a convinced opponent of German rearmament in any form.

Pleven argued that since the simple joining together of national military units would only conceal a coalition of the old type, a united European army would 'bring about as near as possible a fusion of its human and material components under a single political and military authority'. A European defence minister or defence commissioner, who would be nominated by the governments involved, was to be responsible to a council of ministers and a European assembly. The rearmament and equipment programme for Europe would be laid down and carried out under his authority. Furthermore, he would be held accountable for obtaining the contingents, equipment, material and supplies from the various member states. The contingents provided by the countries participating would be integrated into the European army at the level of the smallest possible unit, that of battalions of 3-4,000 men, and the financial contributions of the member states would be harmonised by a common budget. The

---

[211] G. Warner, 'The United States and the rearmament of West Germany, 1950-54', *International Affairs* 61 (1984-85) 2, pp. 110-111.

countries which had part of their forces stationed outside Europe would retain authority over that part. The part declared available for integration into the European force would, however, operate in accordance with the undertakings of the Atlantic pact. Pleven reassured the NATO countries that the European army plan would not in any way delay Atlantic council's plans designed to create national forces under unified command.[212] It was on this basis that the French government suggested inviting some Western European countries, who had already agreed in Strasbourg to share in the creation of a European army, to work out in common the implementation of the proposals at a conference to be held in Paris.

The first comments on the French plan by the Dutch Ministry of Foreign Affairs were downright negative. It was argued that the plan would hinder rather than help improve Western European defence capabilities. Though in the course of 1950 The Hague had become an outspoken supporter of German rearmament, the Pleven plan was not seen as the appropriate framework for tackling this issue. The government felt that national security interests would be better promoted within NATO than within a European army, and feared that the French plan would lead to divisions in the Atlantic community. Moreover, it was anticipated that like-minded partners like Great Britain and the Scandinavian countries would not be interested in becoming involved in a supranational defence structure. It was feared that in a continental European grouping, France would play the dominant partner, not only at the expense of Germany but also of the Netherlands. The initial version of the plan openly discriminated against the Federal Republic. There would be no independent German army or general staff, just small German units operating alongside similar units from other member states. Pleven also denied Germany the right to have its own minister of defence, federal recruiting agency and tactical air forces. Finally, Germany was the only country that was not allowed to have national forces (apart from those meant for the European army) for colonial and

---

[212] E. Fursdon, *The European Defence Community. A History* (London 1980) pp. 89-90.

other purposes. As opposed to the French government, The Hague immediately spoke out in favour of equal rights for Germany.[213]

Foreign Minister Stikker warned that the 'pace of the military build-up in the North Atlantic domain would be needlessly slackened', if the Pleven plan were accepted.[214] The Dutch military had recently started to organise their army in Western Europe in line with NATO's Medium Term Defence Plan requirements, and had promised to build up five divisions, planned to be ready by the end of 1954 (see chapter 1). These divisions would be equipped with American material and standardised and trained along the lines of the US combat system. The Foreign Ministry feared that experiments with an integrated European force would not only hinder the implementation of the Medium Term Defence Plan but also endanger recently developed standardisation plans. Another reason for rejecting the French plan was that mixing small battalions of different nationalities into the basic army unit, the division, would be militarily unsound and would never yield a fighting force. Both the government and the Ministry of Foreign Affairs suspected France of trying to delay German rearmament, especially after Pleven's announcement that negotiations were not to be broached before the signing of the Schuman plan treaty, expected in the spring of 1951. The Netherlands needed the rapid build-up of German armed forces for military-strategic reasons - to facilitate an Elbe rather than a Rhine defence - as well as financial reasons - the availability of German troops would lessen the urgency of building up an expensive standing army in the Netherlands.

In the United States, it was mainly the Pentagon which looked askance at the purport of the French proposal. The American military rejected the concept of integrating small units of different nationalities into one European army. And although the official reaction by the State Department was similarly disapproving, it soon became clear that many officials felt secretly relieved that on the

---

[213] Ministerie van Buitenlandse Zaken (MinBZ), Archief EDG, EDG 921.331, Memorandum Stuyt (DEU/WS), 10-24-1950.

[214] Ibid., Code telegram Stikker, 10-24-1950.

issue of German rearmament, they had not received a point-blank refusal from the French.

Stikker soon discerned that the American view on the Pleven plan was rather flexible. In November 1950, he warned the *Raad Militaire Aangelegenheden van het Koninkrijk* (Cabinet's defence council) of the possibility of a sudden change of opinion in the United States in favour of the European army. Once again, Stikker criticised the French plan, stating that the creation of a European army with political institutions entailed the construction of a completely federal state, consisting of France, Germany, Italy and the Benelux countries. He felt strongly against joining such a state but, anticipating a change of opinion in the United States in support of the European army, he expected that in the long run the Netherlands would be pressured to take part. Stikker lacked confidence in the internal political stability of France, Italy and Germany, and he expressed concern at the size of the French and Italian communist parties.[215]

In an attempt to forestall adverse developments, Stikker suggested a compromise between the official American position (German rearmament within the Atlantic framework) and the French plan for an integrated European army. The Stikker proposal sought to restrict the level of military integration to the troops stationed in Germany. These forces needed to be placed under the command of a NATO High Commissioner, to be appointed by and responsible to NATO's Council of Ministers. Stikker deliberately omitted delicate issues such as parliamentary control and supranational guidance. In stark contrast to prevailing opinion in the Netherlands, the proposal discriminated against Germany, particularly in its initial stages, in order to enlist French support. For example, Germany was allowed to have a special defence agency for recruiting and training troops, but under strict limits and rules set by the High Commissioner. Its

---

[215] Ibid., Code telegram Stikker, 10-26-1950; Ministerie van Algemene Zaken (MinAZ), Raad Militaire Aangelegenheden van het Koninkrijk (Raad MAK), Notulen 10-07-1950, Bespreking van het in het North Atlantic Defense and Military Committee gevoerde overleg.

responsibilities would entail pay, food, clothing and housing. In Stikker's proposal, powers were to be shifted gradually to the German defence agency, 'proportionally, as NATO's confidence in Germany increased'. The duties of the High Commissioner would end as soon as Germany was accepted as an equal partner in western defence.

Stikker's main aims were to placate Paris and to facilitate and speed German rearmament because he felt that his plan could be realised at short notice. Surprisingly, he did indeed manage to enlist Schuman's support, at least for a short while[216]. The proposal did not, however, gain much favour with Acheson or Adenauer, the latter strongly condemning the provisions discriminating against the Federal Republic. In the meantime, NATO's Council of Deputies had made progress towards reconciling the American and the French plans for German rearmament. In December, disappointed by the lack of interest abroad, Stikker decided to drop his plan.

Despite this setback, the government continued its opposition and looked for support from other countries, Great Britain in particular, to garner the requisite critical mass. British Foreign Minister Bevin had made known that he preferred an Atlantic solution to the German problem to a supranational European approach. 'We cannot afford', Bevin wrote, 'to allow the European federal concept to gain a foothold within NATO and thus weaken instead of strengthening the ties between the countries on the two sides of the Atlantic'.[217] The Hague, fearing the prospect of being trapped within a small continental bloc, encouraged Bevin to develop his ideas of a comprehensive Atlantic confederation, including all Atlantic countries as well as Germany.[218] However, to The Hague's

---

[216] V. Gavín (University of Barcelona): first draft of PhD thesis on the roots and causes of the European Defence Community (to be published in 2003). Gavín argues that Schuman's initial backing of the Stikker plan constituted a clear signal that he was by no means a dedicated supporter of the supranational European army.

[217] Quoted from: M. Trachtenberg, *A Constructed Peace. The Making of the European Settlement 1945-1963* (Princeton 1999) p. 117.

[218] Algemeen Rijksarchief (ARA), Notulen Ministerraad (MR), Continentale en Atlantische politiek, 11-29-1950.

disappointment, the British government was reluctant to elaborate these ideas into workable plans for European defence. In December 1950, when the United States allowed the French government to convene a study conference on the European army plan, the British reconciled themselves to the new facts, all the more so as Washington refrained from pressuring them into active participation.

Furthermore, the British government had no reason to feel excluded. In December, the United States, France, Germany and Great Britain agreed to convocate a meeting on the Petersberg near Bonn, starting in January, just before the inauguration of the Paris conference on the European army, to study the possibilities of activating national German troops within a NATO framework.

Early in January 1951, General Eisenhower visited The Hague where he urged the Netherlands to increase national defence efforts (see 2.1). Stikker used this talk with Eisenhower to vent all his grievances about the European army plan. He thought it an error that France was allowed to organise a European army study conference because 'such an army could never be realised and would only aggravate existing divisions in Europe, given the fact that the United Kingdom, the Scandinavian countries and the Netherlands rejected French conceptions of a European federation'. Stikker feared new disagreements on the question of German rearmament, which would complicate and delay the realisation of an Elbe strategy. He argued that 'without German forces, the Rhine-Yssel would continue to be the main defence line, a situation totally unacceptable to the Netherlands'.[219]

3.2 Observer at the conference in Paris

By flatly rejecting the French plan, The Hague had manoeuvred itself into an isolated position, especially after US approval of the study conference in Paris. The government, nonetheless, refused to accept the invitation by the French government (on 27 January) to

---

[219] Foreign relations of the United States (FRUS) 1951, Volume 3 part 1, Telegram Anderson to Acheson, 01-11-1951, pp. 413-414.

participate as a full member at the conference. In spite of the fact that a large group of MPs favoured the European army concept, the government limited national representation in Paris to observer status only. It justified its reticence by hinting at domestic political problems following the fall of the Drees cabinet on 24 January, but it was obvious that the government strongly objected to the principles of the European army plan. Besides, it was convinced that the French plan was so unrealistic that it would never be realised. Consequently, The Hague managed to manoeuvre itself into a difficult position in the international arena, as the government was at that time also being harshly criticised for dawdling on defence expenditure (see 2.1).

During the first half of 1951, the Ministry of Foreign Affairs shared the government's criticism, indicating several inconveniences:

a) For financial and economic reasons the merger of national armies should be considered the copestone of the integration process, rather than the starting point

b) Traditional Dutch interests in the domain of finance, economics and politics were inadequately protected under a purely continental structure without Great Britain's participation. There was a danger of the re-emergence of French and/or German hegemony over continental European affairs, at the Netherlands' expense

c) Although, before the start of the Paris conference, the French government had conceded that the national combat team (regiment with extra armour and artillery support) rather than the battalion was going to be unit of integration in the European army, The Hague found this concession inadequate, arguing that any integration of troops below the level of the – nationally homogeneous – division should be rejected

d) The main argument: German rearmament would be delayed by experiments with a European force, which was dangerous in view of the vulnerable geographical and strategic position of the Netherlands. Moreover, if a quick answer to the question of incorporating Germany remained forthcoming, then American enthusiasm for European defence might well dwindle.

The conviction that national interests would not be harmed by observer status in Paris was strengthened by the full membership of the two Benelux partners, Belgium and Luxembourg. The latter were supposed to act as watchdogs for Dutch interests at the conference table.

During the first months of the Paris conference, the French and German delegations turned out to be strongly divided on certain essential aspects of the Pleven plan, such as the level of integration of army units. The Dutch government realised that, had they fully participated, the national delegation would have been forced to take sides with Belgium against France, with the resultant risk of pushing the latter towards co-operation with Germany. By opting for observer status, the Dutch sidestepped the thankless task of criticising the French plan to the Belgian delegation.

Early in 1951, a few officials in the Foreign Ministry, Max Kohnstamm and Conny Patijn in particular, came out in support of the European army concept, but they represented only a minority in their 'pro-European' views. Kohnstamm, at the time head of the Germany desk and involved in the negotiations on the Schuman plan, found himself more and more isolated in a dominantly 'atlanticist' environment and eventually decided to leave The Hague to occupy a post at the newly created High Authority of the European Coal and Steel Community in Luxembourg.[220]

Events in Paris took a different course from what the government had expected. This was mainly caused by an external factor. From the summer of 1951 onwards, after the failure of the Petersberg conference to find a solution for Germany's involvement in

---

[220] 'Een sneeuwveld in 1942', interview with M. Kohnstamm, in: A.G. Harryvan, J. van der Harst and S. van Voorst (eds.), *Voor Nederland en Europa. Politici en ambtenaren over het Nederlandse Europabeleid en de Europese integratie, 1945-1975* (Den Haag 2001) p. 95.

NATO,[221] the United States became an active supporter of the plan for a supranational European army. Bruce, US ambassador to France, McCloy, the High Commissioner in Germany, and ECSC's president Jean Monnet were said to have converted SACEUR General Eisenhower[222] who, in his turn, had exercised considerable influence on President Truman and Acheson to go along with the French proposals. From then on, the European army plan was accepted and supported by official United States policy as the only avenue open for German rearmament. This was primarily because Paris refused to accept any other solution, but it also suited Washington. The US government pointed to the positive influence the European army might have on European integration in general, a process strongly welcomed in the US ever since 1945. Furthermore, the Truman administration obviously preferred to deal with Europe as a whole - in the Cold War struggle against the Soviet Union - than with six separate countries. Finally, the idea that a European army could bring about a repeal of the German statute of occupation had gained ground, as well as an opportunity - in the longer run - to 'bring American boys home'. The advantages of supporting the supranational army were so obvious that Washington even refused to use the diplomatic trump card of 'Indo-China' against France.

Stikker was very much concerned about the possibility of an American retreat from Europe, feeling that any replacement of American forces, for example by fresh German recruits, would considerably weaken the defence of Western Europe. Once, he asked SACEUR Eisenhower what advice the general would give to his government, after the creation of the European army organisation, on the question - 'so very important to all of us' - of maintaining

---

[221] In June 1951, the Petersberg talks ended without result because France was not willing to accept a NATO solution and the US refused to bring the issue to a head.

[222] T.A. Schwartz, *America's Germany. John J. McCloy and the Federal Republic of Germany* (London 1991) pp. 222-225; see also 'Een sneeuwveld in 1942', in: Harryvan c.s. (eds.), *Voor Nederland en Europa*, p. 112.

American forces in Europe. Stikker added that he had 'never seen Eisenhower so evasive as on this occasion'.[223]

Apart from American support, the Paris conference itself made considerable progress. At the end of June, the Military Committee managed to produce a draft interim report, which was accepted by the conference on 24 July. The report contained general outlines and objectives, and also gave an overview of the outstanding problems. The original Pleven plan had been modified substantially, in that several discriminatory elements against Germany were eliminated. Concerning the level of integration of army units, the French delegation had again made concessions, accepting the *unité de base* of 12,500 to 14,500 men as a national homogeneous unit, to be integrated in the European defence force. The basic unit had now almost reached the size and level of a single-nationality division. The Germans were also permitted to have their own recruiting offices. By way of compensation, Germany said it was prepared to refrain from building up a national heavy weapon industry.

The government was highly suspicious of the progress made at the Paris conference. It became clear that integration would not be restricted to army units but would also encompass armament industries, defence budgets, legal systems, etcetera. Observer status was increasingly seen as a hindrance, but full participation was still not under consideration. The Foreign Ministry argued that the basic error of the European army plan lay in the attempt to federalise a most vital public institution: defence. The consequences were serious because it was 'impossible to federalise one sector while leaving adjacent sectors in national control'. Integration of armies implicitly meant integration of foreign policies, which in its turn would undermine independent policy-making in the Netherlands. It was seen as 'unavoidable' that within a supranational state the bigger powers would dominate the smaller ones.[224]

---

[223] D.U. Stikker, *Men of responsibility. A memoir* (London 1965) p. 303.
[224] MinBZ, EDG 921.331, doos 7, Memorandum Kamerlingh Onnes, Constitutionele opmerkingen bij het Pleven plan, 08-02-1951.

The above observation might seem surprising, given the fact that at a later stage the Netherlands came to regard supranational institutions and decision-making as instruments to *protect* the smaller states' interests. But in 1951 the intergovernmental approach was still dominant, as witnessed by Dutch insistence - during the same period - on incorporating a Council of Ministers in the ECSC structure.

Trachtenberg has argued that the European army 'was to be supranational only in an administrative sense', namely in the areas of recruiting, training and equipping European armed forces. There would be 'no true pooling of sovereignty on the part of the member states'.[225] Even if this observation were correct, it was at least not perceived as such by Dutch authorities during the early 1950s. On the contrary, the conviction prevailed that participating in a European army implied a serious delegation of power to a supranational organisation.

The Hague's chief grievance concerned Washington's moving away from the Atlantic solution, in favour of the European army. A great deal of frustration arose from the 'vague' American desire for European unification. The Dutch ambassador to the United States, De Beus, was annoyed by the fact that the US government asked European countries to transfer part of their sovereignty to the institution of a European army while the Americans themselves were reluctant to delegate any sovereignty to NATO. De Beus perceived a difference between European and American mentalities: 'the first is founded on principles and is directed towards long-term goals; the second is often inclined to be guided by motives of immediate practical and opportunistic importance'. The Foreign Ministry largely shared De Beus's bitterness, but the ambassador warned 'not to overrate Dutch influence abroad', explaining that Washington failed to take much notice of Dutch objections to the European army.[226]

---

[225] Trachtenberg, *A Constructed Peace*, p. 120.
[226] Ibid., Code telegram De Beus, 08-10-1951.

The American change of view compelled the government to reflect on its position. In August 1951, at the 'Ambassador's conference' in The Hague, attended by ministers, ambassadors and civil servants, two different camps could be discerned. Prime Minister Drees and Foreign Minister Stikker stuck to traditional views and reiterated their objections to the European army. Under Drees, the Netherlands had gradually recovered from the losses suffered during the Second World War, and the Prime Minister feared that the process of economic recovery would be endangered by experimenting with European institutions, with 'unstable countries like France, Germany and Italy' participating. However, among those attending the meeting were others who stressed the advantages of full membership at the Paris conference, arguing that only full participation would enable the Netherlands to have real influence on the discussions. One of the most ardent advocates of this line of thinking was Spierenburg, representative of the Ministry of Economic Affairs and Dutch negotiator at the Schuman plan negotiations. He argued as follows:

a) Dutch influence within NATO was limited, mainly because of the dominant position of the Standing Group consisting of the 'Big Three' nations. Presumably, Dutch impact would increase within a continental European framework

b) Europe should do more for its own sake because US foreign policy sometimes overlooked European interests

c) The European army was the only way to make France accept German remilitarization. Also, many Germans considered the French plan as providing the most acceptable form of rearmament

d) Political instability in France, Germany and Italy made it necessary to lend strong support to reliable and stable elements in these countries, particularly the political parties in favour of European integration and co-operation (MRP in France, DC in Italy, CDU in Germany). These parties, all represented in government, were indispensable elements in the struggle against communism.[227]

Spierenburg's speech had a marked effect, at least in the long run. Although many objections remained valid, it became increasingly clear that the Netherlands could not indulge in the luxury of standing aloof at the Paris conference. Benelux co-operation was at stake and, more importantly, the United States threatened to reconsider the allocation of economic and military aid if the Netherlands continued being obstructive. The question of whether Holland could financially afford to remain outside the European army discussions was raised. Despite this, international pressure on the Netherlands to co-operate was tame. It was considered inevitable that the Dutch would eventually participate.[228]

The government still refused to consider participation as a matter of course. To give a clear demonstration of its point of view, The Hague presented a counterproposal to the governments of the 'Big Three' (United States, United Kingdom and France). The proposal emphasised that 'NATO continued to be the best safeguard against aggression and therefore safety should in the first place be sought by strengthening the link between the members of that organisation'. It was also stated that NATO offered the 'proper framework for preventing the resurgence of an aggressive Germany', a passage aimed at placating the French delegation. Dutch objections centred on the impracticability of three elements of the European army: the unified administration (a single High Commissioner or European Defence Minister), the common budget and the common armament programme. In their counterproposal, The Hague sought to simplify the structure of the European Defence Community (from the end of July 1951, the term European Defence Community - EDC - very largely replaced that of European army) by reducing the status and powers of the High Commissioner and strengthening the role of the

---

[227] Ibid., Resumé van de Ambassadeursconferentie over het Europese leger, 08-28-1951.
[228] MinBZ, EDG 999.0, inv. nr. 20 doos 5, Eerste vergadering Interdep. Adviesraad, 10-15-1951.

Council of Ministers. By so doing, the Netherlands acted in a manner consistent with that of the ECSC negotiations, where it had introduced the Council of Ministers to balance the authority of the supranational High Authority. The Dutch view was that the drafting and implementation of the common budget needed to be the prerogative of the Council. Their main aim was to avoid the relinquishment of essential sovereign powers to a supranational authority.[229]

The counterproposal was an act of desperation which failed to attract attention abroad. The government was disappointed but not surprised by this lack of interest. Early in September 1951, The Hague received an *aide-mémoire* from the US government confirming that Washington attached the utmost importance to the creation of an effective EDC and hoped that in the immediate future agreement could be arrived at over Dutch participation.

Ultimately, Stikker came to realise that obstinacy was not the best way to achieve his nation's goals, and he decided to change his position. This was mainly a tactical move rather than the result of a more optimistic assessment of European defence integration. In a letter to Drees, the Foreign Minister observed that the French government had suddenly ceased pressing the Netherlands to active participation, out of fear that Holland, as a full member, would start to team up with Italy and Belgium with the aim of thwarting French initiatives. For this very reason Stikker suddenly advocated active involvement at the conference. He added:

> Unpleasant as it may be, we have to take into account the development of political events, since the 'Big Three' have promised their support for the creation of a European army. It is hard indeed to accept the loss of independence in the making of our own foreign policy.

---

[229] FRUS 1951, Vol. 3 (1), Tel. Webb to the Embassy in the United Kingdom, 10-05-1951, p. 886; ARA, Buitenlands Economische Betrekkingen (BEB), 2.06.10 EDG doos 640, Dutch counterproposal of August 1951.

Stikker mentioned some new objections to a further development of integration in Western Europe. He feared that a continental federation would strengthen protectionist tendencies in France, Italy and Germany, and he complained about the harmful social and inflationary effects of French economic policies. Stikker added that a substantial basis for an advanced process of integration was lacking, arguing that in France, Italy and Germany the parliamentary majority in favour of the European army was very slim, if it existed at all. He feared that a change in government in these countries could have a disastrous impact on European integration in general.

In conclusion to his letter to Drees, Stikker showed great concern about growing tensions between the United States and the Soviet Union. In the event of escalation, Western Europe would suffer:

> Europe must defend itself as adequately as possible. German rearmament is necessary for a credible Dutch defence. It has been proved that such rearmament can only be realised within a European army. Whether we like it or not, we have to concede to it. However, our attitude at the conference will undoubtedly be critical.[230]

3.3 From observer to full participant

Stikker's advice was followed and, early in October 1951, the *Ministerraad* - reluctantly - decided to change their status at the Paris conference from observer to participant. Van Vredenburch, a Foreign Affairs career diplomat, was appointed head of the delegation. Minister Van den Brink of Economic Affairs had initially preferred to nominate the experienced ECSC negotiator Spierenburg, but the Cabinet decided otherwise, following the intervention of Minister Stikker, who considered the European army the domain of Foreign Affairs and not - as in the case of the ECSC - Economic Affairs. Another possible reason was that, because of his involvement in the Schuman plan negotiations, Spierenburg was considered as having been 'Europeanised'; the government, for that reason also, put its

---

[230] MinBZ, EDG 921.331, doos 8, Nota Stikker, 09-24-1951.

trust in the 'atlanticist' Van Vredenburch.[231] The *Ministerraad* gave strict instructions to the delegates in Paris[232]. Firstly, the common budget should cover only a few EDC organs, such as the High Commissioner and the General Staffs, and thus not the whole EDC, and approval of the national parliaments was required before entering into important financial obligations. Secondly, smaller states deserved a strong position within the Community, and should claim their own representative on the High Commission or Board of Commissioners. Instead of one single Commissioner with broad powers, as the French had proposed, the government suggested a collegiate body. Furthermore, the authority of the Council of Ministers should be strengthened through the introduction of the principle of unanimity for important decisions. Finally, NATO's administrative and strategic authorities had to be clearly defined vis-à-vis the EDC.[233]

These instructions aimed at restricting military integration to an absolute minimum and, in this form, Van Vredenburch's mission seemed impossible from the start. In practice, however, Van Vredenburch had some room for diplomatic manoeuvre, and he carefully ensured that the Dutch contribution to the conference was as constructive as possible. In fact, he soon succeeded in removing doubts about the sincerity of the Dutch delegation's intentions after the country's retinence in the first half of 1951.

The conference's chairman, incumbent already from the outset in February, was Hervé Alphand, nicknamed *le renard argenté*, or the silver fox. According to Van Vredenburch, Alphand 'deserved this epithet not only because of his thick head of grey hair but also for his reputation as experienced diplomat and dyed-in-the-wool negotiator'.[234]

---

[231] H.F.L.K. van Vredenburch, *Den Haag antwoordt niet. Herinneringen* (Leiden 1985) p. 593, chapter 16 note 1.

[232] Apart from Van Vredenburch, the Dutch delegates in Paris were Mathon for military affairs, Blaisse for economic affairs, De Groot van Embden for financial affairs and Riphagen for juridical affairs.

[233] MinBZ, EDG 921.331, doos 8, Instructies voor Van Vredenburch, 10-08-1951.

[234] Van Vredenburch, *Den Haag antwoordt niet*, pp. 451-452.

The Dutch change of status was salutary for Benelux co-operation. Earlier in the year, many minor issues had soured relations between the three countries, especially between Belgium and the Netherlands. Brussels resented Dutch obstinacy, and had been reluctant to look after the interests of its absent northern neighbour, while the Netherlands often complained about the 'self-willed, unpredictable policy' of Belgian Foreign Minister Van Zeeland, and about the pro-French views of the Walloons. Moreover, Benelux payment problems had resurfaced with the Korean War, worsening the Dutch deficit with Belgium.

Gradually, The Hague had become convinced of the usefulness of an alliance with their Benelux partners in opposing the supranational provisions in the EDC plans. They perceived that, following the approval of the July interim report, co-operation between the French and German delegations had intensified. The two delegations often met prior to the plenary debates to investigate common positions on important issues. The Hague, fearful of isolation, felt relieved when the Belgian government showed interest in exploring closer Benelux collaboration. Brussels worried that EDC membership required a revision of the national constitution because of the implied transfer of sovereignty to the supranational Community. A more profound reason for Belgian opposition was the fear that within a European framework the country's national identity would be further eroded. This identity was already strongly challenged by the linguistic conflict that divided the country into two separate parts with diverging views and priorities. Although The Hague was sometimes irritated by the confusing manner of policy-making in Belgium (a regular complaint was that Brussels had not formulated a proper standpoint concerning the EDC), it was simultaneously pleased to see Brussels taking the Dutch side in the struggle against the EDC.

At the end of October, the Benelux governments convened in Brussels. Drees summarised his objections to having a single Commissioner and a common budget. Instead of the Commissioner he suggested a council or board of commissioners, with adequate Benelux representation. The installation of a collegiate body would relieve Dutch fears that the French government sought to appoint a fellow-countryman in the position of High Commissioner. As for the common budget, the Prime Minister thought it unacceptable that an international organisation, with 'flippant Frenchmen' and 'irresponsible Italians' in its ranks would take control of one third of the national budget. He further argued that one could not deprive national parliaments of their right to decide defence budgets.[235] The government preferred a simple juxtaposition of the national budgets, with a dominant position for the Council of Ministers and without interference from the High Commission, whereas France and Germany advocated a real merger of budgets instead. Moreover, the Netherlands was headed for a long transitional period, during which national regulations would prevail (see chapter 5). In principle, the Belgian government shared Dutch objections but at the time had not formulated an official view on the financial issues. Although there was no talk of a common EDC policy in the future, at the end of the meeting the Benelux countries promised to 'maintain the closest possible relations'.[236]

Following the Benelux conference, The Hague was surprised but pleased to see that the Belgian delegation, more than the Dutch, became the *enfant terrible* at the Paris conference by adopting a critical, almost uncompromising attitude. For instance, Belgium proposed to restrict the integration of armies only to the forces of the 'Big Three', thus excluding the smaller countries. The Belgian change of attitude raised suspicion among the other delegations, all the more so as, at an earlier stage - immediately following the start of the Paris negotiations - the Belgian delegation had still proved willing to co-operate. As a consequence, the Dutch position at the negotiations improved considerably: Belgium became the

---

[235] Ironically, in March 1951 the government had introduced a multi-annual defence budget, covering the period until 1954, which had strongly reduced the national parliament's control on military expenditure, see also Th.J.G. van den Hoogen, *De besluitvorming over de defensiebegroting. Systeem en verandering* (Leeuwarden 1987), pp. 66-69.

[236] MinBZ, EDG 999.0, inv.nr. 16, Notulen van de vergadering van de Benelux-landen in Brussel, 10-25-1951.

conference's scapegoat, which enabled Van Vredenburch to act as an intermediary between Belgium and the other delegations. Chairman Alphand was obviously annoyed by the creation of what he saw as a firm Benelux front against the EDC. It was remarkable that the original Franco-German dispute was replaced by conflict between the Big Three (France, Germany and Italy) and the Small Three (the Benelux). After French abandonment of the most harmful discriminatory proposals, the German delegation had become much more constructive and co-operative than at the start of the conference. In mid-November, Bonn and Paris expressed their common desire for the rapid creation of a supranational EDC and, by working together, they sought to undermine the position of the Small Three.

The Benelux countries found themselves in a delicate position, concerned as they were about the prospect of being absorbed in an organisation where the three larger partners would predominate. Van Zeeland and Stikker decided to formalise their partnership: in November 1951, at the NATO council meeting in Rome, Belgium and the Netherlands took up a joint diplomatic position for the first time. Both countries feared a future extension of EDC collaboration towards political areas far beyond the original concept, concerns inspired by public statements from De Gasperi and Schuman, the Foreign Ministers of Italy and France respectively, about the creation of a European political association. At the same time, uncertainty grew about the official French position. Early in December, The Hague noticed a certain degree of ambivalence in Paris's approach to European integration. On the one hand, the French government's striving for a political community in Europe became more and more radical-federal. On the other hand, the French parliament was increasingly critical of the drastically pro-integrationist policy of its own government. Minister of Finance Lieftinck had heard from his French colleague Mayer that France 'advocated German EDC membership mainly for financial reasons'. In the early 1950s, a third of the French defence budget was spent in Indo-China, and Paris reckoned that Germany's contribution would help alleviate the country's heavy defence burden.[237]

At the end of the Rome council meeting, the American delegation launched a peremptorily worded resolution, urging the delegations at the Paris conference to finish their work with the greatest possible speed and to produce a vital EDC. The Benelux countries immediately submitted a counterresolution inviting Britain and the Scandinavian countries to 'participate in the European army and contribute to the further unification of Europe'. The Benelux initiative was rejected right away because it was obvious that the recently installed conservative British government as well as its Scandinavian counterparts were not interested in active membership. The Benelux ministers were well aware of the fact, particularly after SACEUR Eisenhower's public statement that, from a military standpoint, such active membership was not necessary, and that a simple association of these countries with the EDC would suffice. But the Benelux aim was to confront the Atlantic council once again with the apparent inevitability of British abstinence. By doing so they manoeuvred Britain and the Scandinavian countries into a position where it was morally impossible for them to vote for the American resolution in its original form. Benelux tactics ultimately succeeded because, as a result of their intervention, the wording of the American resolution was substantially moderated.[238]

In the meantime, the Dutch delegation had started criticising the EDC's common armament programme, which provided for strict control by the High Commission/High Commissioner over production, imports and exports of war materials. The underlying purpose of these provisos was to increase efficiency in the production of war materials by means of an advanced process of standardisation. The Dutch preferred to stick to their national production programme, at least for a long transitional period. They also felt that standardisation policies should continue to be the

---

[237] MinAZ, Raad MAK, Notulen 12-01-1951, De nieuwe status van West-Duitsland en de EDG.
[238] F.C. Spits, *Naar een Europees leger* (Den Haag 1954) pp. 135-136.

privilege of NATO's Defence Production Board, instead of its European counterpart. The Netherlands lacked a real war industry and feared that the High Commission/High Commissioner would use a substantial part of the national contribution to the European budget to place defence orders with foreign industries. The Hague therefore insisted on the inclusion of textile, food and footwear products in the common armament programme, because, instead of weapons production, domestic factories were pre-eminently able to manufacture uniforms, blankets, tinned food and boots for the European army (see chapter 5).

Another cause of concern for the Benelux countries was the decision by the Big Three at the NATO council meeting in Ottawa to make completion of the contractual arrangements[239] with Germany conditional on the realisation of EDC. Stikker said that this placed a particularly heavy responsibility on the shoulders of the smaller countries, who were not consulted on these contractual arrangements and still doubted the wisdom of EDC membership. It was also feared that, without allied control, German policy-making would become too autonomous, and thus potentially dangerous. Stikker urged the strengthening of the Atlantic Community (meaning an increase in NATO responsibilities in economic, political and even cultural areas) to keep a proper check on the Germans. He also pressed for closer links between NATO and EDC. In contrast, France emphasised the independence of the new defence organisation.

By December 1951, the Paris conference was on the verge of collapse. The Belgian delegation remained the main antagonist but the Netherlands likewise refused to cede ground. Duchêne wrote that at this stage 'the Benelux countries were not at all their later federalist selves'[240]. Drees and Lieftinck said they had no scruples in sacrificing the EDC if Dutch wishes concerning the High

---

[239] The contractual arrangements between the Western allies and the West German government aimed at supplanting the Occupation Statute. Under the Occupation Statute the allies had far-reaching authority to intervene in German decision-making.

[240] F. Duchêne, *Jean Monnet. The first statesman of interdependence* (New York 1994) p. 232.

Commission and the common budget were not met. Drees added that he was not afraid of critical reactions in the national parliament, which had always taken a more positive view of the EDC.[241] Indeed, the great majority of MPs belonging to the established political parties - KVP, PvdA, VVD, CHU and ARP -attempted to steer the government in a more federalist direction.

In an attempt to escape the straitjacket of the EDC negotiations, Stikker even investigated the possibilities of closer co-operation with the neutral countries Sweden and Switzerland, but without concrete results.[242]

In Paris and Washington, discussions were held on the possibility of creating the EDC without the Benelux countries. The Americans in particular were disappointed at the lack of progress, and Bruce, one of the US proconsuls in Europe and a convinced integrationist, suggested that Acheson amend US policy on military assistance to Belgium and the Netherlands 'if these countries failed to join an EDC created by the remaining countries'.[243] Acheson, realistic as ever, replied that it would be inappropriate to distinguish between members and non-members of the EDC with relation to the amount of US aid or the manner of its receipt. He thought it objectionable to penalise the Benelux countries for not being willing to join the EDC. In that sense, he strongly differed from his successor, Dulles, who two years later would show no scruples about holding the threat of 'agonising reappraisal' over countries refusing to ratify the EDC treaty. On the other hand, Acheson also stated that the United States would not hesitate to go ahead with an EDC composed of France, Italy and Germany 'if the Benelux countries continued being reluctant'.[244]

---

[241] ARA, MR, De EDG, 12-10-1951; ibid., 12-22-1951.
[242] MinAZ, Raad MAK, Notulen 12-01-1951. See also: M. af Malmborg, ' How can defence issues be avoided in European integration? Sweden, the EDC and the Eden plan', in: M. Dumoulin (ed.), *La Communauté Européenne de Défense, Leçons pour Demain?* (Brussels 2000) pp. 247-264.
[243] FRUS 1951, Vol. 3 (1), Tel. Bruce to Acheson, 12-10-1951, p. 958.
[244] Ibid., Tel. Acheson to American Embassy in France, 12-20-1951, pp. 976-977.

Chancellor Adenauer warned that the time might come that Germany, France and Italy 'would have to have a showdown' with the Benelux countries, and if so, he trusted that the United States would back the larger countries. However, Adenauer also expected that, *if* the Benelux countries persisted in being obdurate and the larger states were forced to go ahead regardless of them, this would confront the German, French and Italian parliaments with serious difficulties in ratification of the treaty.[245] At the US's initiative, the British government put pressure on the Netherlands to drop its resistance. At the same time, Washington urged France and Germany to be more compromising towards Dutch demands during the negotiations.

Eventually, US intervention proved successful. Several questions that could not be solved at the Paris conference were delegated to special meetings of the foreign ministers of the six participating countries. In late December, at a Council of Ministers gathering in Paris, the decision was taken to create a Board of Commissioners instead of a single High Commissioner, with adequate representation for the Benelux countries. The Hague was naturally pleased with this result, and deemed that Benelux co-operation on this issue had yielded results.[246] In return, the Dutch made a concession on the issue of the common budget, saying that they were prepared to accept the European budget from the first day, provided that during a limited transitional period the Council of Ministers would have to determine the budget by unanimous vote. The transitional period had to coincide with the duration of NATO's Medium Term Defence Plan (covering the period until 1954, see 1.2), meaning that national contributions would be fixed according to existing NATO procedures for a while. Previously, in Paris, the Dutch government had

---

[245] Ibid., Tel. Bruce to Acheson, 12-29-1951, p. 982.

[246] According to the French ambassador in the United Kingdom, Massigli, an interdepartmental committee had already (on 9 August 1951) agreed that the French delegation at the Paris negotiations could, if necessary, accept a Board of Commissioners. R. Massigli, *Une comédie des erreurs 1943-1956* (Paris 1978) pp. 287-288.

abandoned its claim that the national parliaments should have to give their approval to the European budget.

By the start of 1952, with these thorny problems solved, the risk of an imminent failure of the Paris conference had disappeared. Early in January, the State Department reiterated its stance that the EDC was not feasible without the participation of the Benelux countries, and offered support to solve the outstanding problems. At that time, the crucial issue for the Netherlands concerned the liaison between NATO and EDC. The American ambassador to France, Bruce, urged the German and French delegations to issue a joint declaration accepting the overall authority of NATO, in order to reassure the Dutch government. Bruce also said that in return for this Franco-German concession The Hague should be willing to respect the authority of the European institutions from the outset, to avoid discrimination against Germany and the creation of a German national army.[247] As described above, with regard to the common budget, the Dutch delegation complied with Bruce's demand.

The German financial contribution to the EDC was a perennial worry for the Dutch government. Experts at the Paris conference, including the Germans themselves, seemed to share the view that during the first year of the EDC Germany would pay more than the cost of its own contingents, but that its contribution would gradually decrease in subsequent years. The Dutch feared that the bulk of the German money would be spent on occupation costs (the maintenance of American and British occupation troops), rather than the building up of its own forces. The government was annoyed at being left out of the discussions on the German contribution. Stikker complained that Holland was considered a *quantité négligeable* at the negotiations. Dutch dissatisfaction did not have much impact, however; ultimately, they had to give in to allied decisions on this matter.[248]

---

[247] FRUS 1952-1954, Vol. 5 (1), Tel. Bruce to the Department of State, 01-03-1952, pp. 572-575.

[248] Private archive prof. Riphagen (Archief Riphagen), Analyse van de onderhandelingen ter Parijse conferentie, p. 23

Another awkward question arose as a result of American plans to change the way financial, economic and military assistance was given to Europe. The United States came out in favour of dealing with Europe as a whole, i.e. by means of the new EDC. The Hague, on the other hand, tried to safeguard its bilateral contacts with America, particularly in the area of financial aid, supplied under MDAP. For some time, the government refused to co-operate, but in the long run they gave in to American pressure. This was done on the vehement insistence of delegation leader Van Vredenburch, who had become increasingly irritated by the stubbornness of his government.[249]

In the meantime, many other obstacles were removed at the Paris conference. After the successful London foreign ministers conference and the North Atlantic council meeting in Lisbon, both in February 1952, everything seemed ready for the signing of the EDC treaty. The Dutch government was pleased to see that the Atlantic Council had provided for close links between NATO and EDC. The Council had decided that members of the two organisations would be bound by reciprocal security undertakings. EDC nations agreed to consider an attack on NATO as an attack on the EDC and vice versa.

Notwithstanding this satisfactory result, the NATO issue kept giving rise to misunderstandings and tension. In March, the German delegation stipulated that the EDC treaty should automatically commit all EDC members to repel an attack on any Community member. Dutch authorities refused to accept this as they could see themselves committed to fighting for German (or another country's) interests without British forces alongside. Furthermore, this would go beyond the provisions of the North Atlantic treaty, because Germany was the only EDC member not involved in NATO. The Paris conference was once more threatened with collapse. The only way out of this disagreement was by appealing to the United Kingdom to commit itself.

---

[249] MinBZ, EDG 999.1, inv. nr. 63, Code telegram Stikker, 01-23-1952; ibid., Code telegram Van Vredenburch, 03-22-1952; Van Vredenburch, *Den Haag antwoordt niet*, pp. 462-463.

The Netherlands had always hoped that the British Conservative government would some day decide to join the Community if the EDC plans were sufficiently diluted, but this had appeared to be an idle hope. The British Foreign Minister, Eden, instead promised to maintain British forces on the continent at existing levels (four divisions and the Tactical Air Force) for the foreseeable future, and to consult the EDC powers in advance if any redeployment was under consideration.[250] Washington made a similar statement and together the Anglo-Saxon countries declared that 'if any action from whatever quarter would threaten the integrity or unity of the Community, the two governments would regard this as a threat to their own security'.

These concessions were welcomed but failed to remove all apprehensions. Just before the signing of the EDC treaty, The Hague put forward another grievance, this time concerning the planned 50-year duration of the EDC. NATO had been given an initial life of 20 years, after which a member could withdraw at one year's notice. As the EDC was to fall within the NATO framework, for how long would the treaty be binding? For the full period of 50 years, even after NATO ceased to exist (formally in 1969), or for a shorter time? To The Hague, these were essential questions, given the suspicion that some countries, particularly France, considered NATO membership as only a temporary commitment. The government wanted to have some freedom of action within the EDC, to be in a position to negotiate autonomously after the first 20-year membership of NATO lapsed. Another option was to extend the Atlantic treaty to 50 years, equal to the EDC's duration. With this intent, the Dutch government approached the UK for a special commitment. Likewise, France put pressure on Washington to provide a formal guarantee for European security, but this would require congressional approval. Drees was sceptical about the value of such a guarantee, explaining that if Germany decided to withdraw

---

[250] ARA, MR, Gesprek met Minister Eden, 03-24-1952. Also: K. Ruane, *The Rise and Fall of the European Defence Community. Anglo-American relations and the crisis of European defence, 1950-55* (New York 2000) p. 32.

from the EDC before the final date of expiration, 'Paris apparently expected the US and UK to take counter measures' against the Federal Republic. Drees feared that the Germans would instead side with the Soviet Union, were they dealt with too severely. The other members of the *Ministerraad* criticised the prime minister's scepticism.[251] Stikker suggested making the resolution to this problem conditional on the development of political integration and the duration of the British guarantee. Acheson eventually succeeded in easing Stikker's mind by proposing that, in the event of a premature demise of NATO (within 50 years), a 'new situation' would arise. Stikker said he was satisfied with the clause 'new situation' because it would enable the government to consult the partners and make an independent assessment. He thought the clause would also make it morally justifiable to withdraw from the EDC if international developments required such a step. Stikker's colleagues in the cabinet remained sceptical but there was no option other than to accept the new formula.[252]

On 27 May 1952, the governments of France, West Germany, Italy, Belgium, Luxembourg and the Netherlands signed the EDC treaty and the related protocols, but Dutch scepticism remained unabated. Drees doubted the degree of sincerity of the rapprochement between France and Germany, pointing out that the treaty still contained discriminatory elements, such as the provision that Germany, designated a 'strategically exposed area', was forbidden from manufacturing heavy war materials on its own territory. This would give France substantial advantages in the field of weapons production. Another significant area of inequality was that Germany was allowed to become a member of the EDC but not of NATO. How would Bonn react to this? Drees expected that German ratification of the EDC treaty would be very unlikely in the event of the defeat of Chancellor Adenauer at the 1953 elections.

A written analysis of the results booked at the Paris conference - drafted by the Foreign Ministry - showed a clear lack of enthusiasm

---

[251] Ibid., De EDG, 05-05/06-1952.
[252] ARA, MR, Verslag van de Ministersconferentie van de EDG, 06-03-1952.

for the performance of the Dutch delegation. Although it was generally acknowledged that Van Vredenburch had headed the Dutch delegation in the best possible way, there was also widespread disappointment with many of the outcomes. According to the Foreign Ministry, the starting position of the French delegation had been so strong that Paris had often been able to assert its will at the cost of the other delegations. Dutch efforts to stir up differences between France and Germany had failed to produce convincing results. The other partners had only occasionally switched to the Dutch standpoint; on many issues the government had been forced to abandon its initial position. In its efforts to forestall the EDC's creation, The Hague had emphasised the priority of NATO obligations, but had often failed to obtain support for this stance, even from SHAPE itself. Likewise, the United States had been extremely reluctant to make concessions to the Dutch government.

On the other hand, the Foreign Ministry welcomed the provision that the navy and the naval industry would not form part of the EDC. Although the naval forces were given European status, they would in practice continue to operate under national and NATO command.[253]

The EDC treaty had come into existence but the real battle, its ratification by the national parliaments, had yet to begin.

3.4 Ratification developments

After the second Drees cabinet, consisting of KVP, PvdA, CHU and VVD, had been dissolved, the general elections for a new Dutch parliament were held in June 1952. The PvdA (Labour party) of Prime Minister Drees won the elections and became the strongest party in the country, followed closely by the KVP (Catholic People's Party). Drees himself was charged with the formation of a new coalition government. On 1 September, the 3rd Drees cabinet was formed, consisting of the PvdA, KVP and two protestant parties, the CHU (Christian Historical Union) and the ARP (Anti-Revolutionary Party). The VVD (Liberal Party) of Foreign Minister Stikker was not

---

[253] Archief Riphagen, Analyse van de onderhandelingen etc., p. 28.

represented in the new coalition and thus, after four years at the foreign ministry, Stikker was replaced. It has been argued that even if the VVD had remained in power, Stikker would not have retained his job. It was clear that in 1952 his position vis-à-vis parliament had become untenable, mainly due to continuous disagreements about the minister's New Guinea policy.[254] Stikker was sent to London to become ambassador to Great Britain.[255]

In the new cabinet, an innovation was made with the nomination of two ministers for foreign affairs instead of one, Beyen (unaffiliated) and Luns (KVP). In reality, it was Beyen who devoted most of his time to EDC and other European affairs, while Luns was put in charge of the 'rest of the world', particularly bilateral relations and the UN. From the summer of 1952 on, the chief discussions of EDC affairs took place in the Foreign Ministry and the *Ministerraad* itself. Beyen played a prominent role in these debates; his impact on national EDC policy soon became evident, and he emerged as a convinced advocate of regional integration in Western Europe.

Beyen's conversion to Europe stands as a telling example of the irony of history. In 1952, Drees had given the job to Beyen, a former IMF official without party affiliation, because he preferred a prudent approach to European integration and simply abhorred the idea of having a Catholic member (of the KVP) as the new minister of Foreign Affairs. The Prime Minister feared the coming of a *l'Europe Vatican*, and he thought that under Beyen, European affairs would be in safe hands. Needless to say, it was an unpleasant shock for him to discover that Beyen turned into the most pro-European minister of the post-war period soon after his appointment, and would later die a devout Catholic. In wry contrast, the KVP minister Luns[256], Beyen's successor in 1956, was rather sceptical of radical integrational

---

[254] FRUS 1951, Vol. 3 (1), Tel. Chapin to the Acting Secretary of State, 11-19-1951, pp. 928-929; P.E. Taviani, *Solidarietà Atlantica e Communità Europea* (Florence 1954) p. 143.

[255] D.U. Stikker, Ambassador to Great Britain, 1952-1958.

[256] J.M.A.H. Luns, Minister without portfolio (within the Foreign Ministry), 1952-1956; Minister of Foreign Affairs, 1956-1971.

developments and developed into a convinced 'atlanticist', thus becoming a man much more after Drees's heart.[257]

After the signing of the EDC treaty, the Paris conference installed an Interim Committee, entrusted with the following tasks: to consider measures to be taken in advance of the institution's being established, to prepare implementation of the treaty's provisions, and finally, immediately after ratification, to carry out such work as would enable the Board of Commissioners, once constituted, to exercise its many responsibilities. The Dutch representative at the interim committee was Tjarda van Starkenborgh Stachouwer[258], who - after the signing of the treaty - succeeded Van Vredenburch as leader of the delegation. Like Van Vredenburch, Starkenborgh was an experienced Foreign Office career diplomat, at that time stationed in Paris as the country's Permanent Representative to NATO. From the summer of 1952, he was entrusted with the responsibility for both NATO and EDC affairs. In the interim committee, Starkenborgh's main task was to be watchdog of Dutch national interests; he was not known as a convinced 'European'. The co-ordination of EDC affairs at the Foreign Ministry in The Hague fell under the responsibility of Lewe van Aduard, the head of the Directorate of Western Co-operation.

Which country would be the first to ratify the EDC treaty? Defence Minister Staf thought it of great importance that the national parliament should ratify the treaty quickly, in order to preclude possible French amendments to it. Staf anticipated growing French resistance to the EDC. Drees added that the US government was convinced of rapid ratification in the Netherlands, but it expected heavy opposition from the French *Assemblée*.[259]

French opposition to the European army had always been present, but following the signing of the treaty, criticism was vented in an

---

[257] 'Door de bank heen hebben wij dat gewonnen', interview with E.H. van der Beugel, in: Harryvan c.s. (eds.), *Voor Nederland en Europa*, pp. 37-38.

[258] A.W.L. Tjarda van Starkenborgh Stachouwer, Dutch ambassador (Permanent Representative) to NATO, 1950-1956.

[259] ARA, MR, Ratificatie van het EDG-verdrag, 10-20-1952.

unprecedented manner. In October 1952 the president of the *Assemblée Nationale*, Herriot, a respected political veteran with great authority himself, spoke out in public—in Bordeaux—against the EDC. Fursdon wrote that

> Herriot's signal from Bordeaux prompted expression of strong views all round. The effect was to reveal a general latent opposition among all French political parties to the negotiated terms, if not all the principles of the EDC treaty.[260]

The three most important French desiderata concerned: adaptation of the treaty, safeguarding British and American guarantees against German predominance, and a definite solution to the Saar problem. From the end of the war, Paris had tried to associate the Saarland with France, but this policy clashed with the German preference for holding a referendum on the future of the Saar area. Paris found itself in an awkward predicament. On the one hand, it wished to keep Germany in check by means of severe and possibly discriminatory provisions in the treaty, and on the other, it tried to mitigate the EDC's supranational powers to protect French national interests and to preserve autonomy for the national army. The contradiction between these two priorities complicated their position at the negotiations.

In October, Belgian Foreign Minister Van Zeeland suggested that the European army discussions be transferred to the Brussels Treaty Organisation (BTO), with Britain among its members. Van Zeeland feared that France would not ratify the EDC treaty in the form it had at that time, therefore he proposed a revival of the intergovernmental BTO, emphasising the importance of British membership of this organisation, not only for Belgium but also for France and the other countries.[261] Although Van Zeeland's plan was certainly visionary - two years later, after the failure of the EDC in August 1954, the BTO was revived to make German rearmament possible - the time was not

---

[260] Fursdon, *The European Defence Community*, p. 202.
[261] Politisches Archiv des Auswärtigen Amts Bonn (PAAA Bonn), Band 2 EVG (1/10/52 – 31/12/52), Tel. Pfeiffer, 10-31-1952 and 11-05-1952.

yet ripe for it. Van Zeeland failed to gain support from his European colleagues, including Foreign Minister Beyen. Benelux co-operation, so successful before the signing of the treaty, soon faded into the background.

Unlike his predecessor Stikker, Beyen turned out to be a moderate advocate of the European army. In his view, the EDC constituted a useful, or even indispensable, intermediate stage on the way to the attainment of the main goal of Dutch European policy: the realisation of a liberal trade regime in Western Europe in the form of a customs union or a common market. Ever since 1945, successive governments had looked for ways to liberalise internal European trade, but to no avail. In September, Beyen introduced his first proposal for a closer economic union on the continent within the framework of the European Political Community (EPC), under discussion then as a result of the insertion of Article 38 in the EDC treaty. This article foreshadowed the establishment of a long-term political structure, functioning as a roof over the ECSC and EDC. The EPC, as envisaged, was so closely tied to the EDC that it was generally assumed that a failure of the latter would automatically lead to the dissolution of the EPC, including Beyen's scheme for regional trade liberalisation. To protect his own plan, Beyen came out in support of the EDC, and he refused to believe that the French parliament was really considering rejection of the treaty.[262] His colleagues in the *Ministerraad* were much more sceptical of French intentions. Although Zijlstra, the minister of economic affairs[263] (successor to Van den Brink), and Mansholt, the minister of agriculture, were in favour of further steps towards European integration, particularly in economic areas, they felt that the EDC was not the right instrument to promote such development. Drees remained as reluctant as he had been before signing the treaty; his reluctance even increased after an announcement by French Foreign Minister Schuman that Spain would soon be welcome as a member of the EDC. Drees said he could not imagine how Spain under the

---

[262] ARA, MR, Ratificatie van het EDG-verdrag, 11-03-1952.
[263] J. Zijlstra, Minister of Economic Affairs, 1952-1959.

current fascist regime could ever be represented in a democratically elected European parliament.[264] Nevertheless, the Prime Minister shared Beyen's view that the Netherlands should ratify the EDC treaty as soon as possible. He had two reasons for doing so: first, it would help 'strengthen the image of the Netherlands as a faithful, law-abiding country that fulfilled its international commitments', secondly, further delays would 'provoke the French government to ask for new concessions from its partners'.

In January 1953, the government started to feel uneasy at the so-called interpretative protocols the new Mayer government[265] in France wished to attach to the EDC treaty. In Mayer's view, some modification to the EDC was necessary because the treaty in its current form would never be ratified by national parliament. The interpretative protocols were intended (a) to determine that the voting powers of the EDC Council of Ministers conformed to the levels current in the ECSC Council (with France and Germany having more votes than the smaller powers), even if French military input was diminished by extra-European responsibilities, (b) to ensure the integrity of French forces, (c) to retain full authority over that portion of the armed forces required for overseas duty, particularly in Indo-China, (d) to ensure that French forces in Germany would have the same status as British and American forces, and finally (e) to retain the ability to manufacture war materials in the French colonies without interference from the EDC Board of Commissioners.

The interpretative protocols aggravated Dutch suspicions that France was looking for ways to back out of the EDC. Drees, irritated by the 'unpredictable and procrastinating' policy of the French government, said that The Hague should 'not refrain from following the French example by introducing its own protocols, aimed at maintaining national salary scales and national criminal law'. The *Ministerraad* felt that the French proposals were so radical that the

---

[264] Ibid., 10-27-1952.

[265] The Mayer government was dependent on parliamentary support of the Gaullist RPF party.

ratification documents sent to the national parliament 'should be accompanied by a list enumerating the cabinet's objections to these proposals'.[266]

However, in April the Dutch government changed tack and agreed to sign the French protocols, probably under American pressure. Washington sympathised with the French demands aimed at extending the freedom of movement for their armed forces, particularly in view of the poor progress of the war in Indo-China. Drees eventually had to accept this, regardless of his reservations concerning the withdrawal of army units from the EDC in the event of an emergency in overseas possessions. He saw this protocol not as a different interpretation but rather as an essential departure from the original text of the treaty.[267] French success on this score was not unqualified, though; Paris was forced to accept that, in line with the treaty, voting strength in the EDC Council would be related to the size of each country's military contribution.

Despite the approval of the protocols, Drees continued to be pessimistic about the likelihood of ratification in France. He witnessed successive French governments dragging their feet on the EDC. In the meantime, Foreign Minister Beyen carefully ensured that adequate progress was made in preparing the national parliamentary debate on the treaty. He realised that the Netherlands would foster considerable goodwill in the United States if the national parliament proved co-operative. US Secretary of State Dulles promoted the process of European integration in an unprecedented way and American policy and prestige became increasingly identified with ratification of the EDC treaty. Eisenhower and Dulles laid emphasis on the political importance of the Defence Community, whereas in the past Truman and Acheson had rather focused on the military-strategic side of the matter. Almost from the moment he took over the Department of State, Dulles used the threat of a reversal of America's European policy in the event of EDC failure. Washington stressed the link between

---

[266] Ibid., Het EDG-verdrag, 01-26-1953.
[267] Ibid., De Franse protocollen bij het EDG-verdrag, 04-20-1953.

ratification and decisions by Congress and Administration on the supply of military and economic aid to Europe. The Netherlands proved sensitive to these American considerations. The country was in urgent need of American aid, particularly after the disaster caused by the floods in the province of Zeeland on 1 February 1953.

Beyen thus pressed for a fast-track procedure, and even some 'pro-European' parliamentarians, who used to criticise the government for its lukewarm stance on the EDC, now suddenly began to worry about Beyen's hurry. The government felt that a pro-EDC attitude was welcomed in the United States, and would yield rewards in financial and economic terms. Moreover, from early 1953 several members of government started to doubt whether the EDC bill would ever pass the French parliament. In their view, this was not a cause for great concern, however. On the contrary, they felt that French hesitancy should be countered by using Machiavellian tactics, implying that the best way to incorporate Germany into NATO - still a Dutch priority - was to have the EDC treaty promptly ratified by the national parliament. The Hague hoped that the parliaments of Germany, Belgium, Luxembourg and Italy would soon follow this example because 'in that case the finger of blame for the failure of the EDC could clearly be pointed at France'.[268] And even if the EDC treaty were ratified by the French Assembly - but, again, this was considered increasingly unlikely - then the Dutch government could not be blamed for having been an unreliable partner. Nevertheless, for the greater part of the *Ministerraad,* the EDC was still only a necessary evil. It was in fact only Beyen who welcomed the Defence Community, mainly because of its connection to EPC and his own plan for economic integration. Curiously enough, his policy for a quick ratification happened to coincide with general opinion in Cabinet.

Beyen obviously took a stronger interest in an advanced process of European integration than his predecessor Stikker. This emerged very clearly from an exchange of letters between the two in March

---

[268] FRUS 1952-1954, Vol. 5 (1), Tel. Chapin to the Department of State, 07-08-1953, p. 795.

1953. Stikker, who had become ambassador to the United Kingdom, wrote that Dutch participation in a European structure under French leadership was futile because of the 'existing lack of sincerity in France to ratify the treaty'. Stikker added that even if France were to adopt the EDC, it would soon turn out that it was unwilling to accept the creation of a common European market, which was, after all, the Dutch government's main policy aim in Europe. Because of this, he dissuaded Beyen from advocating European integration at home and abroad, and from pushing ahead EDC ratification. Instead, he urged closer co-operation with the United Kingdom and the Scandinavian countries, especially for economic reasons. In Stikker's view, intensifying European integration among the Six would push the British towards focussing their economic policy on America, with harmful implications for the European continent. Finally, he suggested that Beyen find another framework for the integration of Germany into the defence of Europe. He realised that his suggestion would not be welcomed by the Dutch parliament, which had 'never woken up to the fact that the French plans were weak and unsound'.[269]

Beyen proved to be irritated by the contents of Stikker's letter. In his reply, he pointed out that the EDC treaty had been signed by the previous Dutch cabinet - with Stikker as foreign minister - and that, consequently, the Netherlands had reached the 'point of no return'. Since the EDC had become a reality, Beyen argued, Stikker's 'retrospective wisdom was useless'. He added that he personally welcomed initiatives aimed at deepening European integration, following the example set by the European Coal and Steel Community. According to Beyen, the EDC was the 'right instrument for solving European defence problems, simply because there were no alternatives left'. He even preferred the EDC solution to the direct admission of German troops into NATO, because he feared the domestic political consequences of the re-establishment of a national army in Germany. Unlike Stikker, he still believed in the general

---

[269] MinBZ, Archief DGEM 6111/1252, Brief Stikker aan Beyen, 03-05-1953.

ratification of the EDC treaty, and he was also convinced that the EDC's realisation would pave the way for closer economic co-operation in Western Europe - along the lines of the EPC and his own Beyen plan. Beyen was 'not biased in favour of far-reaching political integration on the European continent': in his view integration in 'High Politics' was acceptable only if accompanied by progress in the economic field. He failed to understand Stikker's plea for closer co-operation with Great Britain, because thus far London had not shown much interest in developing ties with the continent. He felt that any further attempt to integrate Britain into Europe would lead to disappointment and frustration only, and that the desired solutions therefore 'should be sought within a continental framework'.[270]

Beyen received only lukewarm support from his own government for this stance, and Drees, in particular, continued looking for ways to get rid of the EDC. In June 1953, he pointed to new developments in the relations between the 'free world' and the Soviet bloc, following Stalin's death in March of that year. New Russian proposals concerning Germany, anti-Soviet demonstrations in Berlin on 17 June, and changes in the Soviet hierarchy - particularly the dismissal of Beria as minister of state security - all combined to indicate that there was a 'slender chance of an east-west agreement on central Europe'.[271] Although Drees admitted he could only speculate about the sincerity of Soviet intentions, he clearly welcomed recent changes in the communist world. He cautiously stated that, if the Russians were prepared to withdraw from East Germany and Austria - allowing the creation of a non-communist Germany - and to refrain from strengthening the German military potential, 'improvements in the mutual contacts should not be precluded beforehand'. Such improvements would help to bring about German reunification without risking a war. Drees pointed to the importance of reunification for the maintenance of universal

---

[270] Ibid., Brief Beyen aan Stikker, 03-11-1953.
[271] Fursdon, *The European Defence Community*, p. 219.

peace, and he was even prepared to abandon 'the idea that German reunification should never be realised at the cost of the western military co-operation with Germany'. In other words, the Prime Minister seemed prepared to sacrifice the EDC if East and West Germany could be reunified on an acceptable and peaceful basis. The *Ministerraad* generally shared Drees's views, though Beyen doubted the sincerity of Soviet intentions regarding Germany. The Foreign Minister urged the government to continue its policy of speeding up EDC ratification.[272] In August, following the signing of the Korean armistice, Drees said that if Germany was going to be reunified and if the reunified country was given a free hand in making its own decisions on how to participate in the international defence system, German EDC membership was to be ruled out. Direct incorporation of Germany into NATO would then remain the only credible alternative.[273]

The US government put pressure on the EDC countries to start the parliamentary procedure for ratification. President Eisenhower had made clear that he preferred a country other than Germany to ratify first, and it was obvious that he had placed his hopes on the Netherlands. The Hague was susceptible to American wishes: in May 1953, the national constitution was amended, empowering the government to delegate sovereignty to supranational European institutions. At Beyen's instigation, the Second Chamber of the States General (Lower House of parliament) was prepared to postpone its summer recess to debate the EDC Bill. This was welcomed by the ambassador in Washington, De Beus, who, in a letter to Beyen, once again emphasised the advantages of quick ratification. First, there was the argument of the goodwill the Netherlands would gain in the United States; even in the event of the EDC treaty not being ratified by other countries, quick ratification would still make, De Beus explained, 'a good impression'. Secondly, he warned that Washington threatened to reduce defence

---

[272] ARA, MR, Bezoek Beyen aan Londen en Parijs, 06-29-1953; ibid., Het probleem Duitsland, 07-20-1953.
[273] Ibid., De Europese Gemeenschap, 08-03-1953.

commitments to Europe if ratification continued to be postponed.[274] This was the result of the Richards amendment in the House of Representatives, suggesting a reduction of US military aid to a value of $ 1000 million in case the EDC treaty did not come into force. Congress linked the Richards amendment to the Mutual Security Program for 1953-54, meaning that half of the funds provided for European military aid could be made available only to the EDC or to its member countries. If the Community failed to come into existence the funds would not be made available unless Congress changed its mind on the recommendation of the President.

Beyen was not pleased with this new element of American pressure, fearing that EDC sceptics in the national parliament would consider overt US interference as an argument against ratifying the treaty. Instead, he preferred to show that ratification reflected the free will of the Dutch government and people. He hoped that Eisenhower would ask Congress to suspend the relevant section - the special EDC clause - of the Mutual Security Act of 1953, in order to avoid a delay or decrease of military assistance.

On 23 July 1953, at a plenary meeting of the Second Chamber, the EDC treaty was sanctioned by a safe majority of 75 votes to 11. The noes belonged to parties of the extreme right and extreme left, the Catholic National Party (KNP), the Political Calvinist Party (SGP) and the Communist Party (CPN). There was also one member of the ARP, a party in office, who voted against the treaty: Gerbrandy, Prime Minister during the Second World War.

Just before ratification, the Lower House adopted an amendment, implying that every future international commitment resulting from the EDC would have to be submitted for parliamentary approval. The government regretted this intervention, but complied reluctantly.[275] During the debates, the government was said to have shown a lack of cogency while outlining its arguments in favour of the EDC. Beyen's efforts to dispel misgivings about US influence on Dutch policy-

---

[274] MinBZ, EDG 999.1, inv. nr. 55, Code telegram De Beus, 07-07-1953.
[275] 'Ik kan niet goed tegen ambtenaren', interview with M. van der Goes van Naters, in: Harryvan c.s. (eds.), *Voor Nederland en Europa*, p. 74.

making sometimes lacked persuasiveness. At that time, a rumour was circulating that the US administration was considering an increase in defence (offshore) orders with Dutch industries, were Holland to be the first to ratify the treaty.

Dulles was indeed delighted by the 'constructive step' the Dutch Lower House had taken. At the same time suspicions grew of continuous delays in France. In December 1953, Dulles issued a clear warning to the European government by stating that,

> If the EDC should not become effective; if France and Germany remain apart, so that they would again be potential enemies, then indeed there would be grave doubt whether continental Europe could be made a place of safety. That would compel an agonising reappraisal of basic American policy.

With the term 'agonising reappraisal', Dulles basically meant a re-orientation of American policy away from Europe towards other regions such as the Far East. Concerning European defence, he intended to rely on the US nuclear deterrent and a gradual withdrawal of American conventional troops from the continent–the idea of creating a 'fortress-America'. Dulles obviously made his statement with a view to pressuring France into ratifying the treaty at short notice. As argued before, he clearly differed from his predecessor Acheson, who had always said that outward signs of American pressure and influence would prove counterproductive, especially when dealing with nationalist French opinion. But Dulles had a double agenda. In a private conversation with Adenauer, he reassured the German government that American troops would stay in Germany even in the event of the 'reappraisal' being effectuated. This reassurance was somewhat superfluous because Dulles had no real alternative but to remain on the continent as long as the German occupation statute was in force. Nevertheless, Dulles's speech prompted much criticism in Europe, particularly in France. The Hague was disappointed that, for the moment, the US Congress - generally seen as the evil genius behind 'agonising reappraisal' - refused to consider suspending the special EDC clause in the Mutual

Security Act.[276] The government urged continuation of US military assistance to those countries that had already ratified the treaty or were about to ratify. The Hague even contemplated entering a formal protest against American policies but eventually decided against it, realising that Dulles's remarks were basically meant for French consumption.[277] Paris found itself in an uncomfortable position. On the one hand, it kept being reticent, feeling that a quick decision on the EDC, whether positive or not, would endanger the forthcoming solution of the Indo-China conflict. On the other hand, it had to make sure it did not offend the United States, because by that time Washington was underwriting around 75 percent of the total financial costs of the French war effort in Indo-China.

In January 1954, just before the start of the Four Power conference in Berlin, the First Chamber (Senate) of the States General debated the EDC Bill. The Senate approved the treaty by a sweeping majority of 36 votes to 4, the discontents being the two Communists, one member of the CHU and one of the VVD. The Senate's decision led to the Netherlands, in 1950-1 originally the most hesitant, becoming the first participant nation to ratify the EDC treaty. Taviani praised the Dutch decision as a proof of high political maturity. He was so fascinated by what he saw as the favourable Dutch attitude towards European integration that he even wrote that Queen Juliana had declared herself prepared to renounce the throne if the development of European unification required it.[278]

Reality was different. Also, after ratification the *Ministerraad* continued to show a lack of enthusiasm towards the EDC. Drees still considered the Defence Community a rather unattractive *pis aller*, devised only as a means to make German rearmament feasible and

---

[276] The so-called Richards amendment of 1953 sought to make half the Mutual Security appropriations for Europe in 1954 available only through the EDC, the implication being that if there was no EDC, then US aid would be cut by 50%.

[277] Ibid., Archief DMA 13 inv. nr. 16, Code telegram Beyen, 07-14-1953. In general, it seems that the Dutch cabinet was much less impressed and perturbed by Dulles's threat policy than the Eden government in Britain; compare: Ruane, *The Rise and Fall of the European Defence Community*, p. 6.

[278] Taviani, *Solidarietà Atlantica*, p. 146.

acceptable. With the exception of Beyen, the entire Cabinet retained a preference for direct German membership of NATO. Even US reassurances that the Richards amendment to the Mutual Security Act would probably not apply to countries that loyally proceeded towards ratification could not completely assuage Dutch reservations.

In January 1954, the Four Powers conference in Berlin discussed the options for reunifying Germany on a peaceful basis, but without avail. In Beyen's view, Moscow needed a few years rest, because any weakening of her position in East Germany was going to have an adverse impact on the relationship with other satellite countries.[279] Drees gave up all his previous hopes of a rapprochement between the Soviet Union and the West and a peaceful re-unification of Germany. The failure of the Berlin summit convinced the *Ministerraad* once more of the need for general ratification of the EDC treaty (regardless of French vacillation) and a clear definition of the United Kingdom's commitment.

Although in November 1953, the British government had agreed to integrate the greater part of the army air-force in the EDC,[280] The Hague raised doubts about the continuation of British military presence in Germany, because at just that moment London was experiencing considerable financial problems at home. Until then, the German government had been responsible for financing British troops in Europe, but this would change after the end of the occupation regime and the start of the EDC, because from that moment on the British themselves would have to pay for the occupation troops. Drees pointed to the UK forces in Egypt as a possible solution for this problem; in the event that the government in London decided to repatriate part of these forces to Europe, it would be much easier to maintain troops in Germany, even if the costs were on the British account.

At French instigation, the government asked London for more updated information about the future presence of British troops in

---

[279] ARA, MR, Conferentie in Berlijn, 02-01-1954.
[280] Ibid., Onderhandelingen inzake de vorming van een EG, 11-02-1953.

Germany. Dutch mediation was needed because Britain refused to inform Paris itself of the size of the commitment as long as France continued to attach new demands to the ratification of the EDC treaty.[281]

In April, the Dutch government welcomed the signing of a co-operation agreement between the United Kingdom and the EDC. Beyen said that the British had gone even further than he had expected. The agreement entailed the following elements: firstly, a UK minister would attend meetings of the EDC Council of Ministers and a permanent British representative would have contacts with the Board on a day-to-day basis, secondly, the government pledged to maintain on the mainland of Europe, including Germany, such armed forces 'as were deemed necessary and appropriate', and thirdly, the UK had no intention of withdrawing troops from the continent as long as there was a threat to West European and EDC security.

The United States soon followed the example set by the British, despite continuous rumours about an 'agonizing reappraisal'. In mid-April, President Eisenhower reaffirmed the unequivocal American commitment to NATO and support for the EDC. Foreign Affairs top civil servant Van der Beugel welcomed this step and said that French demands had been largely satisfied by the British and American pledges. After all, the latter had 'indefinitely' extended their commitments beyond the North Atlantic treaty's limit of twenty years to 'encompass the thirty-year mismatch with the fifty years envisaged for the EDC', about which the French hitherto had been much concerned.[282]

By the end of April, four countries - the Netherlands, Belgium, Germany and Luxembourg - had ratified the EDC treaty, and the chances of ratification in Italy seemed rather favourable[283]. France

---

[281] Ibid., Omvang Engelse troepen op continent na inwerkingtreding EDG, 01-25-1954; ibid., Bezoek Beyen aan Brussel, 02-01-1954.

[282] E.H. van der Beugel, *European integration as a concern of American foreign policy* (Amsterdam 1966) p. 296.

[283] A. Varsori, 'Italian diplomacy and the 'querelle de la CED'', in: Dumoulin (ed.), *La Communauté Européenne de Défense*, p. 183.

continued to equivocate. The Hague regretted French recalcitrance, even more so because Paris simultaneously championed the creation of a European Political Community, functioning as a roof for ECSC and EDC. In its European policy, The Hague drew a sharp distinction between developments in the realms of economic and political integration, the former being welcomed, the latter not. The EPC statute was acceptable only if accompanied by economic paragraphs (the Beyen plan), to accomplish the desired customs union. The view held by the Dutch was that abolition, or at least reduction, of tariff barriers to European trade was absolutely crucial to satisfy the national interest.

Paris, on the other hand, increasingly distrusted European proposals with economic implications. In the early fifties, the state of the French economy deteriorated, simultaneously with a boom period for most of the other Western European nations, especially Germany. The contrast between German economic strength and French stagnation 'reduced French readiness to proceed further with the Six-Power organisation of little Europe'.[284] In 1950, French industry was still performing rather well, but between that year and 1954, economic developments followed a course disadvantageous to the country's competitiveness, thereby increasing French criticism of the economic elements of European integration plans. Paris therefore distrusted the introduction of the Beyen plan within the EPC framework - in September 1952 - because this plan was based on low tariffs (or even no tariffs), without adequate protection for the French economy. With the Beyen plan, the process of integration took a turn which was unacceptable to the French government. To a certain extent Paris welcomed political integration, but trade liberalisation was, in their view, quite another matter.

Beyen noticed that, by 1954, France was experiencing profound difficulties with the supranational course of the European integration process. He deemed that France had become intellectually isolated, a problem 'reinforced by the attachment to her glorious past'.

---

[284] Quote from the British Foreign Office, in: Ruane, *The Rise and Fall of the European Defence Community*, pp. 177-178.

According to Beyen, this had led to the curious paradox of Paris taking the initiative for close co-operation between the Six, but simultaneously turning into the most outspoken opponent of such a development.[285]

In June 1954, the French EDC story entered a new phase with the arrival of Pierre Mendès-France as Prime Minister. The general expectation was that under the new government - with the *anticedist* General Koenig as defence minister - ratification of the EDC treaty was very unlikely. Mansholt predicted that the new French government would not last long, and his colleague Zijlstra assumed that Mendès-France would be unable to solve the Indo-China problem unless he combined this with a simultaneous relinquishment of the EDC.[286] The *Ministerraad*, almost reconciled then to a premature death of the EDC, continued to advocate Germany's direct entry into NATO. Beyen was the only dissenter, arguing that German rearmament could be better monitored within the EDC, NATO's main aim being the unlimited increase in fighting potential, without regard to proper monitoring. He warned that in the event of the EDC's failure, a solution to the German problem would be further away than ever. At that moment, Beyen still believed that the French parliament would accept the EDC treaty, a small majority in favour of ratification being sufficient because, in his view, the 'French people were less averse to the EDC than their politicians'. Beyen rejected suggestions aimed at discussing *solutions de rechange*: he thought that the situation would be clarified if the French were finally confronted with the choice of either ratifying the treaty or accepting German membership of NATO.[287]

At the end of June, the government discussed the EDC stalemate with their Benelux partners. The foreign ministers of the three countries, Beyen, Spaak and Bech, proposed the convocation of a conference of the foreign ministers of the six EDC countries, but Mendès-France replied that, for the time being, he had neither the

---

[285] ARA, MR, De EG, 04-13-1954.
[286] Ibid., De EDG, 06-21-1954.
[287] Ibidem.

time nor the inclination to discuss the EDC. At that moment, the French Prime Minister was entirely absorbed by the complicated Indo-China negotiations, which had just entered their final stages.

At the same time, the national parliament rejected a US proposal to investigate the creation of a small EDC without France.[288] The Hague was only partly satisfied by a congressional agreement that those countries which had already ratified the Paris treaty would receive their full share of military aid during the next fiscal year albeit 'only on condition that they have joined with each other in a new organization for collective defense or are jointly developing collective defense programs in a manner satisfactory to the president'. In other words, to a large extent, aid was still dependent upon realisation of the EDC.[289]

On 21 July, the Geneva conference on the Indo-China conflict was brought to a successful conclusion. Mendès-France was considered the main architect of the final solution and, consequently, his prestige on the international political stage increased immensely. Beyen felt that the strengthened position of the Prime Minister improved the chances of EDC ratification in France. Unlike his colleague Zijlstra, who expected the contrary, Beyen was convinced that, following the Indo-China solution, Mendès-France would be willing to submit the treaty to the National Assembly. At the same time, the Foreign Minister wondered why the Soviet delegation in Geneva had been prepared to make concessions to the West. Were they apprehensive of the Indo-China conflict escalating into a world-wide conflict, or was the Geneva agreement an appropriate instrument for blocking further developments in European integration? Beyen was inclined to opt for the latter because, immediately after the Geneva conference, the Soviet Union proposed convening a conference on Europe.

Nevertheless, Beyen continued to be optimistic about the chances of ratification. In the French *Assemblée* he distinguished a group of MPs who were still undecided, and another group tied by decisions taken in the past, and he thought it possible to persuade both groups

---

[288] Ibid., 06-28-1954.
[289] Ruane, *The Rise and Fall of the European Defence Community*, p. 92.

to ratify the treaty. Beyen opposed any modification of the text of the EDC treaty, and he disagreed with Drees who was in favour of modifying the treaty to the Dutch advantage by introducing new amendments. Drees thought that the forthcoming conference of the six EDC ministers in Brussels in August (after 'Geneva', Mendès-France no longer refused to meet his European colleagues) would present a good opportunity to put forward new desiderata.[290] His main grievances against the EDC centred on the inefficiency of multinational army corps troops and the introduction of a uniform system of salaries[291] and promotion for all European servicemen.[292]

Just before the start of the Brussels conference, Mendès-France introduced a *Projet de protocole d'application du Traité instituant la CED*, in a final attempt to bend the treaty to French advantage. To spare sensitivities abroad, the French Prime Minister spoke of 'applications' of rather than formal amendments to the EDC treaty. But his European partners refused to be mollified. The *Ministerraad* felt that the tenor of the protocols was not only strongly anti-supranational, but also openly discriminating against Germany. The French Prime Minister urged, for example, restricting integration of national armies to the troops stationed on German territory, in the so-called *zone de couverture* (forward zone), and to air force units supporting forward troops. This was close to what Stikker had suggested back in late 1950, although in Stikker's plan the NATO High Commissioner was made responsible for the troops in Germany (see 3.1). One of Beyen's main objections concerned the proposal that during the first eight years of the EDC, a member state could suspend - in effect veto - any decision of the Board of Commissioners or the Council that it considered as affecting its vital interests. In Beyen's opinion, it was 'useless' to become involved in a community of six countries 'if there was no general acceptance of joint responsibility'. He also objected to the discriminatory character

[290] Ibid., De situatie in Frankrijk na de Conferentie van Genève, 07-26-1954.
[291] 'De Europese eenwording is geen mooi-weer-zeilen', interview with J. Zijlstra, in: Harryvan c.s. (eds.), *Voor Nederland en Europa*, p. 348.
[292] Ibid., De EDG, 07-05-1954.

of the French protocols 'which had no intention of helping to solve the German question'. Even if Adenauer & co. were prepared to go along with the protocols at this stage, their commitment would not last for long, Beyen expected. Finally, in the matter of the production and distribution of war materials, the Foreign Minister blamed France for trying to exempt their domestic industry from competition with the other five countries. Generally speaking, he was appalled at the change in the fundamental nature of the treaty envisaged. For the first time Beyen even preferred to drop the whole EDC project than to continue on French terms.

Apart from the motives mentioned above, Beyen's disappointment was caused by the protocol concerning Article 38 of the Treaty with its commitment to creating a European Political Community. In Mendès-France's *projet*, this article could be interpreted neither as limiting freedom of action nor as prejudicing the decisions of governments or parliaments with regard to the operations of a future EPC. It was clear that with such a vague compromise both Article 38 and the EPC - including the Beyen plan - would be discarded.

Drees observed that the French protocols included the provision that all decisions related to defence policy would be taken jointly by the EDC council and the NATO council, implying–as the prime minister added–Paris's acceptance of a future German entry into NATO. However, given the history of French opposition to German membership of NATO, Drees doubted the sincerity of this provision.[293]

The Brussels conference turned out to be a fiasco: Mendès-France and his protocols met a solid front of refusal. Beyen once again blamed the French Prime Minister for his lack of willingness to accept an organisation with joint responsibility, and he warned that the protocols could never be sanctioned without a new ratification procedure in the national parliaments. The other delegations supported Beyen in his resistance to Mendès-France and, despite a

---

[293] Ibid., 08-16-1954.

last-minute conciliation attempt by Spaak, the Brussels conference was adjourned without result.

Soon afterwards, in evaluating the conference, the *Ministerraad* expressed the hope that Mendès-France, despite his 'misconduct' in Brussels, would not resign as a result of the EDC controversy because this would 'even further aggravate existing problems'. Drees hypothesised that Mendès-France personally disliked the EDC but knew concurrently that German rearmament could no longer be avoided. If this hypothesis was correct, then 'Mendès-France's hint in Brussels at finding an alternative to the EDC, in the form of Germany's involvement in the Western Union, was of great importance'. Drees presumed that Mendès-France had gone to London to discuss this alternative with Churchill. Beyen concluded that Mendès-France would not stake his government's existence on the EDC, should he fail to obtain a clear majority in the *Assemblée*.[294] He was proved right: at the end of August 1954, when the French National Assembly took its final decision on the EDC, Mendès-France refused to ask for a vote of confidence. The Assembly, voting not on the treaty itself but on a Gaullist motion to remove the treaty from the agenda to pass to other business, rejected the treaty by 319 to 264 votes with 43 abstentions, some of whom included members of the government. The implicit consequence of this vote was the defeat of the EDC.

The decision of the French parliament failed to discountenance the Dutch government, which had never been a supporter of the Defence Community, and for a long time had anticipated its collapse. Beyen was the only cabinet member who showed signs of disappointment, particularly about Mendès-France's categorical refusal to cast his lot in with the EDC. Beyen had always preferred the EDC to direct German membership of NATO, but he had failed to gain adequate support for this stance from his own colleagues.

Following the EDC's collapse, France was the pariah of the international community, and the Dutch government, too, made no

---

[294] Ibid., 08-23-1954.

secret of its irritation at French obstructionism and wilfulness. Despite this, the Netherlands spoke out against an American proposal to convene a conference of five European countries - thus excluding France - plus the United States, to discuss the post-EDC situation. The Hague preferred a meeting of eight countries - the EDC countries plus the United States and the United Kingdom. Isolating France was seen as dangerous and counterproductive, because the government realised that German rearmament - still top priority on the Dutch agenda - was not possible without French endorsement.

Early in September, the *Ministerraad* wondered how far France was prepared to go in its opposition to German membership of NATO. In Drees's view, a blunt French refusal would certainly make Germany's entry extremely difficult. Both as a NATO member and as an occupying power in Germany, the French government could block Germany's return to western defence. If, on the other hand, France decided to give in, it was unclear under which conditions German rearmament was to take place. Drees felt that Germany should be forbidden from having atomic weapons, but it would be wrong, in his view, to put a limit on the number of German divisions (the French had stipulated a maximum of twelve). Minister Luns disagreed, arguing that unlimited rearmament was dangerous in view of the 'strong German desire for reunification with and the liberation of East Germany'. Drees replied that the West German government was 'well aware of the risks of rearmament and knew that adventurous policies would inevitably lead to the destruction of the entire country'.[295]

The abortion of the EDC stirred great diplomatic activity aimed at solving the problem of German rearmament. In September and October 1954 the Brussels pact countries met in London and Paris with the United States, Canada, Italy and Germany. The resulting Paris Agreements regularised relations between members of NATO and the Federal Republic. In May 1955, West Germany was accepted as a member of NATO. Italy and West Germany acceded to the

---

[295] Ibid., De Europese defensie, 09-06-1954.

Brussels pact, and the Western Union of 1948 was thereby transformed into the West European Union. The United States and the United Kingdom again promised to maintain troops on the European continent. Britain renewed her commitment to maintain four divisions and a tactical air force in Germany and even made the promise not to withdraw them unless with the majority approval of the enlarged Brussels Treaty Organisation. Prime Minister Eden realised that this was a far-reaching commitment, and tried to reassure his fellow-countrymen by saying that 'given our close ties with the three Benelux countries, I think we can always rely on obtaining this majority if we have a reasonable case'.[296]

The Dutch government and parliament welcomed the London and Paris Agreements because one of the main goals of Dutch foreign policy, German rearmament in an Atlantic context, had finally been reached. Moreover, the presence of American and British conventional forces on the continent was secured.

Conclusions

The remarkable history of the European Defence Community reveals that though in 1950, when France proposed the creation of a supranational European army, the Netherlands was its strongest opponent, four years later their roles were entirely reversed. In 1954 Holland was the first country to ratify the EDC treaty, whereas France, after tortuous hesitation, rejected its own 'brainchild'.

Between 1950 and 1954, policies concerning European integration had fundamentally changed, mainly for economic reasons: the Dutch economy - based on low wages and high exports - began to prosper, while simultaneously the competitive position of the more inward-looking French economy deteriorated. Through participation in a supranational European market with low tariffs, the Dutch hoped to take further advantage of their comparatively favourable position. This did not entail the government championing an advanced process

---

[296] Quoted from: Ruane, *The Rise and Fall of the European Defence Community*, p. 153.

of defence integration. Although in October 1951 the Netherlands became an active participant at the EDC conference in Paris, the government retained its preference for quick and secure German rearmament within a NATO framework. The EDC was considered a necessary evil, inescapable after the United States had spoken out in favour of the European solution. It then became clear that one of the main aims of Dutch foreign policy, the rearmament of Germany, was possible only within the supranational framework of the EDC, which was supported by the United States. The Hague was left with no other choice but to participate in the discussions, to try to adapt the French proposals to its own advantage, as well as to dilute the most harmful integrative elements. In practice, this was extremely difficult, not in the least because on fundamental issues, France could count on American support.

The Dutch government distrusted American pressure towards European defence integration. Especially after the coming to power of Eisenhower and Dulles, the fear was that the United States would use the EDC as a long-term excuse to withdraw its conventional forces from the continent thus leaving Europe in the lurch. The Hague's main concern was that in the event of war, continental countries would be directly involved with their ground forces, while the United States could remain in the background with its more indirect, nuclear capacity.

Furthermore, the Netherlands worried about the loss of national sovereignty in an integrated European army. Drees, Stikker and Lieftinck were extremely suspicious of sharing control over the national budget and armament programme with financially 'irresponsible' governments like those of France and Italy (see also chapter 5). The history of the negotiations in Paris shows that The Hague was not at all in favour of an advanced process of integration in 'High Politics'. Considering the EDC case, it is quite remarkable that in the literature of post-war European history, the Netherlands is often characterised as the champion of European federation and supranationalism. The negotiations over the European Coal and Steel Community - where the Dutch delegation urged the creation of a strong Council of Ministers as a counterbalance to the supranational High Authority - the European Defence Community and the European Political Community - which the Dutch government was prepared to accept only if the Beyen plan was included[297] - bear witness to the fact that in reality, the opposite was true. The government was prepared to pool small fractions of national sovereignty for the benefit of the country's economic and commercial interests, but in political arenas The Hague's policy was decidedly anti-supranational.

Although large sections of the Dutch parliament welcomed the development towards European unification, in the field of foreign policy-making the government was emphatically in the driving seat. This was clearly the case in January 1951, when Stikker made known that the Netherlands would be represented only at observer status at the start of the Paris conference, and parliament hardly even protested. Moreover, the move towards active participation in October 1951 was caused by the altered international situation, and particularly by the American endorsement of the European army, rather than by interventions from parliament.

After the signing of the treaty in May 1952, the government's attitude towards the EDC became somewhat more constructive. This was mainly caused by the 'pro-European' policy of Foreign Minister Beyen who had succeeded the 'atlanticist' Stikker in September 1952. Beyen saw the EDC as a useful intermediate stage on the road towards the economic integration of Western Europe. He felt that ratification of the EDC treaty would improve the viability and acceptability of his own Beyen plan for regional trade liberalisation - launched within the framework of the EPC. Other cabinet members remained sceptical, but as the treaty had been signed, they felt it useless to thwart the ratification procedure, especially when it became clear that the United States would not hesitate to punish non-co-operative partners by cutting military and economic aid (the 'agonising reappraisal' policy). Moreover, the introduction of the

---

[297] R.T. Griffiths and A.S. Milward, 'The Beyen Plan and the European Political Community', Colloquium paper Doc. EUI Florence 1/86 Col. 1.

'New Look' strategy forced the Dutch to realise that the US was serious in threatening to recall their troops from the continent unless Western Europe acquiesced to the *quid pro quo* of EDC.

The installation of the Mayer cabinet in France in January 1953 convinced the government in its belief that the EDC treaty was marked for death. Foreign Minister Schuman left the stage and the traditional *cedist* section within the French parliament was replaced by *anti-cedist* Gaullists, who saw no benefits to be gained from pooling national sovereignty with other European countries. The implications of European integration developments had gradually become unacceptable to Paris, mainly for reasons of national identity, but also as a result of new plans for trade liberalisation in Western Europe, including the Beyen plan of September 1952. The growing awareness in various European countries of the necessity for economic integration caused confusion in France and was actually one of the reasons - among several others - for Paris to reject the EDC. Even before the signing of the treaty, the Dutch government had questioned the sincerity of French plans for an integrated Europe. In November 1951, Drees observed that parliament in France was far less convinced of the need for new steps towards European integration than the government, and that the former was unlikely to continue supporting the government's policy on Europe. The French government subsequently moderated its policy, but after the signing of the treaty, parliamentary dissatisfaction raised its head again, mainly out of fear of sacrificing national sovereignty within supranational institutions. From then on, the government also began to worry about the prospect of being chained to these institutions, thereby limiting the country's autonomy and room for manoeuvre in situations of international conflict. From early 1953, the realisation grew that the link between EDC and EPC - with its political and economic implications - would be fundamentally detrimental to French national interests.

It was, however, not before August 1954 that the Treaty was finally rejected in the French *Assemblée*. The reason why the ultimate decision was taken after a year and a half of hesitation concerned the French need for American support for their colonial war in Indo-China. A premature decision on the EDC would doubtless have endangered this indispensable support. It was indeed clear that Dulles was highly interested in helping the French, partly to contain Communism in Asia, but also to prop up a government in Paris which might deliver the vote on EDC. However, after the Geneva resolution of the Indo-China conflict, French rejection of the EDC became inevitable, as was also the conclusion of Minister Zijlstra and his colleagues in the *Ministerraad*. Unlike Dulles, whose European policy had utterly failed, the Dutch government refused to worry too much about the French decision. Only Foreign Minister Beyen had cause to be disappointed because the death of the EDC and EPC also affected his own plans for regional trade liberalisation.

Although in general its response was lukewarm, this is not to say that The Hague was entirely optimistic about the state of international affairs in the late summer of 1954. Several risks manifested themselves simultaneously: further delay both of German rearmament and implementation of the forward defence concept, the possibility of a disillusioned West Germany drifting into the Soviet orbit, the danger of an American withdrawal from mainland Europe, etcetera. Hence, the rapid birth of the Western European Union was enthusiastically welcomed in the Netherlands. It secured the approval of the United States and the maintenance of US forces on the continent, it paved the way for West German sovereignty and, soon after, for West German rearmament within the preferred NATO framework. After four years of uncertainty and frustration, the government eventually got precisely what it had aimed for in the summer of 1950.

In chapter 5 further consideration is given to the question of why, after 1952, the French decided to abandon their own plan. I shall argue that besides political and military considerations, economic factors also played an important role in their final decision. Chapter 4 deals with the military views on the EDC.

CHAPTER 4

Defence authorities and the European Defence Community.

Introduction

The present chapter explores the views of the Dutch military concerning the foundation of the EDC. Was the Pleven plan on the European army seen as a viable initiative, or not? To what extent would it affect the position of the national defence organisation? Another focus concerns the reception of military views at governmental level. It is argued that both the government and the General Staff had strong reservations about the European army but, only for a brief period, were civil authorities really interested in the critical observations made by the military. After the announcement of the EDC interim report of July 1951, in which the nationally homogeneous division was accepted as the basic army unit, the government directed its attention to political, financial and economic elements of European defence integration and from then on, military arguments were increasingly ignored.

Unlike their civil counterparts, military authorities in the Netherlands and France held strongly identical views on the EDC. Both wanted to safeguard the traditional, nationally organised army institutions and both wished to integrate German army units directly into the NATO framework, because in military terms, the EDC was considered inexpedient. However, to their utter regret and frustration, the political and economic dimension of the EDC prevailed and eventually undermined the ambitions of the military to leave a stamp on the policies of their governments.[298]

---

[298] The views of the French General Staff are adequately reflected in: P. Guillen, 'Les Chefs militairs français, le réarmement de l'Allemagne et la CED (1950-1954)', *Revue d'histoire de la deuxième guerre mondiale* 129 (1984), as well as in:

4.1 The Pleven Plan and the first comments

In the course of the year 1950 and especially, following the September meeting of the North Atlantic council in New York, German rearmament became more and more acceptable and accepted in Western Europe, leaving France as the only antagonist. Many Frenchmen, still remembering the cruelties of German occupation, resisted any form of German rearmament, and the government in Paris was outwardly sensitive to these feelings (see chapter 3). However, the majority of military leaders entertained divergent opinions. Many officers openly advocated the integration of German divisions in NATO in order to strengthen Western defence against the perceived Soviet menace.

French civil authorities felt that the problem of German rearmament was essentially a political problem requiring a political answer. Early in October, Jean Monnet decided to convoke the faithful and devoted Schuman plan team, Clappier, Reuter and Alphand, to work on a new concept in the *marges* of the Coal and Steel conference. He deliberately excluded military expertise, feeling confident that what he sought was, first and foremost, an acceptable political solution for Europe's defence - one to which later the military expertise could be applied in order to turn it into a workable and effective defence plan.[299] Monnet's team soon produced results, developing a plan presented to the French Assembly on 24 October 1950.

Ph. Vial, 'Le militaire et le politique: le maréchal Juin et le général Ely face à la CED (1948-1954)', in: M. Dumoulin (ed.), *La Communauté Européenne de Défense, Leçons pour Demain?* (Brussels 2000) pp. 135-158. German attitudes towards the military provisions of the EDC are described in: W. Meier-Dörnberg, 'Politische und militärische Faktoren bei der Planung des deutschen Verteidigungsbeitrages im Rahmen der EVG'. In: MGFA (ed.), *Die Europäische Verteidigungsgemeinschaft. Stand und Probleme der Forschung* (Boppard am Rhein 1985), pp. 271-290; N. Wiggershaus, 'German rearmament, 1949-1952', paper given at the EUI Florence, October 1984. Later published in: O. Riste (ed.), *Western Security: The Formative Years* (Oslo 1985).

[299] E. Fursdon, *The European Defence Community. A History* (London 1980), p. 87; J. Monnet, *Memoirs* (London 1978) pp. 344-345.

The Pleven plan was not directed against the deployment of German troops, but attempted to forestall the establishment of an independent command structure in the Federal Republic. The plan proposed a European army in which the West German contribution would be monitored through the formation of small units - battalions of 800 to 1200 men - operating under a unified command structure. German troops were to be recruited and armed not by the Bonn government but by a supranational European authority, headed by a European minister of defence. West Germany was not allowed to have a national ministry of defence, nor a supreme command or recruiting agency. Moreover, according to the French proposal, the actual deployment of German troops had to be postponed until the realisation of the proposed integrated system.

The first comments on the French plan by leading military officers in Netherlands were decidedly dismissive. It was felt that the plan would delay the strongly needed improvement of West European defence capabilities. For military-strategic reasons, the Dutch military were in favour of a prompt German rearmament in an Atlantic context (see chapter 1) and they feared that the plan for a European army would, for a long time, obstruct the availability of German troops.

To discourage the development towards a European army, the Dutch government hoped to convince the allies of the imperfections of the Pleven plan, by initially emphasising considerations and arguments offered to them by the military. The Hague knew that the Chiefs of Staff of the twelve NATO countries - including France - shared the opinion that any attempt to form European forces by mixing small battalions of different nationalities within the basic army unit, the division, was militarily unsound and could never therefore produce a fighting army. The government fully supported opposition to integration below the level of the national division.

Likewise, the State Department and the Pentagon highly distrusted French intentions; there too, the Pleven plan was regarded as a useless and even dangerous device, which had no other aim than to delay the re-establishment of a West German army.

At the meeting of the Defence Committee of the Atlantic pact in Washington (28-31 October), the Dutch government's military objections were put forward by the recently appointed Minister of Defence, 's Jacob. The minister pointed to,

> The smallness of the German units; the amalgamation into a unified force of various national contingents of a small size; the existence, at least for a considerable period, of national armies to which several national standards were applied, alongside the European army which would necessarily be organized on the basis of some assumed general European standard; the denial of the need for a German recruitment and administrative agency; the position of the European Ministers of Defence.

Finally, 's Jacob warned his European colleagues 'German co-operation was attainable and valuable only if willingly given'.[300] Along with the government, the Dutch military stressed the need of equal rights for Germany and opposed the discriminatory provisions in the French plans.

In November 1950, French and American positions seemed irreconcilable. Washington became impatient about further delays and threatened to mobilise two German divisions without authorisation by the European governments, before the end of 1951. On the other hand, French Defence Minister Moch, whose son had been tortured and executed by the Germans during the occupation period, was unwilling to make a move, arguing that France would never agree to the foundation of an autonomous West German army.

In November and December, two attempts were made towards reconciling the American and French plans for German rearmament. Firstly, the Stikker plan (see 3.1), which failed to gain any particular favour with Secretary of State Acheson or Federal Chancellor Adenauer and secondly, the Spofford plan, named after the American permanent representative at NATO in Brussels. The Spofford plan, launched within NATO's Council of Deputies, provided that the core

---

[300] Ministerie van Buitenlandse Zaken (MinBZ), EDG 921.331, Toespraak 's Jacob in Washington, 10-31-1950.

of the joint European forces would consist of combat teams - regiments with extra armour and artillery support - of 5,000 to 6,000 men, rather than the smaller battalions, as proposed in the first version of the Pleven plan. In December, the French government decided to go along with the Spofford requirements and thus gave up the battalion as the only acceptable European army unit. In return, Paris stipulated that there would be five European combat-teams to every German team and that German units would not be equipped with heavy weapons. Moreover, the German army was not allowed to have an independent General Staff.

The NATO Council, convened in Brussels on 18 and 19 December, found additional solutions for the integration of NATO forces. At the Council's request, General Eisenhower was appointed Supreme Commander Europe, a step warmly welcomed in Western Europe, both by military and civil authorities. In return, Acheson pressed the European governments to accept the principle of German rearmament and to accept it openly and readily.

The approval of the Spofford report was a compromise between France and its partners. France was allowed to pursue the European army proposal, in return for accepting preparatory talks on the immediate activation of West German units, within NATO. The outcome was ambiguous with, on the one hand, the so-called Petersberg talks, directed towards strengthening Atlantic defence as soon as possible and, on the other hand, the Pleven plan conference in Paris, embarking upon the preparation of a supranational European arrangement for German rearmament.[301] It was decided that the Paris conference would begin in February 1951, soon after the start of the talks on the Petersberg.

The Dutch General Staff was disappointed with the dual solution and, particularly, with the concession made to France regarding the convocation of the Paris conference on exploring the viability of a European army: they felt that Washington was over-susceptible to French sensitivities regarding German rearmament. Their opposition

---

[301] Wiggershaus, 'German rearmament', pp. 17-19.

centred on military-technical elements of the Pleven plan. They feared that a further delay in the rearmament of Germany would paralyse the national defence effort[302] and, they also suspected, that domestic maritime interests would be damaged if the national navy became part of a continental organisation, without British participation. Early in 1951, the government still shared the critical views of the General Staff; both believed that the Pleven plan was completely unrealistic and therefore welcomed any form of co-opposition.

4.2 The General Staff and the discussions on the European army

At the start of the Paris conference, with the Netherlands participating as only 'observer', the French delegation presented a memorandum, giving a *resumé* of the history, essence and subsequent developments of the original Pleven plan. The memorandum formulated as the most important military aim the creation of a homogeneous European army with a unified structure and administration. This was planned to come about in two phases: firstly, the transfer of national contingents to the European army simultaneous with the re-mobilisation of the first German units; and secondly, the progressive integration of training and administration, leading to a fusion of European divisions and reserves, accompanied by central recruitment and basic training.

Despite these promising intentions, one of the working committees at the conference, the *Comité Militaire*, soon ran into difficulties over the size of the German units. Although the North Atlantic Council had accepted the combat team as the basic unit to be integrated into the European army, Bonn continued to show discontent and urged instead integration at the level of the *unité opérative* (consisting of either a combat-team infantry with tank support plus a combat-team tanks with infantry support, or two combat teams of the same type, embracing about 11,000 men). During the committee's meetings,

---

[302] In the autumn of 1950, the Netherlands had promised to build up five divisions in NATO framework, to be ready by 1954 (see chapter 1).

arguments dealt with the terminology, the political implications of defence integration and the military realities of divisions, brigades and combat teams. France and Germany found it hard to agree on these matters and the pace of the conference slackened.[303]

In April, French Lieutenant-Colonel Le Corbeiller confided in his Dutch colleague Modderkolk that, in the long-term perspective, a re-establishment of German divisions could not be avoided. Contrary to the official French (government's) position at the conference, Le Corbeiller opposed military integration at a level lower than the national division and he assured Modderkolk that all French army authorities shared his opinion, with only Defence Minister Moch dissenting. Le Corbeiller argued: 'Ou bien on fait confiance aux Allemands et on les réarme, ou bien on n'a pas confiance, et alors on ne les réarme pas du tout'. Like Le Corbeiller, Modderkolk preferred to solve the German problem in accordance with the existing NATO plans.[304] Meanwhile, the Army Staff did not deplore the stalemate reached in the discussions of the Military Committee in Paris.

Nevertheless, from the summer of 1951 on, events in Paris took an unexpected turn. After the failure of the Petersberg conference[305], the United States suddenly developed into a staunch supporter of the supranational European army. SACEUR Eisenhower had come to the conclusion that the only way to rearm Germany was by means of accepting the French European solution. Apart from American support, the Paris conference itself made substantial progress and at the end of June, the Military Committee managed to produce a draft

---

[303] Fursdon, *The European Defence Community*, p. 112.

[304] Ministerie van Defensie (MinDef), EDG 36 dossier 3, Nota Generaal Mathon, 04-20-1951.

[305] At the Petersberg conference the discussion centered on the possibility of a German contribution on the basis of the American plan - launched at the New York Council meeting in September 1950 - for an integrated European NATO force. On the Petersberg, the German delegation negotiated with the High Commissioners, rather than with representatives of the national governments, as was the case in Paris. The discussions were purely military-technical and the conference failed because of the inability of the participants to reach agreement on political issues like the German demand for equal rights.

interim report, dealing with operational, organisational, training, administrative and logistic questions and reserving as a matter for political decision, the vexed question of the size of unit and the level of integration of forces.

Just before the presentation of the final report in July, the French government again made a considerable concession, accepting the *groupement* of 12,500 to 14,500 men as the most appropriate unit for integration. Such a unit was rather similar to a single-nationality division and, therefore, militarily much more realistic than Spofford's combat team or other previous schemes for integrating national forces. According to Fursdon, the introduction of the term *groupement* was a 'deeply-laid invention' of the negotiators in Paris. For the new term, 'although to nearly all intents and purposes a division, saved French face vis-à-vis domestic opinion because it was new and carried none of the emotive political stigma attached to the idea of a German division'.[306] In return for this French concession, the German government was prepared to refrain from having a national minister of defence and from building up a defence industry suited to the production of heavy weapons. Another important aspect of the interim report concerned the provision of NATO's overall responsibility, in other words, the European army was to function under operational control of NATO. The crucial position of SACEUR and the proposed close co-operation between NATO and the European army in the fields of organisation and instruction, training, armament programmes, arms production and distribution of the European units, served as guarantees for the fighting strength of the Western European forces (which were planned to consist of 600,000 to 700,000 men).

On 24 July, the Paris conference accepted the Committee's report, which was subsequently circulated to the governments with a special recommendation that a European army be established in the not too distant future. The original Pleven plan had been modified substantially, in that some of the most awkward discriminatory

---

[306] Fursdon, *The European Defence Community*, p. 124.

elements directed against Germany had been eliminated. For example, after initial French opposition, Germany was allowed to have its own recruitment agency. Also, the size of the German contribution - initially planned at one-fifth of ten European divisions - had, by July progressed to one-fifth of twenty divisions, which was regarded in military sectors as a much more realistic figure.[307] These developments induced the Dutch government to drop most of its initial military objections to the French plan. The Hague continued to oppose the European army, but from then on, used other than predominantly military arguments.

The General Staff deeply regretted this change of tack and felt the time was ripe for developing new arguments against the European army. In August, the Chief of the General Staff, Lieutenant-General Hasselman, unfolded his personal views on the European army. Initially, the French plan had not deserved much attention, Hasselman explained, but after America's change of mind in favour of the European army, 'it had become inevitable to make a more careful analysis of its contents'. According to Hasselman, the US administration had two main motives for supporting the European army plan:

a) German rearmament was crucial and Washington had come to the conclusion that this was attainable only through the creation of an integrated European army.

b) For reasons of convenience and efficiency, the US preferred to deal with one European Commissioner instead of six independently acting defence ministers.

Rather than being apprehensive of the US 'bringing their boys home', Hasselman feared that in a European structure, France would attempt to gain supreme control over the German army, as well as *re*gain an influential position in Western European politics. As far as the Lieutenant-General was concerned, the French plan was unattractive for the following reasons:

---

[307] Wiggershaus, 'German rearmament', p. 22.

a) It was essential that the build-up of armed forces in Western Europe would develop in accordance with existing national plans, instead of a new, indistinct European plan. NATO and SHAPE were well equipped to ensure the requisite co-ordination of national defence policies and it would be wrong to change this.

b) A European army was to lead to confusion and duplications, because the process of developing an integrated army into a workable, effective organisation would be intricate, difficult and time-consuming.

c) A European army was impracticable because of differences in languages, mentalities, manners and customs.

Hasselman warned his government against the far-reaching implications of the European army, because the Netherlands would have to integrate nearly all of its land and air forces. The traditional national defence system was going to be eliminated. Unlike the Netherlands, Great Britain and the Scandinavian countries 'could easily invoke geographical arguments to stay outside the European army'. Hasselman feared that a plain Dutch refusal to join the European army would have serious repercussions, particularly in terms of the supply of military equipment from the United States. Hasselman made a plea for intensifying the diplomatic links with Belgium; in Paris, the Belgian delegation sought to set a limit on integrating national forces in the European defence pool and the Lieutenant-General strongly supported such a position.[308] In his view, the two countries combined would have much more clout at the conference table, than when acting as separate delegations. He advised the government to change the diplomatic status at the Paris conference from observer to active participant, because as an active

---

[308] Belgian Defence Minister De Greef and his General Staff fundamentally rejected the plans for creating a supranational European army; see also: P. Deloge, 'L'armée belge et la CED', in: M. Dumoulin (ed.), *La Communauté Européenne de Défense*, pp.161-168.

member, the Netherlands 'would have better opportunities to prevent, or at least delay, the creation of the European army'.[309]

Having arrived at this conclusion, Hasselman was one of the first officials in The Hague who pleaded openly for a direct representation at the Paris conference. It would take more than a month before Foreign Minister Stikker and his cabinet colleagues would arrive at the same conclusion (see chapter 3). There is not much evidence, though, that the Chief of the General Staff had had much impact on the government's decision.

Soon after the Lieutenant-General's personal note, the national committee of Joint Chiefs of Staff (JCS) produced a comprehensive analysis of the European army plan. The JCS foresaw serious problems during the so-called transitional period - the period between the signing of the European army treaty and the actual moment of integrating military forces - estimated at three years. In this period the dangers of duplication would be enormous: SACEUR, SHAPE, the European Commissioner and national chiefs of staff would all claim authority over (parts of) the European units, because at that stage, the distribution of powers was still ill-defined. Other problems expected to arise during the transitional period concerned the harmonisation of military education (and training) systems and the standardisation of weapons. The JCS felt that much valuable time would be wasted if the European Commissioner were given the task of harmonising national systems of military instruction - as was determined in the interim report. 'Prior to harmonising the instruction systems, the countries' weapons systems first needed to be standardised', but given the fact that weapon standardisation was expected to be a time-consuming process, the JCS feared the negative impact hereof on the existing national staff colleges. The latter needed ample time to accommodate to the recently started reorganisation of military units along American lines, meaning a re-training of the army with the American type of organisation and combat (see 1.2). The Army had deliberately chosen for the US

---

[309] MinDef, EDG 36 dossier 3, Nota Hasselman, 08-08-1951.

system, because it facilitated a greater firepower for the lower echelons of army units, as well as increased mobility of infantry divisions.[310] The modernisation process was already thwarted by the Korean War, as a result of which the Netherlands had been forced to accept British and Canadian equipment. The JCS therefore urged placing a limit on integrating training and instruction in a European context. Certain specialised schools could be allowed to integrate at short notice but, apart from these, 'military instruction should, for the time being, continue to be a national affair'. Another JCS worry concerned the extensive powers the European Commissioner was to have in appointing and promoting higher officers. The main cause for apprehension grew at the thought that the Commissioner would use his authority to have a personal hand in the composition of national delegations on the supreme military board, 'thereby affecting the international position of the Netherlands'. The JCS also objected to the proposed instalment of a European command over national territorial troops. The Chiefs of Staff felt that French fears of German militarism were 'unfounded', because,

West Germany, with a population of 48 million people, will never be able to start an aggressive war, because of the lack of manpower and military potential. The Germans will be able to start such a war, only if their forces are integrated into a larger framework and if their military potential is linked to the potential of other countries. The creation of a European army will not prevent an aggressive policy of Germany, on the contrary: it offers the Germans the one and only opportunity to develop such a policy. It is very likely that in the long run Germany will play first fiddle in the European army.

This was quite a remarkable position and, completely opposed to what the French government had aimed at when launching the European army plan. The JCS re-emphasised that the European army was superfluous, since Dutch interests were adequately protected

---

[310] C.M. Megens, *American aid to NATO allies in the 1950s. The Dutch case* (Groningen 1994) 199.

within NATO, which offered the 'only and logical framework for German rearmament'.[311]

4.3 Active participation at the Conference in Paris

In the meantime, continuing international pressure prevailed to convert the Netherlands to active participation at the Paris conference. In the Dutch counterproposal published at the end of August, the government wrote that it supported the idea of bringing together national armies, although on another basis than proposed by France. It was thought that the military objectives of the French plan could be better realised by a European army created along the following lines:

> The armed forces allocated or to be allocated to SHAPE by the states participating in the European defence organisation should be grouped in an integrated European force in accordance with principles to be laid down in a Protocol annexed to the Treaty establishing the European defence organisation. The principles should provide for integration above division level. Integration into a European force should not affect SHAPE control over those forces. Subject to the functions and powers of the Executive Board of the European defence organisation with regard to the armed forces, the administration and maintenance of the national contingents in the European force should remain under control of the competent national authorities. In view of the fact that in every respect the European defence organisation would function within the framework of NATO, the validity of the Treaty establishing this organisation should be dependent on the continued existence of NATO.[312]

The Dutch government thus opposed the integration of army units at the level of divisions (or *groupements*) preferring instead maintenance of the nationally homogeneous army corps. The Hague further wanted to stick to national procedures for organisation, as

---

[311] Ibid., Rapport Baay (VCS), 08-15-1951.
[312] Algemeen Rijksarchief (ARA), Archief Buitenlands Economische Betrekkingen (BEB), 2.06.10 EDG doos 640 (ban 1-10), Dutch counter proposal, August 1951.

well as a supreme role for NATO and SHAPE in European defence matters.

The Joint Chiefs of Staff understood that the government's counterproposal had been devised as a tactical political move: for diplomatic reasons it was deemed preferable not to dissent completely from the Paris discussions. Nevertheless, the JCS was far from happy with the tenor of the government's proposal; as a matter of fact, the JCS still preferred to reject any compromise solution.[313]

The counterproposal turned out to be one the government's last attempts to change the military elements of the EDC plans. To the dismay of the military, who continued their struggle against the military-technical sections, the government shifted its attention to other problems, particularly those concerning the loss of national sovereignty resulting from the introduction of a common budget, common armament programme and single European Commissioner.

The counterproposal had no real impact abroad and, in the beginning of October, the *Ministerraad* reluctantly took the decision to change the status at the Paris conference from observer to participant. Defence Minister Staf (successor to 's Jacob) gave the following instructions to the delegation sent to Paris:

a) The integration of armed forces should evolve slowly. In the short run, the European army would certainly not be an expeditionary force, and for practical reasons the bulk of the nationally homogeneous units destined for the European army would be stationed on home territory. Under those circumstances, a real and complete unification of armies was inappropriate and could be realised only in a very distant future, if at all;

b) The European army organisational involvement in matters like recruitment, pay, appointments and promotion should be restricted to an absolute minimum;

---

[313] MinDef, Archief Comité Verenigde Chefs van Staven (VCS), zeer geheim, Het Europese leger, 08-24-1951.

c) The country's contribution to the European army should be limited to the troops originally meant for NATO, thus not including national territorial units.[314]

At the end of October, the government instructed the delegation in Paris that for reasons of military efficiency and for economic reasons, it was essential to have the navies of the Western European countries organised on a national basis. To defend the position of the national navy, the government referred to existing NATO obligations, but initially, NATO authorities were not inclined to support the Dutch stance. Eventually, however, NATO decided that although sea forces would have a European status officially, they would, in practice, continue to function under national or NATO command - certainly a relief for government and military authorities. Only a small part of the domestic navy fleet, ships for coastal defence, was to be directly integrated at the European level.[315]

The Joint Chiefs of Staff in The Hague formulated instructions for the country's military experts at the negotiations in Paris, headed by General Mathon. Compared to the earlier period, the JCS now slightly changed tack, in that they no longer flatly rejected European defence integration. Instead, they instructed Mathon and his team to help in developing the European army, provided that the national army corps would be left intact as a homogeneous organisation. The Chiefs of Staff still refused to accept the *groupement* or division as the basic European army unit, because integration at that level would, in their view, produce a heterogeneous and thus ineffective army. They were unwilling to place parts of their corps under foreign command and insisted on implementing the existing national army plan, which provided for five divisions, to be ready by the end of 1954. The JCS opposed any influence on the national army by a European Commissioner - at least until the end of 1954, the period covered by NATO's Medium Term Defence Plan. The JCS also promoted maintenance of national staff colleges and military

---

[314] MinBZ, EDG 921.331 doos 9, Nota Staf, 10-03-1951.
[315] Particulier archief Prof. Mr. W. Riphagen (archief Riphagen), Analyse van de onderhandelingen ter Parijse Conferentie, p. 25.

instruction systems, fearing, in particular, the damaging effects the Paris proposals would have on the *Koninklijke Militaire Academie* (Royal Military Academy) in Breda.[316]

In the interdepartmental Advice Council for EDC affairs, General Mathon, national representative at the *Comité Militaire* in Paris, urged the opposition to focus on the proposed *unité de base*. The European *groupements* envisaged in Paris had considerably more tank support than Dutch units, which were organised along American lines and had the character of infantry divisions. The Advice Council thought it remarkable that the proposed European divisions were so different from NATO divisions, not only in character, but also in size, EDC divisions numbering 13,000 men and NATO divisions almost 19,000 men. Van Vredenburch, head of the Dutch delegation in Paris, was not impressed by the Advice Council's suggestions, and argued instead that the Dutch position at the negotiations would improve substantially if the *unité de base* were accepted 'with the possibility of a period of adaptation'.[317]

Dutch military authorities were anxious to preserve the national identity of the army and refused to sacrifice their autonomy for the sake of making 'a relatively minor contribution to a European army when assigning exactly the same force to NATO entailed giving up none of this'. This point of view was also displayed at the Paris conference, by means of a note from the 'Senior Officer' of the Dutch military delegation. The note ran:

> Dans l'opinion de la délégation néerlandaise il est nécessaire que les projets de réorganisation dans le cadre européen se déroulent de façon que le moins de dérangement possible soit causé à la reconstruction nationale. Ainsi les projets généraux élaborés du côté du Commissariat ne doivent pas être exécutés aux Pays-Bas jusqu'au moment que le Quartier Général néerlandais juge propice. C'est pourquoi le Quartier Général néerlandais, au moins jusqu'au août 1954, devra continuer de fonctionner comme à présent et doit avoir

---

[316] MinDef, EDG 12, Memorandum Comité VCS (Carp), 11-08-1951.
[317] MinBZ, EDG 999.0, omslag 20 doos 5, Tweede vergadering Adviesraad, 10-22-1951.

une voix décisive pour ce qui concerne la mise en vigueur des différentes phases de réorganisation dans le cadre européen.

The Senior Officer opposed the assignment of extensive powers to the European Commissioner, particularly during the transitional period, which was expected to last until August 1954. During this period, national military commanders 'should be in the position to supervise the transition from the national to the European organisation and the Commissioner's role in this transition should be limited'.[318]

Furthermore, the Dutch delegation, backed by their Belgian colleagues, rejected the French claim to place national territorial troops under EDC's command structure. Instead of the centralised French approach, the two delegations advocated the greatest possible autonomy for the national reserves, arguing that in a fighting situation territorial troops would be immediately involved, probably sooner than NATO or EDC divisions stationed elsewhere. The Paris conference eventually decided to keep the organisation of territorial troops under national supervision, but as in the case of the navy, the status of these troops was to be European. This was a rather half-baked compromise because it failed to address the remaining problem of responsibility over command and use of the troops. The final decision on the command issue was postponed and, eventually, partly delegated to NATO.[319] As such, it was considered a satisfactory result for the Dutch delegation.

Military commanders were united in their opposition to the European army, with only few exceptions. Unlike the majority of his colleagues, Colonel Gips, member of the General Staff, spoke out in favour of a certain degree of defence integration in Europe. It was his conviction that, in the event of Russian aggression Europe would be indefensible unless it succeeded in creating a united and indivisible army. However, Gips also had reservations: the weak point in the French plan, he said, was that the European army was not presented

---

[318] Ibid., EDG 921.331 doos 11, Nota Senior Officer, 11-30-1951.
[319] Archief Riphagen, Analyse van de onderhandelingen ter Parijse conferentie, pp. 14 and 24.

as an ideal solution for the sake of the ideal itself - European defence co-operation - but rather as an instrument to impose restrictions on German rearmament. The discriminatory provisions were 'illogical and counter-productive', because 'Europe needed Germany and the German military potential for its own security'. The Colonel argued that, in a conflict situation, Germany would have to make more sacrifices than the neighbouring countries because of its vulnerable strategic position in the heart of Europe and that as a consequence, it was 'imperative to grant equal rights to the Federal Republic'.

As an alternative to EDC, Gips suggested establishing a European Ministry of War, equipped with advisory powers, some controlling powers over the member states and commanding powers, over army units. In Gips's plan, the Ministry of War was to be supervised by a non-permanent Council of Ministers, for setting the general lines of policy. Policy implementation would fall under a Council of Deputies, assisted by a Secretary-General. The main task facing the Ministry would be the formation and organisation of armed forces, necessitating close collaboration with the operative Supreme Command. According to Gips, the common budget for the European army should cover only military infrastructure and joint schools.[320]

The Gips proposal implied a less drastic transfer of national sovereignty than envisaged in the original French plan, but it failed to attract attention, even among the national General Staff. According to the GS, the European army, in whatever form, had to be avoided. Suggesting alternatives, like Gips had done, might give the wrong impression that the Netherlands was moving slowly towards the French position. The military feared that the European army would expose them to French leadership and, at the conference table in Paris, they sought to contain French dominance in every possible way. Instead, they emphasised the bond with NATO and the importance of maintaining smooth contacts with the Anglo-Saxon powers.

---

[320] MinDef, JCS 36, Nota Colonel Gips, 12-02-1951.

In December, in an *aide-mémoire* on the use of languages within the EDC, the Senior Officer stated that native languages should have priority, but that,

> Dès qu'il y aura des difficultés de langue, soit dans le contact entre unités, soit dans le contact entre individus dans les Etats Majors intégrés, l'anglais doit être employé.

Apart from an anti-continental motive, this was prompted by the fact that the navies and air forces of the NATO countries were already accustomed to using the English language in their daily work.[321] Until the signing of the treaties, The Hague kept emphasising the bond between the two organisations. For example, concerning the term of military service in the EDC, the cabinet announced that a uniform term (pressed for by the Belgian delegation) was acceptable only if it did not interfere with the fulfilment of the NATO obligations.

Early in 1952, considerable progress was made towards reconciling the various national positions - particularly concerning the common budget and the Board of Commissioners and on May 27th 1952, West Germany, France, Italy and the Benelux countries signed the EDC treaty.

The day before, Minister Staf remarked that, during the negotiations, the military experts' advice had been largely neglected because the European army had become a political, rather than a military matter. German rearmament was seen as a political necessity and military arguments were considered of secondary importance. Staf predicted that the treaty's elaboration would create further problems, especially in those areas - e.g. military schools – where the EDC operated independently from NATO. He feared that, as a result, NATO would figure less prominently in the policies of the member-states.[322]

According to the military section of the EDC treaty, the basic operational unit of the European army was to be the *groupement*,

---

[321] MinBZ, EDG 921.331 doos 11, Aide-mémoire Senior Officer, 12-17-1951.
[322] ARA, Notulen Ministerraad (MR), De EDG, 05-26-1952.

which was in fact similar to a division - consisting of 12,000 to 13,000 men. On French insistence, European army corps would be composed of divisions of different nationalities and would thus lose their national character. The corps' command and the General Staff were also to be wholly integrated. Member-states would eventually contribute a total of 43 divisions to the general military pool: 14 from France, 12 from Germany, 12 from Italy and the remainder from the Benelux countries.[323]

As a logical result of the integration of forces, the Treaty included an 'automatic action commitment', implying that 'any armed attack against one of the member states in Europe or against the European defence forces should be considered an armed attack on all member states', and that 'the member states and the European defence forces should afford to the state or force so attacked all the military and other aid in their power'. This resembled the automatic guarantee clause of the Brussels treaty of 1948, but went much further than the relevant article of the North Atlantic treaty, which only provided for mutual consultation in an emergency situation.

Articles 9 to 18 of the EDC treaty laid down all the principles upon which the constitution and organisation of the European defence forces were to rest. The European army would fall under the command of NATO's Supreme Commander in Europe, thereby securing an operational link with the Atlantic alliance. Units from all member-states were to be made available to the Community 'with a view to their fusion', but no member state could recruit or maintain national armed forces other than those for which the Treaty had made special provision.

Articles 12 to 14 laid down the conditions, under which a member-state might, with the authority of the Board of Commissioners, temporarily withdraw part of its EDG force contribution to meet national contingencies. The problems envisaged were those of disorder or threatened disorder in the member state's own territories, in the event of a major crisis affecting a non-European territory for

---

[323] S. Dockrill, *Britain's policy for West German rearmament, 1950-1955* (Cambridge 1991) p. 89.

which it had assumed responsibility, or to fulfil an international mission entrusted to it outside the EDC area.[324] These exceptions were requested by the French and were deplored in the Netherlands where colonial responsibilities had been heavily curtailed since the independence of Indonesia in 1949. Drees also disliked a treaty provision concerning the establishment of military schools in North Africa, arguing that Paris had added this provision with the aim of involving other EDC countries in her colonial problems.

The greater part of the air force units was to remain organised on a national basis. A certain number of basic units of different nationalities would be grouped together under and supported by integrated higher echelons.

European naval forces would be equipped according to the requirements for protection of the home waters of the member-states' European territories. Contingents were to form groups of the same nationality for single tactical tasks, but would have European status; they could be incorporated in part or as a whole, in NATO commands. In practice, the greater part of the navies would remain nationally organised and fall under NATO's command structure.

Furthermore the Treaty regulated that conscripts from the various member states were to perform a similar period of active service - eighteen months, according to a proposal made by the Belgian delegation - and that the Board of Commissioners and the Council were to act quickly in standardising training. The Board was to be responsible, as from an agreed date, for recruiting the European defence forces. It was also to be responsible for the training of these forces. It was to direct the staff colleges of the member states and to prepare mobilisation plans. The deployment of the European defence forces, within the framework of the recommendations of NATO's Supreme Commander, was also to be the responsibility of the Board, as was the administration of its personnel and equipment. The Protocol regarding relations between the EDC and NATO, provided for reciprocal consultation between the two Councils and for

---

[324] Fursdon, *The European Defence Community*, pp. 153-154.

combined meetings. In the event of a threat posed to the territorial integrity, political independence or security of one of the parties to the two treaties, or if the continued existence of NATO or the EDC was at stake, a combined meeting would be convened at the request of the party concerned, to consider what measures would need to be taken to deal with the situation. As soon as EDC forces were placed under a NATO commander, the latter's headquarters were to have EDC representation.[325]

The Treaty was signed, but the ratification procedure in the national parliaments was yet to begin. It was clear that military commanders in the Netherlands were not happy with the results and would continue to strive for adaptation of the military provisions. In particular, the level of integrating army units, standardisation of training, integration of staff colleges and harmonisation of the conscription period were seen as highly unsatisfactory outcomes of the negotiations.

4.4 Military opposition to ratification

Although the Ministry of Defence and the General Staff were united in their opposition to the EDC, mutual relations between civil and military authorities left much to be desired. In August 1952, Van Hoeve - head of the Ministry's EDC department - and Lieutenant-General Hasselman gave a striking example of the strained relationship between the two institutions.

In an exchange of letters, Van Hoeve explicitly argued that the military should be prevented from meddling in political affairs. As for the EDC, he made a sharp distinction between the responsibilities of military and civil authorities, indicating that national governments should have the final say regarding legal issues, administration and management. He further argued that the Board of Commissioners should be made responsible for policy-making and supervising the Chiefs of Staff, the latter's activities being confined to policy implementation. Obviously, Van Hoeve had little confidence in the

---

[325] Ibid., pp. 160 and 179.

military, as may be inferred from his (rhetorical) question '*quis custodiet ipsos custodes*?'[326].

Hasselman disliked the tenor of Van Hoeve's letter and rejected the explicit distinction therein between military and civil authorities; real authority was, in his view, indivisible. Moreover, Van Hoeve's 'quis custodiet ipsos custodes' was proof of 'unwarranted distrust in the military'. The Lieutenant-General rejected a military role for the Board of Commissioners, arguing that, in operational terms, European forces would fall under NATO's command structure and not under the Board. Hasselman also disagreed with Van Hoeve's preference for civil predominance in the EDC's administration and management. In his view, a substantial role for military experts was necessary, particularly in the areas of personnel, real estate, weapons and equipment.[327]

In November 1952, Lieutenant-Colonel D'Engelbronner even decided to ignore the Defence Ministry, by sending a letter directly to the Ministry of Foreign Affairs, the department most involved in EDC affairs. According to D'Engelbronner, the EDC had one advantage, in that it would facilitate the re-establishment of German troops. Apart from that, the expected effects were purely negative:

a) Building up a European army required an excessive amount of time and personnel. Much work would be superfluous because duplication of the tasks of existing organisations like NATO and BTO was unavoidable. Moreover, unlike the other five participating countries, Germany had no experience with standardising its forces along American lines, which further complicated the organisation of a European army.

b) The formation of one big European army corps consisting of *groupements* of different nationalities would reduce the fighting strength of the European army.

c) The idea of having a German officer commanding a Dutch division was simply unacceptable.

---

[326] 'Who controls the guards?'
[327] MinDef, EDG 25, Nota Hasselman, 08-01-1952.

d) The integration of military schools would be thwarted by unavoidable language problems. The existing national colleges had, in general, a high reputation, and should therefore continue to perform their duties.

e) A conscription period of eighteen months for all EDC forces interfered with the existing NATO commitments.

To avoid all these problems, D'Engelbronner urged direct admission of German troops into NATO.

In a reply to D'Engelbronner, the Ministry of Foreign Affairs wrote that the EDC had become indispensable for political reasons, it being the only acceptable instrument for German rearmament. According to the Foreign Ministry, D'Engelbronner's arguments were perhaps plausible, but, since the EDC treaty had been signed, 'the Lieutenant-Colonel was discussing a might-have-been'.[328]

At the end of 1952, Foreign Minister Beyen - Stikker's successor from September 1952 - carefully ensured that sufficient progress was made in preparing the procedure for the ratification of the EDC treaty in the national parliament.

Hasselman was indefatigable in expressing his grievances. In January 1953, in a note to Defence Minister Staf, he once again gave vent to his criticism of the European army, this time using the following arguments: the impossibility of integrating army units of different nationalities; the impracticability of creating specific European training institutions, given existing differences in languages, habits and mentalities; psychological problems as a consequence of the closure of renowned national army institutions like the *Koninklijke Militaire Academie* (Royal Military Academy) in Breda; and inevitable delays in implementing the existing NATO plans.[329]

During a cabinet discussion on the deployment of German *groupements*, Defence Minister Staf reiterated his stance that integration of Dutch troops into a German army corps was unacceptable. He also endorsed the military view that sticking to the

---

[328] MinBZ, EDG 999.0, omslag 21, Brief d'Engelbronner, 11-20-1952.
[329] Ibid., EDG 999.1, omslag 55, Nota Hasselman, 02-12-1953.

national system of army organisation would be the best guarantee for a solid build-up of the armies in Europe. On the other hand, Staf had no problem in accepting EDC supervision over the training of national troops.[330] In this respect, he differed from the General Staff, which insisted on organising military instruction on a strictly national basis.

Early in 1953, in order to overcome domestic resistance to the EDC, French Prime Minister Mayer introduced additional protocols to the EDC treaty. Defence Minister Staf saw the protocols as a sign that France was looking for ways to get rid of the treaty.[331]

The Dutch General Staff welcomed the new French initiative, being aware of the French military's hostility towards the European army. They probably regarded the additional protocols as an unexpected opportunity to torpedo most of the supranational features of the EDC treaty.

At the end of June, as a result of the growing disagreements between civil and military authorities, the GS was not represented at a Belgian-Dutch meeting in The Hague concerning the military implications of the Mayer proposals. While Colonel Hartenot represented the Belgian GS, the Netherlands sent a strictly civilian delegation: Minister Staf, Starkenborgh (member of the Interim Committee in Paris) and Lewe (head of the Directorate of Western Co-operation of the Department of Foreign Affairs). At the meeting, the Dutch delegates proved reluctant to change the text of the EDC treaty; only minor modifications could be contemplated.[332]

Hasselman kept trying to persuade the government to change its mind and, in February 1953, he recommended the minister of Defence to use the French protocols as a welcome opportunity for adapting the EDC treaty to Dutch advantage. Following the French example, Hasselman suggested instructing the national delegation at the Paris conference to put forward its own protocols. Once again,

---

[330] ARA, MR, De EDG en de opstelling van Duitse legergroepen, 01-05-1953.

[331] Ibid., Het EDG-verdrag, 01-12-1953.

[332] MinBZ, EDG 999.0, omslag 16, Verslag van de Belgisch-Nederlandse vergadering in Den Haag, 01-30-1953.

the Lieutenant-General came out against integrating divisions of different nationalities into one European army corps and, instead, suggested a protocol aimed at safeguarding the single-nationality army corps. Another protocol was needed for changing the term of military service within the EDC. According to the treaty, all military categories and ranks would serve for exactly the same period of time (18 months) but, in Hasselman's view, officers, non-commissioned officers and technicians needed a longer period of training, in accordance with existing practice in the Netherlands. Finally, he suggested a protocol on the size of the *groupements*. The Paris conference had determined that EDC *groupements* would consist of about 13,000 men, but in 1950, NATO had stipulated a size of 19,000.[333] Hasselman feared that the resulting reorganisation of the army would 'lead to disorder and confusion, without demonstrable advantages'. He also felt that the German army would benefit most from this arrangement because, unlike the other five countries (each having NATO responsibilities), Germany could immediately start with building up divisions according to the new plans.[334]

Hasselman failed to acquire support from his government. Although Prime Minister Drees was not averse to certain modifications in the Treaty (see 3.4), the *Ministerraad*, for tactical reasons, urged a quick ratification of the EDC treaty. Once again, the General Staff was confronted with the harsh reality that military arguments hardly played a role in the national EDC debate. For the rest of 1953, they refrained from developing further initiatives on the EDC, discouraged as they were by the neglect of their views in government circles.

In April 1954, the 'agreement regarding co-operation between the United Kingdom and the EDC' was signed in Paris. On the military side, this agreement ensured that the British forces would be present

---

[333] A NATO division consisted of: 3 regiments infantry (at 3 battalions and 1 tank squadron), 1 reconnoitring squadron, 1 tank battalion, 1 military engineering battalion, 4 detachments howitzer artillery, 1 detachment anti-aircraft artillery, 1 technical service company and 1 QMG company.
[334] MinDef, VCS 19, Nota Hasselman, 02-12-1953.

in strength on the continent before aggression began. One UK armoured division would be placed within an EDC corps and Royal Air Force units would participate with EDC air formations in a NATO air group and be controlled by a single integrated Headquarter. In general, the British government was extending and reinforcing its commitments to the European allies, pursuing the policies expressed in the Dunkirk and Brussels treaties.[335]

Defence Minister Staf welcomed the British guarantees and expected no difficulty in integrating British forces into an EDC army corps. In this respect, he pointed to the successful co-operation between the British Rhine army and the first Dutch army corps within the framework of NATO's Northern Army. Moreover, in the autumn of 1953, during the NATO manoeuvre 'Grand Repulse', a British armoured division and a Canadian mechanic brigade had been smoothly incorporated in the Dutch army corps. Together, with a Dutch division and army corps troops, they had operated as one unit under a Dutch army corps commander.[336]

Early in 1954, the national parliament, the first of the six, overwhelmingly approved the EDC treaty. Following ratification, the government hoped the EDC would come into force as soon as possible and it looked askance at developments in France, where EDC scepticism was steadily on the increase.

In January 1954, the French defence council discussed for the first time the EDC and drew attention to the unbalanced preparation of the Treaty, objecting in particular, to harmonised rules for uniforms and pay. Following a critical statement on the EDC by General Juin, Minister Staf interpreted the French military position as 'positive on ratification, but negative on implementation of the Treaty's provisions, except for the involvement of the German army in the defence of Europe'. Like Juin, the entire General Staff in France fought a heavy campaign against the EDC. Apart from influencing their government, officially still in favour of the EDC, the generals also attempted to convert domestic public opinion. Unlike their

---

[335] Fursdon, *The European Defence Community*, pp. 253-254.
[336] C. Staf, *Nota inzake het defensiebeleid* (The Hague 1954), p. 248.

Dutch colleagues (at least in the post-Kruls era), the French military did not shun publicity; they openly utilised the media for disseminating their anti-EDC views.

In January, in an attempt to simplify the structure of the European army, Juin developed an alternative solution to the EDC:

> un simple appareil d'impulsion, de coordination et de contrôle, sans intégration politique ni supranationalité, sous l'étroite dépendance politique et opérationnelle de l'OTAN avec un Conseil des Ministres nationaux, un secrétariat général permanent, des délégués nationaux pour la mise sur pied et la gestion des contingents nationaux.

Other members of the French General Staff suggested creating an intergovernmental European defence organisation along the lines of the Brussels pact of 1948. They argued that the broad resistance to the EDC proved that total integration of military forces required sacrifices public opinion was still not willing to make.

> Il convient donc de partir des accords déjà contractés dans le cadre européen, pour proposer un pacte aux 9, pays d'Europe membres de l'OECE et de l'OTAN.*337*

Dutch military authorities sympathised with these ideas and they were happy to see that in the course of time not only the French military but also the government had become convinced of the EDC's impracticability. Although the official view was still in favour of ratification, the new Prime Minister Mendès-France - inaugurated in June - strove for intergovernmental modifications of the treaty, in order to curtail the transfer of national sovereignty. In August, Mendès-France developed his *Projet de protocole d'application du Traité instituant la Communauté Européenne de Défense*. The general message of the *Protocole* was the creation of 'a European army for the Germans and a French army for the French', as Nutting worded it.[338] The integration of forces would apply only in the *zone de couverture*; in other words, the only part of EDC's forces to be

---

[337] Guillen, 'Les Chefs militairs français', pp. 31-32.
[338] A. Nutting, *Europe will not wait: a warning and a way out* (London 1960), p. 67.

integrated would be Germany's forces and the forces of other participants stationed in Germany. Apparently, Stikker's preferences of late 1950 still found support, also outside the Netherlands. Furthermore, the EDC's collective rules and regulations concerning recruitment, discipline and promotion were to be set aside in favour of the individual nations' arrangements until well into the future.

The *Ministerraad* was appalled at the change envisaged because it was felt that the fundamental nature of the Treaty would be affected, but the Dutch GS openly welcomed Mendès-France's initiative. Lieutenant-General Hasselman - promoted to General in March 1954 - wrote that, from a military point of view, armed forces should remain under national control for a long period prior to being integrated in the European army. Only then, disruption of the military organisation could be avoided. Hasselman applauded the French proposals, because they emphasised preserving the national character of the army by restricting the level and degree of integration.[339]

As before, the General Staff failed to receive support from the government. On 19 August, when Mendès-France introduced his *Protocole* at a conference of the six countries in Brussels, Minister Beyen completely disapproved of the French position. The other governments supported Beyen in his resistance to Mendès-France and the conference was adjourned without results.

At the end of August 1954, the French National Assembly took its final decision on the EDC. After four years of intense discussion, the elaborately drawn plan for a European army died a sudden but not unexpected death.

It is easy to conclude that the Dutch General Staff welcomed the rejection of the EDC treaty, after having criticised the creation of a European army for the entire period of four years. In the end, the opposition proved successful, although it was obvious that the GS's influence on the final decision had been marginal.

---

[339] MinDef, EDG 7 dossier 168, Brief Hasselman, 08-18-1954.

Conclusions

In the early fifties, The Netherlands experienced serious problems in adapting national defence policy to international requirements. Before the War, Dutch authorities had used their army mainly for national military aims, but since becoming member to the Brussels pact and NATO, they were confronted with both European and Atlantic defence obligations. It was mainly the military who had difficulties in adjusting to this new way of handling the country's security affairs. This became explicit after the announcement of the Pleven plan in October 1950; the General Staff vehemently opposed the plan, because they were unwilling to accept supranational interference in domestic army matters. Within NATO, they still had considerable autonomy - the organisation of territorial troops, for example, was a strictly national business - but the expectation was that, within the EDC, this autonomy would be seriously curtailed. Besides the army corps, the army corps' command and the General Staff were also to be integrated in a European army and army commanders consequently feared that the supranational framework would leave them with little room for manoeuvre. They were also concerned about the creation of European military schools, leading to the closure of national colleges with their traditional and NATO oriented instruction methods. The military also worried that their recently introduced system of army organisation along American lines - with American equipment - would be thwarted by the creation of the European army and the development of European standards. Finally, it was clear that the vaunted five-division plan, developed in accordance with NATO's Medium Term Defence Plan, would have to be modified if the EDC came into operation. To illustrate one of the differences: EDC divisions consisted of 13,000 men, in comparison with NATO divisions of almost 19,000 men.

Until the summer of 1951, the Dutch government gratefully took advantage of the critical arguments offered by national military authorities and used these arguments to explain the country's absence from the Paris negotiations. But, following the approval of the Interim Report at the Paris conference in July 1951 and the rejection of the Dutch counterproposal in August 1951, the government directed its attention to other problems related to the integration of European defence: the common budget, common armament programme, board of commissioners, etcetera. The government was particularly satisfied with the agreement made in Paris that the greater part of the navy would remain under national control and was less concerned about safeguarding the identity of the national army.

Although the General Staff continued to be critical of the EDC, military views were increasingly disregarded, especially after Foreign Minister Beyen took office in September 1952. The JCS embraced the opportunities presented by the French Prime Ministers Mayer - in January 1953 - and Mendès-France - in August 1954 - to mitigate the supranational impact of the EDC treaty, but, by that time, the government was no longer interested in the arguments put forward by the military. Beyen preferred to speed up the ratification procedure and to safeguard the supply of military and economic aid from the US.

Compared to the Foreign Office, the Ministry of Defence kept a rather low profile during the EDC discussions. As regards EDC, Foreign Affairs was in charge of policy-making, especially in the period until the signing of the Treaty in May 1952, when the Defence Ministry was headed by the ministers Schokking and 's Jacob. After September 1952, with the energetic Minister Staf in charge, the Defence department became somewhat more assertive and regularly clashed with the General Staff about the tactics to be employed during the EDC negotiations. Staf was not afraid to stand up against his generals if the Cabinet interest required it. And although he distrusted Foreign Minister Beyen's overtly European ambitions and the latter's support of the EDC, tensions between the two ministers and ministries were largely kept under control.

The primacy of the Foreign Ministry was caused by the fact that the European army was designed as a political solution for what was seen as a political problem: a German military contribution to the defence of the West. The consequence was, that when purely military questions were discussed at the Paris conference, resolution of these questions often became a matter of national political decision. Osgood has argued that,

> In the eyes of the military, EDC was a single strategic imperative, but the subsequent history of the Treaty showed that NATO's military security had become inextricably entangled with substantial political issues concerning inter-allied relations, issues which could be resolved within the new strategic imperatives only by a readjustment of allied commitments. The central feature of the readjustment was the firmer commitment of American and British troops to the Continent in order to counterbalance the accession of West Germany to NATO, especially for the benefit of France. Indeed in the eyes of its principal architects EDC became as important as an instrument of Franco-German reconciliation as of military security.[340]

Despite sharp differences of opinion between civil and military authorities, there was one issue upon which all agreed: the safeguarding of the closest possible links between NATO and EDC. Government, ministries and supreme military command therefore welcomed the relevant provisions in the EDC treaty on NATO's primacy in operational matters, although they also felt that the Atlantic-European relationship was still not tight enough.

During the EDC negotiations, the Dutch and French military views often coincided. Like the Dutch, French generals attempted to forestall the foundation of a European army organisation with wide supranational powers and supported the immediate involvement of German divisions in an international framework. On many technical points, French and Dutch generals agreed; both emphasised the independence of the national navy, the non-involvement of territorial troops in the European army and the retention of national schools and training methods. In other words, both French and Dutch military authorities were anxious to safeguard national military traditions and practices. There were also differences: the French generals' main concern was keeping the German army in check,

---

[340] R.E. Osgood, *NATO. The Entangling Alliance* (Chicago 1975), p. 92.

whereas their Dutch counterparts welcomed the incorporation of strong German units on a non-discriminatory basis. Furthermore, the French military looked for the WEU as a framework for making German rearmament possible, whereas the Dutch military solely concentrated on NATO involvement.[341] The opposition of the French military had a considerable effect on domestic public opinion. In the Netherlands, military authorities hardly played a role in the public debate and failed to gain widespread support for their views. When Marshal Juin criticised the EDC openly, he was supported by large sections of the French population, whereas in the Netherlands, where the army is generally considered more a necessary evil than a source of pride, military criticism was largely disregarded.

At the same time, we may argue that all through the period 1950-1954 the Dutch military were remarkably consistent in their views on the EDC. They rejected the European army, in whatever form, because they preferred a less complicated solution: German participation in Western defence through the NATO framework. They had to wait until 1955 before this could be realised.

According to Meier-Dörnberg, the EDC's rejection in the French parliament was aggravated, if not caused, by continuous modifications in the military provisions in favour of Germany. In the course of the negotiations in Paris, France had made so many concessions to Germany in military terms, that the main advantage of a European army, gaining control over German rearmament, was outweighed by an important disadvantage, losing autonomy as a result of incorporation in a supranational organisation.[342]

After the signing of the treaty in 1952, Paris, indeed, became highly sceptical regarding its own European initiative. The government's change of view was caused by military factors, but

---

[341] Guillen, 'Les Chefs militairs français', pp. 13-33.
[342] Meier-Dörnberg, 'Politische und militärische Faktoren', p. 290.

also, and maybe even more so, by political and economic factors; this latter element will be dealt with in the next chapter.

CHAPTER 5

The financial and economic background to the negotiations on the European Defence Community

Introduction

In the literature on the European Defence Community, only scant attention has been paid to the economic side of the discussions and their consequences at the Conference in Paris. In the EDC volume by the *Militärgeschichtliches Forschungsamt*[343], which is awash with political and military-strategic arguments, economic and financial aspects have been largely neglected. Fursdon[344] refers obliquely to the common armament programme - the proposed armament pool within the EDC - but he obviously considers this issue to be of minor importance. The same can be said of Noack's work[345] on the failure of the EDC and the Ruane volume on Anglo-American policies towards the EDC[346]. Aron and Lerner's book[347] paints a similar picture of the EDC debate and enumerates predominantly the 'High Politics' arguments for the initiation and rejection of the Treaty, but it has one valuable contribution to the understanding of the impact of economic factors on French EDC policies. Although the author Jacques Vernant seems to belittle his own observations by pointing to the overall importance of political factors, he refers to several

---

[343] Militärgeschichtlices Forschungsamt (MGFA) (ed.), *Die Europäische Verteidigungsgemeinschaft. Stand und Probleme der Forschung* (Boppard am Rhein 1985).

[344] E. Fursdon, *The European Defence Community. A History* (London 1980).

[345] P. Noack, *Das Scheitern der Europäischen Verteidigungsgemeinschaft* (Düsseldorf 1977).

[346] K. Ruane, *The Rise and Fall of the European Defence Community. Anglo-American Relations and the Crisis of European Defence, 1950-55* (London 2000).

[347] R. Aron and D. Lerner, *La Quérelle de la CED* (Paris 1956).

alternatives as explanation for the Community's failure. Vernant pays particular attention to the role of French industrialists, and to the lack of competitiveness of French industry in the early fifties. In the English translation of Aron and Lerner's book[348] is another 'Low Politics' article, written by André Philip. A more recent contribution to the debate is Paul Pitman's work on the armaments industry in France at the time of the EDC.[349] The importance of French objections to the economic provisions of the EDC treaty will be considered in section 5.5.

The main part of this chapter (5.1-5.4) deals with the positions of the Dutch government and the business community concerning the EDC's common armaments programme and common budget. The Hague was outspoken in its opposition to the treaty's financial provisions, the fear being that within the EDC a substantial part of the national budget would be entrusted to a supranational body dominated by countries like France and Italy with 'traditionally questionable monetary policies'. This notion was not entirely new. In August 1950, a month before the announcement of the European army proposal, The Hague had already clashed with Paris over the Petsche plan, named after the French minister of finance of the time. Petsche had hinted at creating a common defence fund within NATO, a kind of clearing-house aimed at spreading the financial burden of defence equitably between the member countries. The Dutch government responded negatively, fearing that Petsche implicitly strove for a privileged position for France on the continent, given that the governments of the United States and United Kingdom would not be willing to participate in such a fund. The Petsche plan soon fell flat, but the Dutch government surmised that the EDC

---

[348] Ibid., *France defeats EDC* (New York 1957).

[349] P. Pitman, 'Interested circles: French industry and the rise and fall of the European Defence Community (1950-1954)', in: M. Dumoulin (ed.), *La Communauté Européenne de Défense, Leçons pour Demain?* (Brussels 2000) pp. 51-62.

common budget proposal was another French attempt to impose its financial preferences on the European continent.[350]

As far as the common armament programme was concerned, the government's policy was more ambiguous. On one hand, it was hoped that the EDC would offer domestic firms new markets for their products. At that time, the country's industry was well positioned: thanks to modest wage rates, Dutch products were generally cheaper than foreign-made products. On the other hand, government and industrialists worried about the real impact of the common armament programme on domestic firms, considering that during the early fifties, defence production in the Netherlands was still underdeveloped. In other words, a genuine weapons industry, capable of producing heavy equipment, was then non-existent. This was the main reason why, during the negotiations, the Netherlands advocated the insertion of 'soft' goods (food, textiles, leather) into the EDC armaments programme, because national industry was geared towards the production of those goods rather than heavy war materials like tanks, guns, missiles, *et cetera*.

Following rejection of the EDC, the Netherlands refused to play along with Mendès-France's plan for a European armament pool within the framework of the WEU, fearing that the principles of free and fair competition would not be safeguarded in such a pool.

5.1 Observer in Paris

During the first months of the Paris conference, the Dutch government enjoyed its position as an outsider at the European army discussions. The Americans promised to continue the supply of military aid to the Netherlands in line with the Mutual Defence Assistance Agreement signed between Holland and the United States on 27 January 1950. Until August 1951, Dutch criticism was focused on the military-technical imperfections of the French Pleven plan, rather than financial and economic elements (see chapter 4). This

---

[350] F. Lynch, *The impact of rearmament on French reconstruction* (Florence, EUI colloquium paper 4 1986) pp. 7 and 15; MinAZ, Raad MAK, Notulen 09-15-1950.

was caused by the fact that at the start of the conference nobody really knew what the latter exactly entailed. When launching his plan, Pleven had said nothing more than that the rearmament and equipment programme for Europe would be laid down and carried out under the authority of a European Defence Minister or Defence Commissioner, accountable for the acquisition of contingents, equipment, material and supplies from the various member states. As for the financial section, Pleven only vaguely alluded to harmonising the contributions of the member states by means of a common budget. More details were not provided.

Initially, The Hague mainly argued in broad terms that, prior to achieving a defence community, the countries' economic, trade, financial and foreign policies had to be harmonised. In February 1951, this strategy was further developed in a presentation given by the Deputy Secretary-General of the Ministry of Defence, who stated that:

a) Military integration without financial, economic and political integration was unacceptable.

b) Defence was secondary to policy matters with economic and financial impact.

c) Realising economic and financial integration was a long process, as economic and financial policies depended on national restrictions, ways of living, social circumstances, traditions and historical backgrounds.

d) Military matters should not interfere with economic and financial developments.[351]

In other words, financial and economic integration had to be seen as a long-term development, and defence integration was even more remote.

During the first half of 1951, Dutch observers at the Paris conference concentrated on the military aspects of the discussions and paid only little attention to the common budget and the distribution of the financial burden. There was also no need to do so.

---

[351] Ministerie van Defensie (MinDef), EDG 29, 'Individual reflections in regard to the problem of the integration of Western Europe', Lezing Duyverman, Febr. 1951.

The Financial Committee, under the chairmanship of the Frenchman Sadrin, had 'difficulty in doing useful work'. Before the first meeting, Sadrin asked his Minister of Finance for policy direction and instructions: he was merely told 'débrouillez-vous!' (Figure that out for yourself!). Fursdon wrote that there was a touch of '*mysticisme*' about starting discussions on financial matters without first knowing the aim of the discussions. At that early stage, there was no real concept, neither political nor military, around which a financial base could be constructed.[352] Furthermore, economic aspects of military integration, such as production programmes and production control, were only incidentally raised for discussion.

This would suddenly change in the summer of 1951, and as a result The Hague increasingly focused its attention on the financial-economic elements of the European army plan. A JCS report, published in August, dealt with the expected implications of an integrated European armaments programme under the authority of a European Commissioner. The Commissioner was assigned the task of standardising military production, but in the JCS's view, real standardisation was impossible because of the six participants, France was the only country with a substantial armaments industry, while the others simply lacked potential. As a result, European standardisation would unilaterally benefit French industry, but the latter on its own was too small to supply the armies of the other countries with the requisite war materials. The Chiefs of Staff doubted the feasibility of standardisation among the Six, and called to mind the ineffectual attempts made in the United States, France and the United Kingdom to standardise war production. Finally, the JCS predicted that a revival of the German armaments industry was inevitable because 'only the German industry was able to fill the gap which the French industry would necessarily leave behind'.[353]

From the summer of 1951 on, the Paris conference gained in importance after the American U-turn in favour of the supranational European army. The Dutch government continued to be

---

[352] Fursdon, *The European Defence Community*, p. 112.
[353] MinDef, EDG 36 dossier 3, Rapport Baay (JCS), 08-15-1951.

unenthusiastic and, to demonstrate its point of view, formulated a counterproposal in response to the draft interim report produced by the Paris conference on 24 July. In the proposal, presented to the governments of the United States, Great Britain and France, the government focussed on the plans for a common defence budget and a common armament programme.

In The Hague's view, a common European budget was simply superfluous because the level and size of the national defence budgets of the countries involved were effectively determined by the commitments made within NATO. The government argued that common financing could very well be extended to expenditure resulting from special international obligations, in the same way as was practised in NATO, but it was illogical to authorise the European defence organisation - the government disliked the French proposal for a single Commissioner and therefore used the collective denominator 'organisation' - to determine the budget, without simultaneously delegating the responsibility for finding the means to cover common expenses. As a consequence, 'an outside authority was going to interfere with a substantial part of national defence expenditure', a development unacceptable to the Dutch government. The latter felt that 'even a minor change in the pattern of public spending would have an adverse effect on the whole fabric of economic, financial and social conventions' in the Netherlands. The Hague feared that a centralised European budget contravened the national constitution, and also affected the authority of national parliament, which would, at least legally, lose control over a substantial part of the national budget. A European structure, the government argued, was acceptable 'only if economic, social and financial policies were also harmonised, requiring complete freedom of movement (trade, migration, inter-convertibility of currencies, etcetera) between the participant states'. The government added that - especially in the short term - such far-reaching harmonisation of policies was entirely unrealistic.

In their counterproposal, the government also disagreed with the French-inspired suggestion to grant the European defence 'organisation' the power to integrate and expand defence production in the six countries. In The Hague's view, such a structure was unlikely to solve the problem of the alarming financial deficits, mainly caused by the sharp price increase in raw materials following the start of the Korean War, found in the small group of nations involved in the discussions on the European army. It was therefore advisable to 'leave balance of payments issues to the relevant NATO agencies', the Financial and Economic Board and the Defence Production Board. In the government's view, both the common budget and the common armament programme were 'incompatible with the acquired level of economic and monetary integration in Europe', and in general the French European army concept was 'incompatible with the state of co-operation within NATO'.

Contrary to what was written in the Interim Report, the government wanted the European budget to be prepared by an Executive Board - instead of a single High Commissioner - and settled by unanimous vote in the Council of Ministers. In the Dutch view, the budget should cover administrative expenses only, while the member states 'should retain complete control over the financing of the national contingents integrated in the European force'. Moreover, expenditure on the deployment, administration and maintenance of European army units should be regulated by separate arrangements between the contributing states.[354]

The counterproposal failed to gain attention either in Western Europe or in the United States. Early in September 1951, the American government made known that it attached the utmost importance to the creation of an effective EDC, also for economic and financial reasons.[355] This was particularly disappointing for Foreign Minister Stikker, who in July 1951 had launched a plan for the creation of an Atlantic community, involving an extension of the

---

[354] Algemeen Rijksarchief (ARA), Archief Buitenlandse Economische Betrekkingen (BEB) 2.06.10 (bau 1-10), 'Dutch counter proposal and commentary', August 1951.
[355] MinDef, EDG 36 dossier 3, 'Aide-Mémoire from the United States', 09-06-1951.

activities of NATO to economic, financial and social areas.[356] Washington immediately made clear that it was not interested in such a concept, preferring the EDC to any other arrangement. As a result, at the beginning of October, the *Ministerraad* reluctantly took the decision to change status at the conference in Paris from observer to participant.

5.2 Opposition to the common budget

The government gave the following instructions to the national delegation in Paris:

a) The Netherlands must retain absolute sovereignty over determining its financial contribution to the EDC.

b) The country's social policies must not be affected by decisions taken within the EDC.

c) The ceiling on national defence expenditure (NLG 1,500 million per year) must be left unaltered.

d) The execution of NATO's Medium Term Defence Plan must not be delayed by experiments with a European army.[357]

The decision in favour of joining the conference was encouraged by the desire to harmonise Dutch policy with that of Belgium and Luxembourg. From August 1951 on, the Dutch became convinced of the usefulness of an alliance with its Benelux partners in the struggle against the supranational EDC proposals.[358]

At the end of 1951, the most controversial issues at the Paris conference were related to financial and economic issues: the nature and content of the common budget, the method of determining

---

[356] Foreign Relations of the United States (FRUS) 1951, Volume 3 part 1, Telegram US delegation at the seventh session of the NAC to Webb, 09-17-1951, pp. 664-665. It was not the first time that Stikker looked to the NATO framework to find an alternative to the European army plan. The Stikker plan of late 1950 constituted an earlier attempt to steer the discussion in an Atlantic direction (see 3.1).

[357] MinDef, EDG 12, 'Instructies aan de Nederlandse delegatie in Parijs', 11-16-1951.

[358] A.E. Kersten, *Maken drie kleinen één grote? De politieke invloed van de Benelux, 1945-1955* (Bussum 1982), p. 11.

national contributions, the Commissioner's control over expenditure, and the latter's authority in matters of armaments production and supply, including the distribution of US military and economic aid to the EDC countries. Problems arose as a result of fundamental differences between the 'Big Three' and the Benelux countries, the latter being determined to stick, at least until 1954, to national armaments programmes and financial commitments under NATO, as well as to national control over the EDC budget. The government envisaged a low-key framework for the EDC: military integration was possible to a certain extent, but financial integration should be ruled out, at least during a long transitional period. The Netherlands, supported by Belgium, preferred a mere juxtaposition of national budgets, without special authority for the European Executive Board, while France and Germany advocated a real merger of budgets. Italy shared the Dutch view that national parliaments should retain ultimate authority over national defence expenditure. In October, the Italian delegation suggested the scope of the European budget be limited only to the integrated General Staff and staff colleges. This was welcomed by the Foreign Ministers of Belgium and the Netherlands, Van Zeeland and Stikker, but flatly rejected by their French colleague.[359] The Dutch-Italian understanding on a 'confined' budget did not mean that the two countries agreed on the complete range of financial issues. A substantial difference was that Holland sought to hinder integration while Italy advocated the introduction of some sort of common income policy in Europe. Predictably, the *Ministerraad* considered the latter desideratum 'many steps too far'.

Prime Minister Drees thought it acceptable that staff and staff schools would be organised on a supranational basis and that uniform rules would be applied to organisation, instruction and terms of service. However, wages and payments were, in Drees's view, to be nationally determined, 'at least for a long transitional period'.[360] France, Germany and Italy, on the other hand, insisted on having a

---

[359] P.E. Taviani, *Solidarietà Atlantica e Communità Europea* (Florence 1954), p. 138.
[360] ARA, Notulen Ministerraad (MR), De EDG, 11-05-1951.

common budget from the first day of the treaty's effect, and on giving the EDC Executive a free hand in utilising the national contributions for common armaments and supply 'in the best interests of the Community'.

Disagreements between the 'Big Three' and the 'Small Three' were irreconcilable, and, in December The Hague realised that some form of supranational European budget was unavoidable. However, eager to defer its actual implementation, the government reiterated its preference for a transitional period of at least two years during which national standards would be applied. Likewise, national rearmaments programmes were to be respected until 1954, and national parliaments should continue to be involved in determining financial contributions.[361]

At the *Ministerraad* meeting of 22 December, Prime Minister Drees sought to bridge the gap with his European partners by conceding that the desideratum of parliamentary involvement could be dropped if the Council of Ministers was given the final say over the common budget on the basis of a unanimous decision.[362]

Early in January 1952, the US Ambassador to France, Bruce, appraised the Dutch position at the Paris conference as being based on:

a) Concern that France and Germany would dominate the small countries, particularly if substantial authority were given to the central institutions.

b) Worry that the Netherlands would have to make a considerable financial contribution to the build-up of German forces. Experts at the conference, including the Germans, seemed to share the view that Germany would contribute more than the cost of its own contingents during the first year but that it would contribute less in subsequent years.

---

[361] FRUS 1952-1954, Vol. 5 (1), Background paper prepared in the Department of State, January 1952, pp. 600-601.
[362] ARA, MR, De EDG, 12-22-1951.

c) Belief that the Dutch could obtain more US end-items and other military support if the aid were handled on a bilateral basis.

In Bruce's view, the United States could help to solve the problems of the Netherlands and their Benelux partners by making it clear to them that:

a) American aid would be distributed in a manner most likely to promote effective defence.
b) The EDC was in line with the views of Congress, which favoured the political and economic unity of Europe.
c) The Franco-German agreement presented an historic opportunity for the fundamental solution to the problems of the continent. Public opinion in the United States would become very indignant if this opportunity were missed because of Benelux opposition.

Bruce felt it would be much easier to dispel Dutch concerns about the EDC than Belgian ones. He urged Bonn and Paris to concede that during the initial period Dutch EDC contributions were to be determined by NATO, to ensure that the Netherlands would not pay more to EDC than the country had become accustomed to spending on NATO obligations. Bruce further argued that, in return for Franco-German acceptance of the transitional period, the Dutch government should be willing to 'accept from the outset the authority and responsibility of the European institutions'. Bruce concluded that the Netherlands had no reason to complain because,

> The voice of the smaller countries within the Community would be determined when the weight of votes in the Assembly and in the Council of Ministers was agreed on. If the Schuman plan institutions were a precedent, the Benelux countries would probably obtain a larger voice than was desirable or justifiable.[363]

Bruce's intervention had its desired effect and, at the end of January 1952, most of the financial-economic issues were cleared up

---

[363] FRUS 1952-1954, Vol. 5 (1), Telegram Bruce to the Department of State, 01-03-1952, pp. 572-575.

at the meetings of the Steering Committee in Paris. The common budget, though operative from the first day, would be determined in accordance with existing NATO procedures, at least during the first two fiscal years, and the budget as a whole required the Council's unanimous approval. In the event that the Council was unable to act, the budget for the previous year would be carried over. There was also accord on the expenditure side of the common budget, which was to be approved by the Council, deciding by qualified majority. NATO commitments and existing contracts would be respected in executing the common budget. There was no agreement reached on the procedure to be adopted should national parliaments refuse to accept the national contributions determined by the Council of Ministers.

Although the final outcome contained some positive results for them - particularly the link to NATO during the first two years and the voting procedure on the budget - the Dutch delegation had good reason to be dissatisfied because it had not succeeded in preventing the European budget from becoming reality. The Netherlands had even been obliged to accept the budget from the first day of the treaty coming into effect; moreover, pleas for a longer transitional period had failed to achieve the desired result.

Until the signing of the treaty - in May 1952 - the common budget had been the main target of the country's EDC opposition in financial and economic areas. Closely monitored by Prime Minister Drees and Finance Minister Lieftinck, the delegation in Paris attempted to block schemes for a common financing system while seeking to preserve control over national military expenditure. In practice, it turned out that the French and German delegations often succeeded in imposing their will at the expense of the smaller countries.

5.3 The common armament programme until the signing of the treaty

At the outset, The Hague's assessment of the common armament programme was slightly more positive than that of the common budget. Although the government strove for the continuation of US military aid supplies under the Mutual Defence Assistance Program (preferably without EDC involvement), it also hoped that the European army would offer new opportunities for domestic industry to increase production. Industrialists urged the government to ensure that the European armaments programme would not be restricted to weapons, tanks, ammunition, etcetera, but that it would also include food, footwear and clothing because of their ample capacity to produce 'soft' articles. (For a comparative survey of the importance of the various sectors of industry, see Appendix VI). Right at that time, industrialists expected a drop in the sales of shoes, textiles and food products, and the European armaments programme was therefore welcomed as a means to further the industry's and the country's interests.[364]

At the same time, the *Ministerraad* was unhappy with the sweeping powers the European Commissioner was to have in his dealings with national industries.[365] It was thought that centralised policy-making by a supranational high authority would have a detrimental effect on domestic defence production, partly as a result of the dominant position of the French armaments industry, which had a near monopoly in the production of heavy defence material. In October 1951, the chairman of the Steering Committee in Paris, Alphand, installed a so-called Armament and Mobilisation Committee, chaired by his compatriot Hirsch, an armaments industrial expert. The committee would deal with all questions raised by the Commissioner's economic role, in particular the preparation of the armaments programme, the exercise of control over production

---

[364] MinDef, EDG 12, Instructies aan de Nederlandse delegatie in Parijs, 11-16-1951.
[365] Ministerie van Buitenlandse Zaken (MinBZ), Directie Militaire Aangelegenheden (DMA) 71 inv. nr. 128 doos 18, Nota Blaisse, 04-16-1952.

and trade necessary to ensure the implementation of this programme, and the problem of industrial mobilisation. In introducing Hirsch, Alphand stressed the conference's agreement, recorded in Article 10 of the Interim Report (of 24 July, 1951), that the common armament and equipment programme for European forces would be determined and implemented by the Commissioner. The Interim Report also provided that the Commissioner would be responsible for collecting and distributing end-items supplied under the US assistance programme.

At its first meeting, the Hirsch Committee came with the following guidelines for further negotiations:

a. Implementation of the armaments programme:

  i) The Commissioner would have to work closely with the Council of Ministers - representing the member governments - because the programme was expected to have serious impact on the domestic economies of the member states. To ensure efficiency, no formal limitations should be placed upon the work done by the Commissioner. The Commissioner should be required to consult, on certain questions, a consultative committee representing producers, workers and interest groups.

  ii) The Commissioner should be in the position to obtain and verify information to the extent required for the implementation of the armaments programme.

  iii) The Commissioner should have direct supervision of the placing of contracts with European industries.

  iv) The Commissioner would need to collect comprehensive information on all forms of production, export and import of armaments carried out by the member states. Deliveries from non-EDC countries should be reported to the Commissioner by the member government in question. To avoid manufacturing or imports being affected by the armaments programme, the Commissioner should explore with the respective governments which practical measures would have to be taken to prevent their national programmes from being in conflict. The manufacturing of military goods meant for export should be subject to prior authorisation by the Commissioner.

v) The Commissioner should obtain special powers during emergencies and during periods of shortages in military goods and raw materials. Such powers should include the placing of compulsory orders for special products.

b. Military research: the Commissioner should have the authority to determine research programmes and to centralise and utilise the information thus obtained.

c. Contacts with outside organisations on armament and mutual aid programmes: concerning armament questions affecting the EDC, the Commissioner should be the intermediary between the Community and NATO, as well as between the Community and non-member countries. The Commissioner should also be empowered to allocate and distribute equipment received under mutual aid programmes, as well as to secure liaison with international organisations such as the European Coal and Steel Community.

d. Fiscal problems: when dealing with armaments it would be impossible to ignore national fiscal policies, particularly taxation. The Armament Committee's first aim should be the establishment of a single purchasing agency for the whole of the European army's weapon requirements. National fiscal policies should neither disrupt the workings of such an agency, nor distort the system of free competition.

e. Standardisation: the Commissioner should strive for complete standardisation of weapons and equipment throughout the European army.[366]

At the end of the Armament Committee's first meeting, Hirsch added, in answer to a question by Dutch delegate Blaisse,[367] that the

---

[366] Fursdon, *The European Defence Community*, pp. 113-114.
[367] P.A. Blaisse was employed at the directorate-general for foreign economic relations (*Buitenlands Economische Betrekkingen*) of the Ministry of Economic Affairs in The Hague.

committee would also have to study the transitional problems relating to the armaments programme, and set the date at which the common programme could be established.[368] As in the case of the common budget, the Netherlands was in favour of a long transitional period to delay the programme's realisation. The reasoning behind this was that during the transitional period the goals set by NATO's MTDP could be safeguarded and, meanwhile, the Netherlands could fence for time to build up a domestic defence industry, which was still in its infancy then.

The guidelines of the Armament Committee, as sketched above, were fairly ambitious and led to fierce discussions in the member-states. At a Committee meeting in early November, the Belgian delegate said he had serious reservations about the powers granted to the Commissioner in the field of arms production, given that Belgium preferred to keep training and equipment of EDC forces under strictly national supervision. The Belgian delegate acknowledged that his position was radical and not in line with the general tenor of the discussions in Paris, but his instructions left him no other choice than to block the negotiations. An embarrassed Hirsch immediately replied that the Belgian view was so completely at variance with the current negotiations on the common programme that the committee would merely have to note the Belgian objections.

Blaisse, the Dutch delegate, made a more positive contribution, saying that at a later stage the Netherlands might have to introduce certain reservations, but not at that moment. According to American Ambassador Bruce, one of the observers at the meetings, Blaisse was extremely active in developing constructive proposals for the establishment of the armaments programme; on the whole, Bruce continued, the Dutch position was rather similar to that of the French chairman. This was not surprising as, in the Netherlands, Blaisse was known for his European-integrationist convictions. Soon after finishing his tasks at the negotiations in Paris, he was appointed a member of the European Parliament for the Catholic Party (KVP).

---

[368] FRUS 1951, Vol. 3 (1), Telegram Bruce to Acheson, 10-22-1951, pp. 895-897.

The government in The Hague was less inclined to welcome the proposals made by the Hirsch Committee and closely monitored Blaisse's contribution to the debate.

The Italian delegate also came out in support of Hirsch, while the German delegate's position was, in Bruce's view, not altogether clear.[369] According to Fursdon, 'one small worry was that the German representative, from Herr Erhard's Department of Economic Affairs, was personally not in favour of the European solution; from time to time Hirsch had to appeal to the German head of delegation[370] who invariably succeeded in clearing the blockage'.[371] The position of the German delegate was delicate since, in July 1951, Germany had voluntarily waived its claim to the establishment of a national war industry for the production of heavy weapons in return for a French concession on the level of integrating army units within the EDC. At that time the French accepted the *groupement* or division as the basic unit for integration.

On 12 November, when the *Ministerraad* discussed the common armament programme, it was assumed that the Commissioner would be dealing with purchasing rather than with production. The government was happy to see that he was not allowed to interfere in the national production process (as was the case with the High Authority in the production of coal and steel). The Minister of Economic Affairs, Van den Brink, took the view that the Council of Ministers should decide on the common programme by unanimous vote; the 'Big Three' had proposed a two-thirds majority. Van den Brink further pointed to an Italian proposal, aimed at making the member states' financial contributions proportional to their share in the orders placed by the Community. The Italian delegation had suggested that the amount of money spent on defence orders in a member state should be equal to at least 90% of that member's total financial contribution to the EDC. Van den Brink welcomed the Italian initiative, but Drees thought it dangerous to mention such a

---

[369] Ibid., Telegram Bruce to Webb, 11-08-1951, p. 914.
[370] Th. Blank, a Christian-democrat trade union leader.
[371] Fursdon, *The European Defence Community*, p. 114.

precise percentage, fearing that introducing a 90% clause would encourage national producers to resort to monopolistic behaviour, 'with rising costs as an undesired and inescapable consequence'.

Furthermore, the *Ministerraad* was confronted with the dilemma of whether or not food and clothing should become part of the common armament programme. As mentioned above, the inclusion of the two items would undoubtedly yield the country commercial rewards, and as such it was welcomed by domestic industrialists, but it would also augment the scope and size of the common budget, a development the government wished to avoid. No decisions were taken at that meeting.[372]

In an analysis by the national interdepartmental Advice Council, Blaisse advocated using the broadest possible definition of defence goods, thus including food and clothing in the EDC programme. The Advice Council further discussed the Commissioner's responsibility in allocating defence production to the member countries. The French delegation had launched the proposal that the Commissioner should be given the authority to decide on military grounds where, at which location, new factories were going to be built. The French rationale behind this was to prevent weapons factories from being situated in the EDC's borderland, meaning Germany, because of the latter's advanced and exposed geography, making it likely that it would be overrun in the event of a hostile invasion. The Hague, on the other hand, rejected reinforcing the Commissioner's authority in this area, fearing that discriminatory measures taken against Germany would backfire on the Netherlands (boomerang effect), because of the country's strategic vulnerability.[373]

At the end of December 1951, Foreign Minister Stikker underlined the disadvantages of the Commissioner's involvement in domestic military production, indicating that industries in Norway, Denmark, the United Kingdom and the United States retained their freedom of operation, while the Dutch economy would be hamstrung by EDC

---

[372] ARA, MR, De EDG, 11-12-1951.
[373] MinBZ, EDG 999.0, omslag 20 doos 5, 7e vergadering van de Interdepartementale Adviesraad, 12-17-1951.

regulations. EDC membership was expected to have 'serious financial and social (employment) implications, quite apart from those of strategy and dependency'. Initially, the Netherlands had rejected any form of European control over domestic production, import and export, but at the negotiating table in Paris this position had become untenable. Stikker conceded that a certain degree of European interference was acceptable, and he proposed drafting a small and detailed list of articles falling under the Commissioner's authority, leaving all other items to national discretion. He had 'no objections to inter-European control over the production of atomic bombs and tanks', which was easy to say for him, because neither of the two was produced in the Netherlands. Van den Brink made clear that centralised production control was not only a negative thing, arguing that it also helped impede the revival of the German war industry. The Cabinet meeting concluded that a short enumerative list should be drafted, a kind of *Kompetenzkatalog* with items subject to European control in the areas of production, import and export. Additions to the list would have to be made subject to unanimous approval by the Council of Ministers.[374]

Notwithstanding initial Belgian reservations and Dutch reticence, the Armament Committee in Paris made considerable progress. Early in December, the French delegation introduced a revised armaments plan, which succeeded in moderating Belgian opposition. In February 1952, the North Atlantic council meeting in Lisbon was informed of 'general agreement on many questions concerning the production of arms, equipment and supplies'.[375]

Soon after the Lisbon meeting, the Steering Committee in Paris produced a draft treaty containing the following provisions. The Board of Commissioners -the original plan for a single Commissioner had been abandoned - would be charged with the preparation and implementation of common programmes for the armament, equipment, supply and infrastructure of the European

---

[374] ARA, MR, De EDG, 12-22-1951.
[375] FRUS 1952-1954, Vol. 5 (1), Report of the Conference for the Organization of the EDC to the North Atlantic Council, 02-19-1952, pp. 243-246.

defence forces. These programmes would span several years, and would require the Council of Ministers' two-thirds majority approval for the necessary financial arrangements (article 95 of the draft treaty). In carrying out its work, the Board should firstly make the best possible use of the technical and economic capabilities of the member states and avoid creating serious disturbances to their economies, secondly, it should take account of the size of their contribution, and finally, in co-operation with NATO, the Board was to simplify and standardise armaments, equipment, supplies and infrastructure 'as much and as rapidly as possible'. The Board would also accept responsibility for the placing of contracts in support of the various programmes and for supervising and accounting for their implementation in all respects (article 96). Concerning the execution of the programmes, it was stipulated that the placing of orders and the invitation for tenders should take place in free competition and in a context of complete impartiality (article 97). Furthermore, the Board would prepare a common programme and plans for scientific and technical research in the military field, and ensure that these were put into effect (article 99).

When settling an account in a member state in the course of executing the common budget, the Board was to use up at least 85% (and thus not the 90% previously suggested by the Italian delegation) of the contribution paid by that state, but it was not to settle therein more than 115% of the state's contribution. In other words, there was going to be a 15% margin, to be decided on at the Board's discretion. The interpretation of this clause was to become subject to intense debate in the Netherlands and abroad (see 5.4 and 5.5).

Article 100 forbade 'the production, import and export of war materials from or to third countries, measures directly concerning establishments intended for the production of war materials, and the manufacture of prototypes and technical research concerning war materials'. In line with Stikker's preferences, the categories of war materials and equipment to which this article was to be applied were listed, and included small arms and artillery, ammunition and rockets for all military purposes, propellants and explosives for military purposes, armoured equipment, all types of warship and military aircraft, atomic, biological and chemical weapons, and component parts and machines (those suitable only for the construction and production of the weapons listed above, also including ammunition, armoured equipment, warships and military aircraft). Exceptions to the ban on the comprehensive range of activities, which art.100 imposed, included only 'such conduct of these activities by member states as the Board of Commissioners had authorised by grant of a permit'. In other words, the Board's special permission was needed for the production, import and export of certain well-defined defence items. The Board was not empowered to grant permits for the production of atomic, biological and chemical weapons in the so-called 'strategically exposed zones'. This term was deliberately not defined but was obviously drafted with West Germany in mind. With regard to war material intended for forces retaining their national character, the Board would deliver a general permit and establish a control mechanism to ensure that countries with such a permit would not make use of it beyond their specified requirements.[376]

Many of the above provisions were controversial for the Dutch government, and one of their main worries concerned the Board of Commissioners' autonomy in the placing of orders with national industries. The Hague thought that harmonising policies under a European Board would favour the defence industries of the large three countries at the expense of the smaller ones.

In February 1952, the Ministry of Economic Affairs aired its doubts about the effects of the 85-115% clause (see above) on the status of domestic industry. This provision was expected to have profound consequences for the smaller countries because they spent a relatively large part of their defence budgets on wages and services, leaving only a small amount for military production. Dutch authorities thought that the 85-115% rule was likely to benefit domestic textile and food industries - also because of the strong competitive position of these sectors - but it would be damaging to

---

[376] Fursdon, *The European Defence Community*, pp. 165-166.

the country's small − fledgling - weapons industry.[377] The Hague urged a more substantial role for the Council of Ministers (decisions on the placement of orders should be taken by consensus) because this would help curtail the Board's powers.

Furthermore, the Netherlands worried about the provision in the draft treaty (art. 100) stipulating that the export of war materials to third parties - outside the EDC - would be made subject to control by the Board, which was to supply export licences. The government argued that, as a result, rival firms in other EDC countries would acquire detailed information about the amount and size of orders placed in the Netherlands by third countries. Their concern was that the armaments producers of the larger countries would use this information and seek to outbid Dutch firms by offering lower prices, possibly with the help of government subsidies. Admiral Stam, the Flag Officer of the Navy, indicated that domestic shipyards were accustomed to the practice of initiating production - often in collaboration with firms from non-EDC countries - on the condition that third parties (even NATO allies) were kept uninformed about the project until a prototype was ready. According to Stam, industrial production required a high degree of secrecy which - he feared - was not guaranteed within the EDC, 'because members of the Board of Commissioners were national representatives who would never lose sight of their country's economic interests'. Stam expected that non-EDC countries would be encouraged to renounce further co-operation with Dutch industries, should the latter be forced to give public notice of their production plans. Major General De Bie, commissioner for military production at the Ministry of Economic Affairs, agreed that after the EDC's realisation, 'national secrets would no longer exist'.[378] On the other hand, Schoenmaker, national

---

[377] The few firms involved in purely military production were *Artillerie Inrichtingen* (ammunition), *Ned. Springstoffenfabriek* (gunpowder), *Organisch Chemische Industrie* (TNT), *Hispano Suiza* (guns), *Holland Signaal* (fire guidance), *Nefra* (cartridge cases), Van Doorne (jeeps) and *De Kruithoorn* (ammunition). For a more detailed survey see Appendix V.

[378] MinBZ, DMA 220, inv. nr. 32 doos 5, Vergadering AMP, 02-14-1952.

representative at NATO's Defence Production Board in London, pointed out that within NATO, too, 'production secrets had a short life, because of regular leaks to American and French industries'.

Another worry concerned the impact of one of the draft treaty's provisions stating that national scientific and technical research in the military domain was permitted only after prior notification of the Board of Commissioners. Duyverman, deputy secretary-general to the Ministry of Defence, criticised Blaisse for having accepted this clause at the Paris conference. Duyverman saw it as a 'serious infringement of the country's autonomy' and was surprised to see that the national industrialists represented in the Advice Council for Military Production refused to share his apprehensions regarding this issue. In particular, Philips, with its renowned research laboratory in Eindhoven, was expected to feel the effects of the Board's interference in military research.[379]

Moreover, the provisions concerning the production and import of war materials were a source of apprehension and contention. The Hague disagreed with the ban on some categories of war materials and equipment as provided for by article 100 of the draft treaty. A memorandum by the Ministry of Economic Affairs stated that article 100 was prompted by the political desire - particularly on the French delegation's part - to keep a proper check on German rearmament. The Netherlands called for equal rights for Germany, for fear that in the long run the treaty's discriminatory provisions would backfire on the smaller countries' industries. During negotiations, the north-east part of the Netherlands was mentioned as a 'strategically exposed area', and the government therefore urged limiting the list of war materials unfit for production in certain zones. The Hague was particularly apprehensive of the harmful effects article 100 could have on the domestic electronics industry (producing fire control and proximity fuses), aircraft industry and explosives industry. The majority of domestically produced explosives was used for purposes other than military, mainly in coal mines, hence the government's

---

[379] Ibid., 03-13-1952.

insistence on inserting a special clause on the civil use of explosives.[380]

One of the main aims of the common European programme was to achieve a more efficient form of production by means of standardisation. In Dutch eyes, standardisation should be done 'exclusively under the supervision of - rather than in co-operation with - NATO'. The Hague feared that the underdeveloped domestic weapons industry would have to pay the price for a successful standardisation process in Europe. The other European partners, however, flatly rejected the Dutch desideratum, indicating that standardisation efforts within NATO had thus far failed to produce encouraging results, and that the 'European alternative should therefore be taken seriously'.

At the meetings of the Armament Committee in Paris, Dutch opposition centred on two issues. Firstly, they disliked the French plan to give the Board a monopoly on determining the location of new gunpowder factories. The underlying French motive was that, in the near future, a substantial number of gunpowder factories would have to be constructed in Germany, and Paris wished to have a voice in this matter through the EDC. The Dutch government considered it another French attempt to extend geographical control over EDC territory, with possibly harmful implications for Dutch national interests. In April, due to lack of support, the French delegation decided to drop the plan and instead suggested placing newly built factories under the authority of a controller to be appointed by the Board. The Dutch delegation considered this a substantial improvement compared to the original plan. Secondly, for social reasons The Hague opposed another French proposal, which aimed at closing down enterprises transgressing the regulations of art.100 concerning the production, import and export of military goods. Instead, it wanted the Community to take control of these enterprises, but in practice this appeared impossible on juridical grounds. In the end, a compromise was found: companies transgressing the

---

[380] ARA, BEB 2.06.10 doos 687, Rapporten van het Directoraat-Generaal voor de Industrialisatie, 02-20 1952 and 03-27-1952.

regulations of article 100 would have to pay substantial fines to the Community.[381]

In the *Ministerraad*, it was mainly Prime Minister Drees who opposed the plans for a common armament programme. The Minister of Economic Affairs, Van den Brink, proved a moderate advocate, hoping that the national food and textile industries would profit from EDC co-operation. To the relief of the Dutch, the Paris conference did indeed decide to bring 'soft goods' within the scope of the armaments programme.

In February and March 1952, problems arose as a consequence of American plans to change the system of economic and financial assistance to Europe. The United States came out in favour of arranging these affairs with Europe as a whole, by means of the new EDC, instead of bilaterally with the European countries. The Netherlands desperately tried to safeguard the bilateral relationship with America, particularly in the field of dollar aid and offshore procurement.[382] The government feared losing its privileged position if bilateral arrangements were to be abolished. Foreign Minister Stikker was of the opinion that EDC authorities should be prevented from becoming involved in economic policies. He was prepared to make an exception for military end-item aid, but with regard to purely economic issues, like offshore orders, he refused to sacrifice the bilateral links with Washington. For a short while, he even threatened to withdraw the Dutch delegation from the Paris conference if the US government decided to go ahead with this idea.[383]

---

[381] MinBZ, DMA 71 inv. nr. 128 doos 18, Nota Blaisse betreffende het opstellen en uitvoeren van het bewapeningsprogramma, 04-16-1952.

[382] These were orders placed by the United States with European defense industries and paid for in US dollars. The ordered equipment was meant either for the producing country itself or for one of the other NATO members. During the period 1951-1954, the US placed offshore orders with Dutch industry to a total of NLG 663 million, mainly used for the procurement of foodstuffs.

[383] Ibid., EDG 999.1 dossier 63, Code telegram Stikker, 01-23-1951, and Code telegram Van Vredenburch, 03-22-1952.

As so often before, Dutch objections failed to have the desired impact. Although for some time The Hague struck to its opposition - especially with regard to financial aid - in the long run it had to concede to American wishes. Their only solace was that the new arrangement would come into force after ratification of the treaty by all the member countries, which was seen by many as a protracted process.

On 27 May 1952, the governments of West Germany, Italy, France and the Benelux countries signed the EDC treaty. After its negative stance at the end of 1951 and during the beginning of 1952, the Dutch government now reconciled itself to the inauguration of a common European budget, and hoped that national control over the country's financial contribution to the EDC was sufficiently safeguarded in the treaty. Following the signing of the treaty, The Hague increasingly directed its attention to the common armament programme instead of the common budget.

The economic provisions of the EDC treaty were rather similar to those referred to in the draft treaty (see above). Of the whole section, articles 104 and 107 were the most important and controversial. Article 104 (article 96 of the draft treaty) 'specified the procedures concerning the Board's responsibility for the placement of contracts in support of the various programmes, and for supervision of and accounting for their execution in all respects'. Article 107 (article 100 of the draft treaty) stated that the production, import and export of war materials should be arranged under the strict control of the Board of Commissioners. This article laid down guidelines to be applied by the Board in exercising its authority to grant permits. The Board was not empowered to grant permits for some specific items (atomic, chemical and biological weapons) in 'strategically exposed areas'. The 85-115% rule was inserted in the final treaty as it appeared in the draft treaty.[384]

In June 1952, at a meeting of the Advice Council for Military Production, the general opinion was that the national government

---

[384] Ibid., pp. 165-166.

should not keep waiting for further developments in Paris but immediately proceed to action, and that national industry, for its part, should do everything to be prepared for starting up military production. By doing so, Dutch industrial products would attract attention abroad, which was all the more necessary because of Germany's rapidly growing industrial potential. The Advice Council expected that with the EDC coming into existence, Germany would emerge as a 'supreme rival in the production of soft military goods', which was exactly the niche where domestic industry hoped to book good results.[385]

The government was generally satisfied with the treaty provisions on financial and economic co-operation between NATO and EDC, although they also felt that the mutual links should be made still stronger. The Hague once again urged the Board of Commissioners to take full account of NATO's experience and activities, and to avoid duplications. Under the treaty, the problem of determining agreed member state contributions to the common budget was solved for a short interim period by basing these contributions on the NATO contributory procedure (according to the so-called 'Annual Review'). The advantage of this was that national governments were relatively autonomous in drafting these annual reviews without EDC involvement. The *Ministerraad* appreciated the short-term continuation of this procedure, but the EDC treaty also pressed the Council of Ministers to develop a more integrated method for the longer term. The Hague had not succeeded in convincing the partners of the necessity of a prolonged transitional period.

Furthermore, the EDC treaty prescribed that the Board simplify and standardise armament, equipment, supplies and infrastructure in co-operation with NATO. The Hague particularly welcomed the last part of this provision, realising that the development programme for the build-up of the national army was more secure within NATO than within a supranational organisation like the EDC. By tying the EDC to NATO, the government hoped to safeguard the direct link

---

[385] MinBZ, DMA 220 inv. nr. 32 doos 5, Vergadering AMP, 06-06-1952.

between the country's defence contribution and the expenditure made on the maintenance and equipment of national contingents.[386]

5.4 Domestic industry and the common armament programme

On 1 September 1952, the third Drees cabinet was formed. Minister of Finance Lieftinck, (PvdA) and Minister of Economic Affairs Van den Brink (KVP) were succeeded by Van de Kieft (PvdA)[387] and Zijlstra (ARP), respectively. Lieftinck's departure, in particular, was an important moment in national politics. In the preceding years the Finance Minister had succeeded in making a strong mark on the government's policy towards European integration and defence. It soon turned out that his successor, Van de Kieft, had a very different personality, whose impact on the common budget debate and on the government's strategy in general was clearly less forceful than his predecessor's.

In November 1952, the Advice Council for Military Production discussed the impact of the 85-115% clause on the domestic economy and domestic firms. According to this clause, the Board of Commissioners could decide to spend a maximum of 15 percent of the country's total financial contribution to the EDC budget in another member state. Duyverman (Ministry of Defence) calculated that 'in the current situation 93% of the national budget for military acquisitions was spent within the indigenous industry', and that the allocation of a mere 85% thus meant a deterioration in the Dutch position. He expected that the amount of orders placed with Dutch industry by the European Board of Commissioners would not surpass the equivalent of 85% of the country's financial contribution. A higher percentage was of course welcome but deemed unlikely because of low foreign prices resulting from fierce competition between Germany and Italy, two countries with rapidly increasing industrial capacity. Like Duyverman, Van der Beugel (Foreign Affairs; charged with the distribution of US aid in the Netherlands)

---

[386] ARA, BEB 2.06.10 doos 656 (bau 7-1), Rapport Kymmell (DMA), 08-26-1953.
[387] J. van de Kieft, Minister of Finance, 1952-1956.

was pessimistic about the implications of the 85-115% clause, and emphasised that American assistance continued to be of great importance to the development of the national army. With the EDC coming into being, this assistance - the attractive US offshore orders in particular - was to be co-ordinated by the Board of Commissioners instead of the national governments. Van der Beugel thought this was a serious problem because domestic industrial structure lacked the capacity for advanced defence production. He warned that the Dutch voice in the EDC was going to be weaker than in NATO. At the time, the Netherlands was one of the main beneficiaries of US offshore procurement, a position it was going to lose if the EDC took over the management of such tasks from NATO. He suspected Washington of 'luring France into the EDC' by an increase in offshore orders with French firms, a development supposedly detrimental to new production initiatives in the Netherlands.

Compared to the national civil service, industrialists were more optimistic about the financial and economic implications of the EDC treaty, but their contribution to the discussion was minimal, at least for the rest of 1952. Their optimism was based on the fact that in 1952 the domestic defence industry started to perform considerably better than before, also due to US offshore orders and the use of counterpart funds[388] (see 2.3). Although the industry was still unable to produce heavy military equipment, in many other fields it had capacity to meet home requirements, and sometimes even managed to produce for export. It was calculated that the industry absorbed about 85% (NLG 850 million) of the annual procurement budget; 60% of the NLG 850 million was spent on orders with the metallurgical industry (including the important shipbuilding sector), 25% with the construction sector (mainly barracks building), and the remaining part on foodstuffs, textiles, chemicals, rubber, leather, etcetera (see also Appendix VI). Dutch and foreign orders together represented a military-industrial activity worth NLG 1,030 million a

---

[388] The counterpart funds for armaments production amounted to NLG 600 million over the period 1951-54 and were spent mainly on motor vehicles, aircraft and minesweepers.

year. Given the fact that one-third (NLG 343 million) was destined for wages and social costs, it was calculated that, with an average wage level of NLG 4,000 per year (including social costs), the domestic defence industry employed a total of about 84,000 workers.[389]

The beginning of 1953 witnessed an increase in the number of reports and memoranda by national authorities involved in the debate on the common armament programme. This was partly caused by the so-called 'additional protocols' attached to the EDC treaty by French Prime Minister Mayer. In the economic field, Mayer asked the participating countries for an extension of the provisions regarding arms production and export, to be applicable also to overseas forces. Furthermore, he tried to reduce the influence of third parties (non-EDC countries) over the EDC armaments programme.

In March 1953, the French employers' organisation (*Conseil National du Patronat Français*, CNPF) wrote a letter to Mayer to push the Prime Minister to do more for French business interests. In the letter, the CNPF gave vent to its dissatisfaction with the 85-115% clause, arguing that

> Si l'on considère d'une part de cette fraction de 15% correspond à des montants qui sont loin d'être négligeables en raison de l'importance des budgets de défense, et, d'autre part, qu'aucune disposition n'interdit pratiquement au Commissariat de priver de commandes tout une branche d'industrie dans un pays membre, on peut en conclure qu'une mise en application brutale du Traité risquerait d'entraîner d'importants bouleversements économiques dans la structure des Etats membres.

In an effort to forestall detrimental influences resulting from the 85-115% clause, the CNPF proposed a transitional period of at least five years before the clause would take effect. It was expected that this period would allow the participants to adapt gradually to the common armament programme, because, as the CNPF proposal

---

[389] MinBZ, DMA 02 inv. nr. 3, Rapport Schoenmaker betreffende productie van militair materieel in Nederland, 07-09-1952.

made clear, the Board's authority would be limited during this period. The CNPF further criticised the treaty's provision concerning exports of certain war materials to third countries, which necessitated special permission from the Board. In the letter to Mayer, the CNPF wrote that,

> En ce qui concerne les importations, il conviendrait de préciser que les programmes devraient être soumis à l'approbation du Comité consultatif. En ce qui concerne les exportations, il ne semble pas opportun de les soumettre à l'autorisation du Commissariat. Il pourrait être convenu que sauf avis unanime des Etats membres, aucune modification ne serait apportée, aux conditions règlementant, lors de la mise en vigueur provisoire du Traité, les exportations de matériel militaire vers les Etats tiers.

The French employers basically wanted to retain national control over exports of defence material.

Finally, the CNPF worried about the provision determining that the Board would take control of the manufacturing of prototypes and the conduct of technical research. The CNPF doubted the Board's capacity to inform itself adequately of the level of technical research in each of the member countries.[390] From all this, it appeared that French and Dutch authorities had remarkably similar apprehensions and expectations of the workings of the common armament programme.

This was also true as far as internal divisions were concerned. Like in the Dutch case, it was difficult for the French employers to speak with one voice, given the fact that leading sections of the French industry - including aircraft manufacturers, the electrical industry and producers of heavy weaponry - favoured the 'Europeanisation of military procurement.[391]

From January 1953 on, the French sought to augment the role of national governments within the EDC, while simultaneously reducing the power of the Board. Although in principle the

---

[390] MinDef, EDG 4 dossier 52, Brief Nederlandse ambassadeur in Parijs, 03-20-1953.
[391] Pitman, 'Interested circles', p. 58.

Netherlands was sympathetic to this approach, government and industry rejected the protectionist undertone of the French proposals. The Hague feared the cartelisation of European arms production. They argued that prior to concluding the contracts, the Board of Commissioners should guarantee the highest level of industrial competition, not only within but also outside the EDC. Unlike France and Italy, the Netherlands welcomed an open EDC policy towards third countries, and domestic industrialists stipulated maximum publicity for the Board's purchasing policy. The general conviction was that the Dutch economy would benefit from international economic liberalisation because domestic firms produced at relatively low and competitive prices. Industrialists also disagreed with the French assertion that the application of the 85-115% rule endangered the economies of the member countries.[392] This was further proof that the private sector in the Netherlands was more optimistic about the EDC's impact than the public sector, whose doubts about the Board's purchasing policy was similar to those of French employers. The industrialists had also higher expectations of the competitiveness of indigenous firms vis-à-vis German and Italian rivals.

In March, the government finally accepted the additional protocols on the condition that the French gave up looking for more favourable exceptions for themselves, to the detriment of the EDC.[393]

In May 1953, the Ministry of Economic Affairs recommended that in all circumstances the Board should deal with the cheapest contractor, assuming that a high product quality was guaranteed. Firms in EDC countries were not to be given preferential treatment unless the economy of the country in question was in serious danger. Economic Affairs further stated that the Board should refrain from pursuing autonomous commercial and industrial policies. A central political role for the Board would 'reinforce industrial protectionism', which was deemed both expensive - because of discrimination against (possibly cheaper) third countries - and

---

[392] MinDef, EDG 3 dossier 43, Nota Van Hoeve, 06-19-1953.
[393] ARA, MR, Bijlagen 487, Nota Beyen, 03-13-1953.

dangerous - because of the likelihood of venal practices. The Ministry of Economic Affairs concluded that the Council of Ministers should occupy itself with economic policy-making - protectionist or otherwise - rather than the Board.[394]

Liberal economic thinking prevailed in the Netherlands but failed to provoke enthusiasm in most of the other EDC countries, particularly France and Italy. The government was aware of this and started searching for a compromise to appease these countries. At the end of May, it suggested that all parties -including third countries - should be invited to compete for orders, but that in certain well-defined cases the Board could decide to confine the tender to participating countries only.[395]

In May 1953, the *Defensie Studie Centrum* (defence study centre; a think-tank of the Ministry of Defence) published an analysis of the problems relating to the Dutch EDC contribution, which helped to clarify the impact of the 85-115% clause. It was estimated that the country would contribute NLG 1,100 million to the EDC - the defence budget of NLG 1,500 million minus NLG 400 million for expenses made outside the European framework. With this contribution, the Netherlands accounted for about 3% of the EDC's total revenues.

The number of Dutch soldiers participating in the EDC was estimated as follows:

Army:	67,000	conscripts
	17,000	regulars
Air Force:	20,000	regulars
Navy:	(the navy would remain nationally organized).	
	104,000	

A total of 104,000 soldiers accounted for some 6 or 7% of the entire EDC force. Pay and provisioning of these soldiers was calculated at NLG 375 million a year. Furthermore, overhead

---

[394] MinDef, EDG 4 dossier 52, Nota Cramer, 05-02-1953.
[395] Ibid., Rapport Interdepartementale Commissie, 05-28-1953.

expenses were estimated, specifically, the costs of the EDC's administration (NLG 25 million) and local expenses for maintenance and exploitation (NLG 50 million). Together, these sums for domestic consumption amounted to NLG 450 million. As a result, the sum of NLG 650 million (NLG 1,100 minus NLG 450 million) would be available for acquisitions and purchases by the Board of Commissioners. This sum, however, would fluctuate because of the 85-115% clause, which implied that NLG 165 million (15% of the total contribution of NLG 1,100 million) could be added to or subtracted from the amount of NLG 650 million. The Dutch share in the EDC's purchasing policy would thus come to a maximum of NLG 815 million and a minimum of NLG 485 million. In both cases the amounts were considerably lower than the NLG 1 billion reserved in the annual national budget for military acquisitions.

The report concluded that the projected financial contribution - 3% of total EDC income - was low, in proportion to the country's high population figures and its substantial manpower contribution to the EDC force (some 6 or 7%). Hence, it was feared that the European armaments programme would have a negative impact on the national defence industry, the more so as the latter benefited considerably from existing purchasing practices within NATO. The report recommended that all parties involved in the country's defence production (government, parliament, ministries and industry) establish the closest possible contacts, to be well prepared to defend the position of the national industry at the European negotiations.[396]

In the meantime, industrialists started to complain about the neglect of their views by public authorities. More than once, they insisted on having their voice heard, but the most appropriate forum, the AMP, hardly dealt with the Paris negotiations. Top civil servants from the ministry of Foreign Affairs, Everts and Van der Beugel in particular (both DGEM, Foreign Affairs), were reluctant to give the EDC a place on the AMP agenda. In Everts's view, AMP discussions

---

[396] MinDef, EDG 12, Rapport Defensie Studie Centrum, May 1953.

were so 'unprofitable' that it was useless to involve this council in the national EDC debate.[397]

In mid-May, 1953, the Ministry of Economic Affairs attempted to improve the atmosphere by organising a meeting with representatives of government, trade and industry. Many national CEOs attended the meeting,[398] with even the shipbuilding industry represented (by Van der Graaff of *Cebosine*), although the navy and the naval industry would, for the larger part, remain outside the EDC.

The two principal questions discussed at the meeting were:

a) Should the Board of Commissioners be allowed to exclude certain producers in EDC member countries from participating in a public tender

b) Should the Board allow preferential treatment of EDC countries over third countries?

In dealing with the first question, the industrialists preferred an open and free system of public tenders with as many participants as possible. In any case, the greatest possible publicity needed to be given to military orders placed by the Board. The meeting refused to accept a system of preferential treatment within the Community. As far as question (b) was concerned, the CEOs felt that, in certain well-defined areas, the Board should have the freedom to restrict tenders to EDC countries only. They rejected the option of automatic third-country participation in a public EDC tender. In other words, the industrialists preferred a completely liberal system within the Community but a more closed system with regards to outsiders. Economic considerations prevailed at the meeting. The industrialists realised that political motives also played an important role at the

---

[397] MinBZ, DMA 220 inv. nr. 32 doos 5, Vergadering AMP, 03-13-1952, 05-08-1952 and 06-06-1052.

[398] Among those at the meeting were Hijzen (Ministry of Economic Affairs), Amsterdam (*Philips*), Brethouwer (*Holland Signaal*), Daams (Cotton, Rayon, and Linen industry), Van Everdingen (Electrotechnical industry), Van Gerwen (Wool industry), Van der Graaff (Shipbuilding), Jüngeling (*Artillerie Inrichtingen*), Küpfer (Fokker), Quarles van Ufford (Wholesale trade, *Verbond van de Nederlandsche Groothandel*), Rosen Jacobsen (Engineers and architects, *Ingenieurs- en Architectenbureau*) and Weurman (Metal and Electrotechnical industry).

discussions in Paris, but they felt that a political judgement on the EDC fell outside their competence.[399]

A week later, Küpfer (Fokker), one of the participants at the meeting, expounded his personal view on the common armament programme in a letter directed to the government and the Ministry of Defence. Küpfer wrote that the process of European integration, as embodied in the EDC, offered Dutch industries new and unknown opportunities to acquire orders for military products. Within the EDC, Dutch industries would be in a position both to compete for orders in a large geographical area and to obtain technical information on the articles required by the Board. Küpfer added that, in contrast with traditional practices, technical requirements and data should be made public to all interested parties, prior to the Board's decision on allocation. Küpfer further warned of the possible drawbacks of a centralised European programme, such as restricting tenders to only a small group of interested parties. Finally, he pointed to the EDC provision determining that the Board should place orders with only one of the interested parties, preferably the firm with the cheapest tender. As far as the aircraft industry was concerned, Küpfer preferred a system whereby several parties were asked to hand in prototypes based on identical specifications. Strict examination of the prototypes should then determine the type of aircraft to be selected for mass production. Küpfer thought this was the best procedure because it suppressed the temptation to select on criteria other than the purely technical.[400] He expected that within EDC, Fokker's sales potential would expand because Germany - designated a strategically exposed area - was denied the option of producing several types of fighter planes on its territory. The EDC treaty thus offered a framework for protecting the aircraft industry against German competition.[401]

At the end of June 1953, Otten (Philips) joined the paper discussion on the common armament programme, in anticipation of

[399] MinBZ, 999.0 inv. nr. 25 doos 6, Rapport Dir.-Gen. BEB, 05-20-1953.

[400] MinDef, EDG 3 dossier 43, Brief Küpfer (Fokker), 05-22-1953.

[401] Pitman, 'Interested circles', p. 57.

the parliamentary debates on the EDC treaty. Otten was rather pessimistic about the impact of the European programme on domestic industry, fearing, in particular, far-reaching influence by the Board of Commissioners on the member- states' economies. He expected that the Dutch 'presence and influence on the Board were going to be modest, with the consequence of decreasing exports, and increasing imports'. The Philips chairman added that the country's 'civil production was likely to be hit by a recession in the defence industry because of the lack of spill-over of military R&D to civil areas'.

Otten also anticipated that the 85-115% clause would fail to protect the position of domestic industry because, in a small country like the Netherlands, a substantial share (an estimated 45%) of the defence budget would have to be spent on pay and provisions for servicemen, leaving relatively little space (funds) for domestic production. He called on national authorities to intensify the co-operation between government and industry, and to secure EDC orders to a level exceeding the corresponding 85% of the country's financial contribution. While realising the maximum of 115% was naturally the preferred outcome - also because of the expected impact on the country's balance of payments position - Otten felt that such a high target was unrealistic. He even believed that in the given circumstances, the Netherlands would have difficulty reaching the minimum of 85%. Problems could be kept within bounds, Otten concluded, if the member states were given a free hand in producing for and exporting to third countries, but 'this was difficult because of the influential position of the Board in these matters'.

Otten's rejection of the European initiative was understandable because, in 1950, NATO's Task Force electronics Commission had issued a positive assessment of Philips' signal communications equipment, and had stimulated production of these items.[402] Philips was happy with the existing NATO arrangements and reluctant to start experiments with a centralised European programme. Moreover,

---

[402] C.M. Megens, *American aid to NATO allies in the 1950s. The Dutch case* (Groningen 1994) p. 189.

as one of the few domestic firms in the sector, Philips had developed into a substantial exporter of defence equipment, a position which it might lose if the Board was given far-reaching authority in these matters. Otten also feared competition from the French electronics industry in a closed European market, as well as interference from the Board in the company's research activities.

Despite his reservations, Otten realised that the Netherlands had to be prepared for the EDC, and gave the following advice to his government:

a) As long as the EDC treaty had still not been ratified, military authorities must be encouraged to place the bulk of their orders for defence equipment with domestic firms. This would help not only to stimulate the acquisition of future EDC orders, but also to attract orders from third countries, including US offshore orders.[403]

b) To attain these goals, government and industry needed to intensify mutual consultation. Moreover, domestic industry must be given more autonomy in establishing contacts with purchasing authorities abroad; common practice until then was that government mediated between the contracting parties.

c) Information on EDC product requirements must be obtained at the earliest possible moment. Such information was needed for a thorough analysis of the country's military production and research potential. This made it all the more important to monitor carefully developments at the conference in Paris.

d) For reasons of efficiency, a larger number of industrial experts should become involved in national decision-making on the issue. Only close collaboration between government and industry would yield results and avoid disaster.[404]

Otten's letter provoked lively discussion. One of the respondents was the Minister of Economic Affairs, Zijlstra. Zijlstra defended the government's policy, arguing that within the EDC, the Council of

---

[403] Ibid., pp. 189-192. According to Megens, Philips had not been very successful in acquiring offshore orders from the US.

[404] ARA, BEB 2.06.10 doos 683 inv. nr. 2, Nota Otten (Philips), 06-29-1953.

Ministers would have adequate powers to prevent discriminatory policies by the Board. He refused to share Otten's fear of a preponderant Board, pointing to several treaty provisions designed to check the Board's authority. Zijlstra also remarked that export opportunities were not restricted to the EDC area. Apart from the EDC, potential clients for the defence industry were the strictly nationally operating forces (including the main part of the Royal Navy) and third countries outside the EDC (other NATO members, but also countries like Sweden and Brazil[405]). Unlike Otten, Zijlstra denied that the Board would have ultimate control over the export of war material to third countries.[406]

Zijlstra's colleague, Defence Minister Staf, also replied to Otten's letter. In reaction to Otten's first recommendation, he wrote that military authorities traditionally placed the bulk of their defence orders with domestic firms, which made Otten's suggestion less pertinent. Concerning advice b, Staf said that the government had recently started to mediate between domestic firms and third countries at the special request of Philips itself. He disagreed with Otten's implicit criticism that interested parties abroad would feel frustrated and discouraged by the mediating role of the Dutch government; on the contrary, 'government mediation generally helped boost the value of domestic products'.[407]

The Chief of the Navy Staff, Vice-Admiral De Booy, shared Staf's view on the importance of mediation, not only by the government but also by military authorities. He deemed it logical that military authorities should have a voice in the matter since the orders concerned products with purely military significance.[408]

Flag Officer of the Navy Stam concurred with Zijlstra that the EDC treaty ensured satisfactory control of the Council over the

---

[405] During the period 1951-1954, the bulk of Dutch military exports went to non-EDC countries: the United States, the United Kingdom, Sweden and Brazil. The exports mainly concerned ships and radar products.
[406] MinDef, EDG 1 dossier 5, Brief Zijlstra, 09-02-1953.
[407] Ibid., Brief Staf, 08-24-1953.
[408] Ibid., Brief De Booy, 08-08-1953.

Board of Commissioners. On the other hand, Stam shared Otten's doubts about the impact of the 85-115% rule. He wrote that recent developments in European integration had proved that 'national autarchy was becoming the rule rather than the exception'. Like Otten, he was sceptical about the likelihood of domestic appropriation of the flexible 15%, because of Dutch firms' inability to produce various categories of military equipment. Stam's reply to Otten went further. Reacting to point a, he wrote that national industry needed to take more risks and initiatives to ensure competitiveness vis-à-vis foreign firms. Instead of waiting for new orders, firms should immediately start production of ready prototypes, given the fact that foreign governments would only consider dealing with Dutch firms if specific product examples were available. Entrepreneurial and inventive firms would have considerable advantages over 'wait-and-see firms'. Stam rejected the industry's complaint that the national fiscal burden was too heavy to take risks. He argued that compared to other countries, Dutch interest rates were reasonably low (between 4 and 5%), and that some risk-taking was therefore justifiable. On the other hand, Stam agreed with Otten on the issue that European governments - the British and French in particular - were over eager in helping their industries obtain foreign orders by means of subsidies and loans. Foreign interventionism 'ran counter to the Dutch principles of reliability and objectivity'. Although Stam, like Otten, urged close co-operation between government and industry, he thought there were grounds for pessimism because 'Dutch industry occupied itself too often with some narrow-minded commercialism instead of a more broad-minded industrialisation programme'.[409]

The different perceptions of Küpfer (Fokker) and Otten (Philips) with regard to the common armaments programme were understandable, given the fact that at that time the aircraft industry was roughly 90% dependent on military orders, and Philips less than 20% so (see Appendix V). In previous years, Fokker had managed to

---

[409] Ibid., Brief Stam, 08-08-1953.

develop valuable contacts with the Belgian firm *Fabrique Nationale* for the co-production of military planes, but according to prognoses it would be difficult to have a full order book in the next coming years.[410] The EDC thus brought new opportunities, also because of the discriminating provisions against German aircraft production. In general, Fokker mainly focused on the national and European market, whereas Philips also had ample extra-European commitments.

The interdepartmental committee studying the economic provisions of the EDC treaty drafted a report on the common armament programme, and concluded that:

a) Public tenders should not be restricted to only a part of the Community but should always be open to the entire Community. In certain cases the Board should be allowed to pass over the lowest tender. This was in line with article 102 of the EDC treaty, which provided that the Board would give account of the best use of technical and economic capabilities of the member states, the avoidance of serious disturbances to their economies, the size of their contributions, and their commitments to NATO.

b) All interested parties–also from third countries - should be invited to participate in EDC public tenders but in some cases, the Board should be permitted to confine itself to EDC firms.

c) The 85-115% rule should be seen as a useful instrument for protecting the status of domestic industry.[411]

These optimistic interdepartmental conclusions were subject to heated disputes. In July, at a meeting of the secretaries-general and the directors-general of the departments involved in the European army discussions, objections to the EDC project prevailed.[412] In a

---

[410] Megens, *American aid to NATO allies*, p. 185.

[411] ARA, BEB 2.06.10 doos 655 (bau 6-5), Rapport Interdepartementale Commissie, 06-01-1953.

[412] Among those at the meeting were Duyverman (Defence), Brouwers (Economic Affairs), Van der Beugel (DGEM, Foreign Affairs), Fock (*Algemene Zaken*, the prime minister's department), Van Lennep (Finance), Teppema (BEB, Economic Affairs) and Franke (Agriculture).

communiqué drafted at the end of the meeting, the top civil servants wrote that the EDC was likely to affect the country's social and economic stability. The treaty's economic provisions were formulated in such a vague manner that their implementation had to be regarded with the utmost suspicion. The meeting pointed to three specific flaws:

a) Economic relations between the Netherlands and the United States were expected to deteriorate if the US went ahead with the plan to terminate bilateral agreements on end-item and financial aid. The Netherlands would become overly dependent on the EDC Board if the Americans channelled their assistance directly and exclusively through the Community.

b) National policies on incomes and prices would be affected by the 'exorbitantly high wages' the EDC's highest military authorities were going to earn (in some cases 35 to 40% higher than traditional wage rates in the Netherlands).

c) There was a real danger that the Board would interpret the 85-115% clause in a 'creative manner', for example by assigning extra administrative tasks to Dutch EDC officials, at the expense of orders for domestic firms.

The communiqué also indicated that the Dutch delegation at the Paris conference 'gave' more than that it 'took'. Finally, it warned the government against sacrificing an important part of national sovereignty to 'an organisation that did not at all harmonise with the Dutch national character'.[413] This was a rather forceful statement, coming from a highly distinguished group of national civil servants.

In the summer of 1953, national positions on the common armament programme were still strongly divided. Hijzen, one of the most qualified experts (as Dutch representative to the *Comité d' Armement* in Paris), felt that integration of armaments production was supposed to have a beneficial effect on European economic integration in general, a Dutch priority following the introduction of the Beyen plan in September 1952. Hijzen expected that the pooling

---

[413] MinDef, EDG 29, Brief coördinatie-commissie EDG, July 1953.

of responsibility over purchases and tenders within one body, the Board of Commissioners, would help to boost future exports of Dutch defence products. He felt that the Board's position and powers were adequately articulated in the EDC treaty, although this position 'should again and again be carefully checked by Dutch authorities'.[414]

In November 1953, Hijzen gave a slightly different explanation when he compared the European Coal and Steel Community (ECSC) with the EDC. In the ECSC, coal and steel markets were integrated, with the consequence that 'certain national powers, for example, the power to interfere in the system of economic regulations, were transferred to a supranational body'. Hijzen observed that the EDC's scope was different because this organisation was not created with the intention of promoting European economic integration. With the exception of article 107 of the EDC treaty (control over production, research, import and export of war materials), the Defence Community would have only few independent powers over national industries. The Board of Commissioners would only act as a buying agent because it lacked the authority to act as regulator on the market, as was the case with the ECSC's High Authority.[415]

One of the national EDC committees dealt specifically with the position of the Board of Commissioners and, more in particular, with the question of whether the Board's tasks and activities should become centralised or decentralised. This was a rather complex issue. The committee, under the leadership of Baud (Ministry of Defence), observed that EDC policy-making was going to be centralised at the Board level but that policy implementation would remain the responsibility of the member-states, and thus decentralised. The committee stipulated that central policy and direction organs were required for safeguarding free competition and smooth implementation of the 85-115% rule, but that for the rest, the majority of tasks should be delegated to a lower level. In the committee's view, the various tasks had to be organised as follows:

---

[414] ARA, BEB 2.06.10 doos 651 (bau 6-2), Nota Hijzen, 07-17-1953.
[415] MinDef, EDG 4 dossier 52, Vergadering Werkcomité Adviesraad, 11-12-1953.

Tasks	Performance
Tender:	centralised
Appropriation:	centralised
Fixing of contracts:	as decentralised as possible
Control of production:	as decentralised as possible
Offtake, sale:	decentralised

The committee concluded that the EDC treaty was not a good basis for industrial integration, but, at best, an incentive for further economic integration.[416]

In the meantime, Dutch authorities continued trying to convince France and Italy of the importance of allowing free competition within and outside the EDC ('world-wide bidding'). In their view, price, quality and delivery time, rather than national preferences, should be the determining criteria for granting an order to a firm. They indicated that 'wide competitive bidding' already existed, though subject to many stipulations, and functioned rather well within NATO. The Ministry of Economic Affairs therefore urged the extension of 'EDC-wide bidding' to 'NATO- and EDC-wide bidding', as well as incorporating Germany in the system as a full competitor. The Economic Affairs report expected France and Italy to oppose the plans for free competition, but 'not for long, given their recent experiences within NATO'.[417]

Until the end of the EDC, financial-economic experts in the Netherlands continued to be divided on the possible implications of the common armament programme. In a radio discourse on 24 June, 1954, Schoenmaker, director of the firm *Artillerie Inrichtingen* (after his resignation as Dutch representative at NATO's DPB), stated that although it was impossible to predict the precise consequences of the common armament programme, the only certainty was that the EDC

---

[416] ARA, BEB 2.06.10 doos 651 (bau 6-4-1-1), Conclusies Werkcomité Organisatie Commissariaat, 11-23-1953.

[417] Ibid., doos 647 (bau 5-2-2), Nota Dir.-Gen. BEB, 11-09-1953.

offered a new, interesting sales potential in terms of deliveries of material and engineering of military works. Schoenmaker added that, to be successful, government and industry needed to monitor carefully the preparatory activities of the Interim Committee in Paris, particularly of the *Comité d'Armement*. He thought it expedient to find out as soon as possible which types of products the EDC would designate as standardised products. Schoenmaker urged national authorities to 'do their utmost to convince EDC authorities of the country's many-sided industrial potential'.[418]

Related to this, Everts (DGEM) argued in the AMP that good national performance depended heavily on the individual quality of the personnel appointed to the Board of Commissioners. It was calculated that the Dutch delegation to the Board would consist of 125 military and 50 civil officials. Everts felt it would be difficult enough to find 50 qualified civil servants to be delegated to the EDC, and he therefore suggested an intensive training course for capable candidates from Trade and Industry. He added that other countries had deliberately overstaffed their delegations at the Interim Committee in preparation for a future seat on the Board. On the matter of the required qualities of suitable candidates for a position on the Board, Hijzen wrote that 'strength of character and impartiality' were to be considered crucial assets.[419]

In January 1954, the Dutch parliament ratified the EDC treaty. From then on the main question was whether France was willing and able to follow this example.

5.5 French opposition to the economic provisions of the EDC

One of the arguments put forward in chapter 3 was that the dislike for the EPC's economic provisions constituted a vital reason for the French parliament's opposition to the ratification of the EDC treaty.

In the early fifties, the French government became increasingly dissatisfied with the course of economic integration in Western

---

[418] Ibid., doos 655, Radiotoespraak Schoenmaker, 06-24-1954.
[419] MinBZ, DMA 220 inv. nr. 32 doos 5, Vergadering AMP, 11-19-1953.

Europe. The competitive position of the French economy worsened, while at the same time the economies of most of the other Western European countries - and especially Germany - substantially improved. The time factor played an important role. By 1950 French industry still produced at competitive prices, but between 1950 and 1954, industrial output lagged far behind that of German industry, in both relative and absolute figures. The balance of trade and the level of investment in France and Germany showed similar trends. In February 1952, Paris was forced to suspend the liberalisation of foreign trade for fear of international competition, mainly because French industrial prices were substantially higher than those of other Western European countries. Vernant has written that French industrialists failed to appreciate the development towards a European common market because in France,

> les prix de revient étaient plus élevés que ceux des produits étrangers pour plusieurs raisons: le coût des matières premières; les salaires et charges annexes (dont l'impôt sur les salaires supporté par les entreprises et inclus dans les prix); les charges fiscales incorporées au prix de revient à l'échelon de producteur et au prix de vente à l'échelon du consommateur; les frais de transport, amont et aval; les charges financières; les frais de commercialisation; les frais généraux fixes; les récupérations pour la vente de sous-produits éventuels.

The EDC's Interim Committee developed a table of theoretical selling prices of a standardised product in five of the six EDC countries (plus the United Kingdom). The calculations were based on the assumption that all the countries involved had similar industries buying their energy, transport and raw materials at the same prices, and producing the same products with the same efficiency and by the same means.

Theoretical selling prices (all taxes included) of a standard product in five EDC countries, plus the United Kingdom.

	France	Germany	Belgium	Holland	Italy	U.K.
Wages of the workers (Inclusive of social charges)	30.00	25.95	31.50	19.50	22.50	24.60
Wages and salaries of staff and executives	5.00	4.38	5.49	3.39	3.56	4.59
Amortisation and attached matters	9.00	7.13	8.04	5.46	6.24	6.40
Benefits	3.00	2.38	2.68	1.99	2.08	2.13
Property-tax	0.50	1.45	0.45	0.46	0.35	0.36
Export prices	83.65	76.18	85.41	63.14	67.30	71.06
Taxes on transportations	1.00	3.05	3.94	3.03	2.02	-
Taxes on production	15.35	-	-	-	-	-
Internal prices within the European Community	100.00	79.23	89.35	66.17	69.32	71.06

Source: J. Vernant, 'L'Economie française devant la CED', in: Aron and Lerner, La Querelle de la CED, pp. 112-113.

The above calculation shows that the French price (fixed at 100) was the highest, while the Netherlands sold their products at the lowest price of all EDC countries. This was mainly caused by the modest wage levels in the Netherlands, as well as by the level of indirect taxes to be added to French product prices.

French industrialists feared that within the EDC, their firms would become subject to the rules of free competition, with damaging effects, not only for their armaments industry, but also for their civil industry. Moreover, like certain groups in the Netherlands, Paris suspected that the Board of Commissioners would spend a substantial part of the 'flexible 15%' of the French EDC contribution on foreign industries.

On the other hand, two branches of French industry reacted in favour of the EDC's common programme: the aircraft industry and the electronics industry. They expected a growing market potential, mainly because rival industries in Germany - being a strategically exposed area - were not allowed to produce certain types of aeroplanes and electronics. The government was more pessimistic, fearing that the possible advantages for these two industries would be outweighed by the implications of the 85-115% clause, meaning that the gains in aeronautics and electronics production would be accompanied by grave losses for other branches. German steel industry, for example, was expected to have the lion's share of orders in that area, while the textiles industries of other countries, Italy and the Netherlands in particular, would fill the requirements for uniforms and other clothing products in the Community. Hence, there was a fair chance that French metallurgy and textile production would fall back to pauper status. The implications of the 85-115% clause were manifold. The French contribution to EDC budget was estimated at FRF 750 billion per year (the annual amount France spent on defence); a loss of 15% on military purchases implied a decrease of about FRF 100 billion in French industrial sales. To make matters worse, some French industries (e.g. textiles) were already in a difficult position because of their inability to sell at competitive prices. Since these industries employed a considerable proportion of the national labour force, it was clear why large segments of the French public sector worried about the potential threat posed to their welfare by the economic clauses of the EDC treaty.[420]

At the negotiations in Paris, the French delegates proved tough negotiators and consistently tried to adapt the treaty's provisions to their advantage. Dutch representatives were often annoyed by the 'typically national French idea to make the EDC subservient to the national interests of France'. They were, for instance, piqued by attempts on the part of General De Larminat, the French chairman of the Armament Committee since May 1952, to exempt France from supranational obligations during the transitional period. De Larminat defended himself by pointing to the need of an extra check on German industry, but the Dutch delegation suspected that French intentions prejudiced not only Germany, but also the Benelux countries and Italy.[421] They felt that Paris was trying to empty the EDC treaty of its basic content without making any constructive gestures in return.[422]

In the meantime, French opposition to ratification was building and, to save the EDC from collapse, new amendments were put forward. The Radical Senator Maroger was convinced that the United Kingdom should consider some *solution de rechange*, and advocated developing an alternative to the EDC, in the form of creating a special organisation, with equal representation for France, Germany and the United Kingdom. In Maroger's view, this organisation would be less rigid and federalist than the EDC but smaller and more authoritative than NATO. Concerning armament and infrastructure, Maroger wanted the member states to have more leeway than within the EDC, and promoted the Council of Ministers as the highest authority. The Dutch authorities mistrusted Maroger's intentions, arguing that the Senator only sought ways to further

---

[420] J. Vernant, 'L'Economie française devant la CED', in: Aron and Lerner, *La Querelle de la CED*, pp. 121-122.

[421] MinBZ, EDG 999.0 inv. nr. 18 doos 5, Nota Beerman, 10-21-1953.

[422] Ministerie van Financiën (MinFin), DDA (NATO + MHP), Externe nota's 701-1709, Nota Oudshoorn, 10-23-1953.

French industrial interests and to exempt France from foreign competition.

For the same reason, they rejected another French plan (by Lapie) aimed at creating a community of European armament industries and a joint purchasing policy for aircraft. Lapie advocated realising a sound economic foundation prior to initiating plans for political and military integration. He proposed a *communauté de matériel*, arguing that,

> ce qui existe pour le moment, c'est une Communauté économique, une mise en commun de deux matières premières: le charbon et l'acier. N'est-il pas relativement normal de passer de ce stade à une communauté de produits manufacturés, et parmi ces produits manufacturés de se limiter au matériel de guerre lourd (grosse artillerie, blindage de chars et de navires, gros appareils de levage)?[423]

In the Dutch view, Lapie's ideas were not 'relatively normal' because the latter aimed at limiting armament integration to heavy weapons, a sector in which France had a comparative advantage vis-à-vis the other participating countries.

Paris continued the fight to delay competitive freedom at the EDC level. In July, the Vice President of the *Comité pour la Défense des Intérêts français en politique étrangère* (CDI), Guy de Carmoy, tried to contact Dutch Foreign Minister Beyen to discuss economic amendments to the EDC treaty with a view to weakening the treaty's supranational content. Beyen, however, refused to meet De Carmoy because he 'did not want to give the impression that Holland was prepared to renegotiate the EDC treaty, and certainly not with private organisations'.[424] The CDI was not taken aback, and at the end of July suggested a more flexible interpretation of the 85-115% rule. The *Comité* made the optimistic calculation that, since French industry would be charged with the production of aeroplanes and guided missiles for the German army, more than 115% of France's

---

[423] P.-O. Lapie, 'La Communauté Européenne de l'Armement', *La Revue des deux mondes* (Sept. 1953) p. 23.
[424] MinBZ, EDG 999.1 inv. nr. 50 doos 10, Nota Beyen, 07-27-1954.

EDC contribution would be spent at home. This ran counter to the original intention of the 85-115% rule, which was meant to spread production with general equity over the EDC countries. The CDI therefore suggested that in certain well-defined cases the Board should be given carte blanche to ignore the 85-115% clause, and that the Board should also be instructed to buy all the equipment destined for French forces in France. Predictably, The Hague dismissed this idea, arguing that most of the French troops in Germany were not paid for from the French but the German budget. The Dutch also felt that the production in France of guided missiles and aeroplanes would not endanger upholding the 85-115% clause, because France simply had no monopoly on producing heavy equipment for the German army; the other EDC countries, and also Great Britain, would be serious candidate contractors. Moreover, the Netherlands claimed a favourable position for itself in the acquisition of orders for 'soft' defence items.

Another far-reaching CDI proposal sought to curtail the Board's powers in the field of procurement. With this proposal, the CDI tried to make the Board buy 100% of the QMG goods (such as uniforms) and 85% of the remaining defence equipment in the country where the articles were going to be used. The Dutch government vehemently opposed this initiative, for both economic reasons consideration and as a matter of principle. Regarding the latter, The Hague reiterated the need for respecting the principles of free and fair competition (article 104). The economic consideration was that the EDC offered domestic industry additional sales potential in QMG goods, particularly textiles - because of French industry's inability to compete in this sector - and the government was not prepared to sacrifice this advantage. In short, the CDI proposals were far too radical to be attractive to the Dutch government.[425]

During all of 1954, The Hague refused to consider alternatives to the EDC. Although the additional French clauses offered certain advantages in the field of heavy equipment - a relatively

---

[425] Ibid., Nota Kymmell, 08-03-1954.

underdeveloped sector in the Netherlands - they did not square with the Dutch preference for equal treatment of the countries involved. In the government's view, the Board should always buy at the cheapest possible price, unless one of the interested parties—one of the member countries—was experiencing budgetary problems.[426]

In August 1954, the French Prime Minister Mendès-France developed his *Projet de protocole d'application du Traité instituant la CED*, the tenor of which was again strongly anti-supranational. According to Pitman, the CNPF (French employers) had managed to incorporate some of their demands in the protocols.[427] The common budget was no longer to be truly 'common'. It would be composed of the sum of monies individual national parliaments were prepared to vote to it, taking into account each country's circumstances. The protocol on the EDC's economic implications provided that the Council of Ministers should issue a general directive permitting the Board of Commissioners to order defence products net of production taxes. This was important to France, which, compared to other EDC countries, had high taxes on production. In the French view, the Council should also instruct that expenses on heavy military items, listed in an appendix to article 107, would not be included in the 85-115% transfer provisions. Instead, the proposal was made to budget these expenses separately, with payments that would be freely transferable. The obvious aim of this protocol was to safeguard the production of soft military supplies (textiles, etcetera) in France.[428]

The Hague felt that Mendès-France's 'economic protocol' sought to reserve the entire 100% (instead of a more flexible amount between 85 and 115%) of each nation's financial contribution for domestic production. Dutch authorities now pronounced themselves strongly in favour of upholding the 85-115% clause, and they once again blamed France for trying to evade foreign competition. The government stressed that without supranational guarantees the large countries would overrule the smaller ones. Dutch experience with the

---

[426] Ibidem.
[427] Pitman, 'Interested circles', p. 61.
[428] FRUS 1952-1954, Vol. 3 (1), pp. 1034-1035.

ECSC had shown that supranational institutions, 'because of their impartiality, were the best promoter of the interests of smaller countries'.[429]

It seemed that in the run-up to the final French decision on the Treaty, the Netherlands increasingly came to support the approval of the common armament programme. Apparently, industry had convinced the civil authorities of the advantages of having a European production pool.

If accepted, the *Protocole* would indeed fundamentally change the content of the EDC treaty. On 19 August, when Mendès-France introduced his plans at a conference of the six countries in Brussels, Minister Beyen completely disapproved, saying that

> These proposals involve the whittling away of the supranational elements of the treaty and thus affect its real character. Now the French parliament is making conditions on so many issues, one can frankly say that the French do not at all want an organisation with joint responsibility.[430]

Beyen's criticism was shared by the other delegations, and Mendès-France's protocols were subsequently rejected.

While these dramatic events unfolded, the Armaments Committee faithfully continued to meet and managed to produce a complete blueprint for a central organisation governing the research and development, production and programming of EDC armaments. It met for the last time on 25 August.

At the end of August 1954, the French *Assemblée* took its final decision on the EDC. Eventually, the *cédists* lost the battle; the treaty was defeated even before it was put to the vote.

How important were economic arguments in the final rejection? As we have observed, in the period following the signing of the EDC treaty and especially from late 1952, European developments had followed a course strongly disadvantageous to the French economy. It was therefore hardly surprising that Paris started to criticise plans

---

[429] ARA, BEB 2.06.10 doos 640, Nota Hijzen, 08-17-1954.
[430] MinBZ, 999.1 inv. nr. 40, Code telegram Van Lynden, 08-20-1954.

aimed at opening the European markets. To defend their national interests, the French government rejected the Beyen plan (launched within the EPC framework), because it was based on low tariffs or even no tariffs. As far as the EDC was concerned, Vernant argued that in France, both the advocates of *dirigisme* and of *libéralisme* opposed the treaty:

> Les dirigistes arguaient de l'impossibilité d'appliquer sans préparation le traitement de choc de la libération des échanges à une économie aussi structurée et aussi fragile que l'économie française, sans courir le risque de la plonger dans le chaos. Ils faisaient remarquer que pour être efficace et éviter les bouleversements, le Commissariat devrait pouvoir égaliser les conditions de la production d'armement dans les pays de la Communauté, c'est-à-dire assurer leur ravitaillement en matières premières aux même conditions, harmoniser leurs systèmes fiscaux, leurs charges sociales, etc.; bref disposer de pouvoirs très étendus sur l'ensemble de la vie économique des Etats. De leur côté, les tenants du libéralisme dénonçaient dans le Commissariat un organe de direction technocratique, inconscient par définition des réalités et des intérêts nationaux, et qui ne pouvaient que mener à des catastrophes.[431]

Given this widespread opposition in France, it is easy to conclude that the financial-economic problems of the EDC influenced the ultimate rejection of the treaty in the French parliament. As a result of the 85-115% clause, France would have suffered a decrease in the production of uniforms, light weaponry and munitions.[432] The textile and steel industries in particular had begun to fear competition from other EDC countries. For the steel industry, this was not the only reason for rejecting the EDC. Previously, steel producers had violently opposed the Coal and Steel Pool, because of their dislike of sacrificing the old venerated system of international cartels. During the Schuman plan negotiations, the French government had deliberately overlooked the interests of the national steel industry for fear of lack of co-operation. Following the ECSC's foundation, an

---

[431] Vernant, 'L'Economie française devant la CED', pp. 122-123.
[432] Pitman, 'Interested circles', p. 59.

important segment of the steel industry had tried to re-establish the old cartel in an attempt to escape the supranational direction of the High Authority. This segment also financed the campaign against the EDC in the hope that its failure would help undermine the authority of the ECSC. Pierre Ricard, the head of the French Steel Association, said that Monnet had become 'far too involved in the politics of Europe - code at the time for the EDC - and far too little involved in coal and steel'.[433] It was another sign that from 1952 on, the popularity of Monnet, with his plans for 'integration from above' had declined substantially. This was also the feeling in the French *Assemblée*. Taviani wrote that quite a number of MPs began to see Monnet as 'una sorta di spaurracchio' (a kind of scarecrow, JvdH) because of the seemingly unstoppable Monnet-inspired flow of supranational initiatives.[434]

The importance of the various branches of industry can be illustrated by listing the military expenses per sector of the French economy in 1954 (in billions of francs):

Agricultural products	273
Textile and leather	109
Cars	156
Electronics	10
Aircraft	119
Shipbuilding	60
Public works	144
Chemicals	86
Transport	56
Miscellaneous	122
	1,135

Source: J. Dofing, 'Les dépenses militaires', in: La Défense Nationale - Centre de sciences politiques de l'Institut d'Etudes Juridiques de Nice (Paris 1958)

---

[433] Duchêne, *Jean Monnet*, 239.
[434] Taviani, *Solidarietà Atlantica e Communità Europea*, p. 149.

The table provides proof of high military expenditure on aeronautics and textiles, sectors with equal significance for the French economy. At the time, the share of electronics was still rather modest, but the expectation was that this would change if the EDC became reality. Given the special status of Germany and the preferences of the smaller countries, it was calculated that aircraft and electronics production would benefit from the EDC at the expense of textile and leather. As a result, French industry - like its Dutch counterpart - was heavily divided internally about how to respond to the European programme.

Such ambiguity was also visible in Mendès-France's position on a European armaments programme. He clearly disliked the EDC but he was not against other forms of co-operation, even in the area of weapons production. Immediately following the rejection of the Treaty, he launched a plan for an armaments pool within the WEU, meaning, in essence, a copy of the EDC's armaments programme (including control over German production) but now within the intergovernmental Brussels treaty framework. To protect the position of French national industry, Mendès-France sought to limit supranational concepts and to curtail the principles of fair and free competition. What he was basically trying to do was retain the attractive parts of the common armament programme and get rid of the rest.

5.6 The armament pool of the Western European Union

A few weeks after the rejection of the EDC treaty, Mendès-France proposed creating a production control authority within the framework of the Western European Union (WEU; the former Brussels pact). This authority was to ensure the prohibition of certain types of agreed armaments and control the stock-levels of certain specified armaments held by each member state. The actual list of weapons affected was largely borrowed from Article 107 of the 'old' EDC, thus including atomic, biological and chemical weapons.

Another, more controversial, Mendès-France initiative concerned the creation of a European pool for those weapons falling outside the scope of Article 107 of the EDC. Mendès-France reasoned that if the WEU countries managed to reach agreement on standard types of weapons and on quantitative needs, it would generate both technical and financial advantages to arrange for mass production. Moreover,

> From this it follows that it is essential to entrust an Agency with the task of drawing up co-ordinated production programmes to be carried out by the industries of each country either annually or, preferably, covering several years.

In brief, Mendès-France made a plea for mass armaments production on the European continent at the lowest possible costs. The Agency would deal with the production of weapons, the placing of orders with weapon industries, and the distribution of weapons among participating countries. The Agency would be a monopolistic buyer of all the weapons produced in Western Europe. Provisions were made for widespread interference in the production process by means of centralised control on investment. The Agency would also be charged with the establishment of new - and the enlargement of existing - factories, and with the administration of American end-item aid and offshore orders.

The French plan undoubtedly had several advantages: European standardisation was imperative because of the imminent need for weapons as a result of German rearmament and the expected decrease in American end-item aid. Furthermore, it was anticipated that increasing activity in the military sector would have a favourable impact on industrial development in general (the spill-over effect), including civil production. Moreover, efficiency in organisation would help to reduce costs for equipping military forces.

Despite this, the Dutch government was extremely hesitant about indicating approval for any armaments pool scheme. This stemmed largely from their lack of belief - following the EDC's rejection - that France was ready to agree to an arrangement that did not discriminate against Germany, and that did not give preferential treatment to French industry.[435] At the time, France was dealing with substantial over-capacity in weapons production and, simultaneously, German industry was being allowed to produce weapons of several types. And although Germany was still thoroughly held in check by several prohibitions - limitations imposed on strategic zones progressively decreasing from east to west - France still feared competition. Again, France and the Netherlands were diametrically opposed to each other, the latter being in favour of both free competition and non-discrimination towards Germany. As in the EDC period, Dutch suspicions concerned France, not Germany. Prime Minister Drees worried about rumours of French weapon production in North Africa - falling outside any form of European control - and Zijlstra, minister of economic affairs, thought it was impossible to integrate weapon production in the WEU, as long as there was no collective arrangement made for the financing and programming of such production.[436] As distinct from the EDC plans, Mendès-France had made no provision for the creation of a WEU common budget.

During the London discussions on the armaments pool, Foreign Minister Beyen remarked that, under the French proposal, national governments would be in charge of raising and supplying armed forces without having authority over the manufacturing of weapons for these forces. He expected constitutional problems because the national ministers of defence would be accountable to their parliaments for supply and training but not for the equipping of forces.[437] Such a division of responsibilities was, in Beyen's view, the basic difference between the new French plan and the EDC. The Foreign Minister was confused by the French proposal, wondering whether its purpose was control or increased efficiency. Furthermore, he wanted to know to what extent the United Kingdom was prepared to participate in the pool, pointing out that one of the major benefits

---

[435] This was not only a Dutch concern, see: Ruane, *The Rise and Fall of the European Defence Community*, p. 162.

[436] ARA, MR, De Europese defensie, 09-20-1954.

[437] MinBZ, DMA 220 inv. nr. 32 doos 5, Vergadering AMP, 10-28-1954.

resulting from the failure of the EDC was the likelihood of a closer association between the United Kingdom and the continent. But would the UK's involvement in the WEU also extend to matters of weapon production? The original French proposal was rather outspoken on this issue, in that it made a clear distinction between continental production and production for forces assigned to NATO.

At the same time, the British themselves did not seem to be interested in becoming involved in a European structure. Their permanent representative at the NATO Council in London, Steel, stated that Great Britain had strong reservations on not only the weapons pool, but also the creation of a WEU research agency. In the field of research, the British were far ahead of continental Europe, and they 'were not prepared to share their military-scientific secrets and discoveries with other, less advanced, countries'. The Dutch government was annoyed that the Six went ahead with discussing an arrangement which did not include the United Kingdom.[438]

Beyen sought to forestall long, complicated negotiations and urged the French to find some simpler way to meet their objective of controlling armament production.[439]

In early autumn, French delegates tried hard to sell the arms pool plan, but at the end of October after tough discussions, with the Netherlands emerging as their main opponent, a decision on this issue was postponed until January 1955, when a Working Group would convene to further study the French proposals.

This French concession was a temporary relief for the Netherlands, but it soon became linked to another issue at the London conference: a request, directed at the Benelux countries, to make a voluntary statement that they would refrain from the production of atomic, biological and chemical weapons. The Benelux partners were asked to do this because a formal declaration by them would make it easier for Germany to renounce producing certain types of heavy weapons.

---

[438] Ibid., DMA 81 inv. nr. 130 doos 18, Brief Starkenborgh, 11-18-1954.
[439] FRUS 1952-1954, Vol. 5 (2), Telegraphic summary by the US delegation, 09-29-1954, p. 1306.

Adenauer had said he was willing to co-operate on the condition that the Benelux countries made a similar concession. Beyen had no objections; he remarked that the Netherlands had no inclination to produce ABC weapons and that effective control of the German weapon industry would also serve Dutch interests. Zijlstra, on the other hand, argued that certain domestic firms possessed some capacity to produce chemical and biological weapons, and a public statement would therefore interfere with national economic interests. Zijlstra further pointed to the danger of the Benelux declaration being used by foreign controllers to raid domestic research centres, for example the Philips lab in Eindhoven, which conducted research on nuclear fission for civil use.[440]

However, at the end of October the Benelux countries yielded to foreign, predominantly French and American, pressure. Following Adenauer's declaration that West Germany would not produce ABC weapons, the Benelux ministers also renounced the right to manufacture these weapons, but insisted on continuing research in national laboratories.

Ruane wrote that the French, 'in the face of this show of German self-containment', had dropped their demand for a European arms pool.[441] If this is true, it was not immediately perceived this way by policy-makers in The Hague. In December 1954, the Ministry of Foreign Affairs drew up several memoranda on the European weapon issue in preparation for the Working Group, which would convene in Paris on 15 January, 1955.

With EDC memories still fresh, the Netherlands worried about the danger of isolation during the negotiations in Paris, also because the British government refused to become part of the weapons pool. Belgian support of the Dutch position was still not clear. Foreign Minister Spaak had made known that he considered the European weapons pool a useful starting point for economic and political integration, but his compatriot Baron Snoy, president of the Steering

---

[440] ARA, MR, De Europese defensie, 10-04-1954; ibid., De West Europese Unie, 10-18-1954.

[441] Ruane, *The Rise and Fall of the European Defence Community*, p. 163.

Board of the OEEC, appeared more sceptical. Instead of a continental armaments pool, he advocated a *zone de libre échange* within the OEEC framework. Dutch authorities endorsed Snoy's argument that it would be easier to form a free-trade zone with countries like Denmark and Switzerland than with the WEU partners.[442]

Gauging the Italian position, The Hague surmised that this country was opposed to a European weapons pool but nonetheless inclined to go along with it 'as a consequence of persistent worries about intensifying Franco-German co-operation both in agriculture (cereals and sugar) and industry', especially as the latter was expected to have damaging influence on the competitiveness of Italian industry, which was already in dire straits. According to Dutch observers, the negotiations in Paris offered Italy at least the opportunity to become involved in the deliberations between France and Germany.[443]

To sum up, Dutch objections to the European weapon pool were of mainly political purport:

a) British participation was considered of crucial importance but - as in the case of the EDC - London refused to enter the pool.

b) French proposals were seen as a confusing mix of supranationalism and intergovernmentalism (or 'multilateralism'). France had copied a few articles from the EDC treaty without accepting the EDC's constitutional structure. The WEU treaty was a multilateral treaty in the sense that governments continued to be responsible for managing their budgets and equipping their forces in accordance with NATO directives. This was contrary to EDC regulations, which had provided for joint troops, a common budget and joint responsibility for troop equipment.

c) The proposed weapons agency was not transparent, as a result of lack of control by the Council of Ministers and lack of accountability to a parliament. The agency was likely to

---

[442] MinBZ, DMA 81 inv. nr. 130 doos 18, Memorandum Van der Beugel, 11-23-1954.
[443] Ibid., Brief Boon, 11-30-1954.

'develop into a powerful and unverifiable international bureaucracy'.

d) The French desire to keep Germany in check was superfluous because control over German armaments production was assured by the revised Brussels treaty and by the protocol on the production control authority in particular.

e) The WEU would develop separately from NATO, with the resultant risk of duplicating the tasks assigned to NATO. Such a risk was 'acceptable within a supranational framework (EDC) but not within multilateral organisations like NATO and WEU'.[444]

The Ministry of Economic Affairs made a calculation of the expected impact of the weapons pool on the national economy in general and domestic industry in particular. At the time, the main part of the country's defence budget earmarked for procurement was spent on orders with domestic industry. In the period 1951-54, procurement funds amounted to NLG 3,700 million, NLG 3,380 million of which was spent at home, and only NLG 320 million abroad. Common practice was to invite foreign industries only in the event that the lowest domestic quotation was more than 10 percent over a foreign tender. It was calculated that in the period 1 January to 30 September, 1954, about one-third of the domestic orders placed abroad was with industries of the future 'pool countries', and the remaining two-thirds with third countries (Sweden, Switzerland, United Kingdom, United States). Restriction to the WEU area would thus curtail the national freedom of action.

As far as Dutch competitiveness was concerned, it was calculated that in the period 1951-54, exports of military goods, mainly 'soft' items, amounted to NLG 300 million. It concerned goods also produced in the countries placing the orders but where a Dutch firm had come with a lower bid due to favourable wage and price levels in the Netherlands. Imports from abroad (at NLG 320 million)

---

[444] Ibid., Nota De Graaff, Mogelijke betekenis ener bewapeningspool voor Nederland, 12-13-1954; ibid., Nota Van der Beugel, Instructie voor Nederlandse delegatie in Parijs, 12-21-1954.

concerned goods - mainly 'hard equipment' - not produced in the Netherlands.

The Netherlands' main economic worry was that France was looking for ways to distort free competition within the WEU weapon pool. The Hague was concerned about the level of subsidies given by other governments to their armaments industries - state enterprises in particular. The government rejected the French plan for investment control within the weapons pool. Drawing on the analogy of the OEEC dealings in investments in the iron and steel industries, they felt that such control would hinder free and fair competition, unless the countries involved limited themselves to a mutual exchange of investment plans alone. Another impediment to free competition was held to be the 'strategically exposed area', which the French wanted to use as an instrument for investment control.

The Dutch delegation at the negotiations on the weapons pool in Paris received the following instructions:

a) The conference should deal not only with heavy weapons, but also with 'soft' goods.

b) The Netherlands should make its participation dependent on the willingness of the member states to observe and respect the principles of free and fair competition. History taught that governments were extremely protectionist in the field of military production, by means of a 'hardly traceable system of state subsidies'.

c) Concerning armaments production, the Netherlands should not become tied to the group of seven WEU countries. Statistical information proved that the Netherlands placed most of its military orders with non-WEU countries like Switzerland, Sweden, Denmark, Canada and the United States.

d) The European pool should not interfere with existing NATO activities in production and standardisation. NATO should continue to be the dominant organisation in these areas and its activities should not be duplicated by a European organisation.[445]

In January 1955, a compromise was worked out at the negotiations of the Working Group in Paris.

A new WEU organ, the Agency for the Control of Armaments, was to supervise the stocks and, to a limited degree, the production, of 10 conventional weapons classes ranging from heavy guns and tanks to guided missiles and military aircraft. In the light of French objections, the Agency was empowered to control all ABC weapons stocks only after 'effective production' had begun on the continent. The level, which any state - except Britain - could achieve, was to be determined by a simple majority vote of the WEU Council.

Another result was the creation of a Standing Armaments Committee, which was charged with the establishment of some sort of European armaments pool; in reality, it was closely related to NATO. From the Dutch point of view, this was a satisfactory solution, and it soon turned out that the Standing Armaments Committee had only limited powers with regards to the member states' industries. The opposition to the establishment of a common armaments pool with wide-ranging powers had eventually proved successful.

Conclusions

During the period 1950-1954, the Dutch economy began to perform better than previously. Labour costs in the Netherlands were relatively low, mainly because of modest wage levels. Thanks also to its efficiency, domestic industry managed to produce goods at low costs. In short, the competitive position of the Netherlands was strong.

Dutch authorities saw good opportunities to sell their products on a broad European market, and they welcomed plans aimed at economic integration in Western Europe. The opening up of foreign markets

---

[445] Ibid., Nota Economische Zaken, Armament-Pool besprekingen te Parijs op 17 jan. 1955, 12-13-1954.

would, in their view, lead to an improvement in national living standards, which were not high at the time - in 1951, for instance, consumption was cut by 5%, because of the tax burden for the fulfilment of NATO obligations for the build-up of the Dutch army. Within a supranational European organisation, The Hague hoped to realise the abolition, or at least the reduction, of trade barriers in Europe. The government advocated fair and free competition as a logical consequence of the structure and openness of the national economy, and aimed at achieving a *union douanière* and a common market in a regional European setting. At the same time, it was realised that the pursuit of this goal was going to be a very slow and laborious process which would require patience. In November 1952, the Dutch stated that, for the time being, they would content themselves with a more efficient division of labour and the acquisition of larger and more standardised markets. In the Dutch view, a supranational authority was needed as an honest broker, to bring about the abolition of trade barriers and the liberalisation of markets. Such an authority should however, manoeuvre cautiously, without raising too many illusions in its initial stages.

Although national authorities favoured an advanced process of economic and commercial integration, they doubted whether the EDC was the most effective means to realise this. Until the signing of the Treaty, they feared the economic, and particularly the financial, consequences of European co-operation in defence matters. The financial-economic aspects, rather than the military (see chapter 4), played an important role in the discussions on Dutch EDC policy. The government was more interested, therefore, in the opinion of financial-economic than of military authorities.

After the signing of the treaty, attitudes towards the common budget and the common armament programme started to become more constructive, even among industrial circles. Although Philips (radio, radar) feared that mainly only France would profit from the 85-115% rule and the provisions concerning strategically exposed areas, other branches of industry (nutrition and textiles in particular) welcomed the opportunities presented by the EDC armaments programme. The textiles industry was in considerable difficulties at the time because of its predominantly national orientation and, through the EDC, it had hoped to become a player on the European market. Dutch authorities successfully urged the inclusion of 'soft' goods in the common armaments programme. The aircraft industry (Fokker) also welcomed the programme because of the possibilities it offered to supply the German army and air force with Dutch military planes.

Another advantage was that the main part of the Dutch navy - which placed very lucrative orders with the national shipbuilding industry (see chapter 2) was to remain outside the EDC. The naval industry was so significant that, if involved in the EDC, this sector would doubtless have mopped up the greater part of the orders placed by the Board of Commissioners under the 85-115 percent rule. Due to US offshore and Royal Navy orders domestic shipyards disposed of a full order book until the end of the fifties.[446] It was expected that, with the dominant shipbuilding industry *hors concours*, other industry sectors would benefit from the possibilities offered by the EDC programme.

However, there was also a lot of uncertainty about the implications of the European common armament programme. A major problem was the near absence of a heavy weapons industry in the Netherlands. One of the few firms in this sector, *Artillerie Inrichtingen*, was still in the development phase and charged prices too high to compete on the European market. As said above, Philips was also downright sceptical, fearing both the loss of exports to third countries and of favourable production arrangements within NATO.

Similarly, the government and civil service never enthusiastically embraced economic integration within the EDC. They had obviously been looking for other, more explicit, economic instruments - like the Beyen plan - to realise the desired customs union. This also explains the lack of disappointment on the part of the government when the French *Assemblée* refused to ratify the EDC treaty. Soon afterwards,

---

[446] Megens, *American aid to NATO allies*, p. 165.

the Western European Union was formed - without supranational features - an event welcomed in the Netherlands. French Prime Minister Mendès-France's proposal for an armaments pool within the WEU did not, however, meet with Dutch approval. French protectionist tendencies conflicted with Dutch preferences for free and fair competition. The Hague even preferred the EDC armaments programme to the WEU armaments pool, because the former was expected to provide better guarantees for the industrial performance of the smaller countries. In the early 1950s the idea had gained ground that the export-oriented economy of the Netherlands benefited from supranational 'Low Politics' arrangements in a Western European context. This also confirms the sharp contrast the government made in its approach of political and economic integration; the latter was welcomed, the former not.

During the discussions, the Netherlands emphasised the importance of maintaining a close bilateral relationship with the United States. American offshore orders and counterpart funds were considered crucial to the build-up of a national armaments industry in the early fifties. The government feared that a multilateral European initiative would thwart the country's 'special relationship' with the United States.

Final conclusions

In the period 1950-1954, the post-war foreign policy debate in the Netherlands between Atlantic co-operation and European integration came to an early climax. Following the creation of the Brussels Treaty Organisation in March 1948, the country's main policy objective in the field of security was to ensure a permanent American involvement in the defence of Western Europe. This aim was achieved with the signing of the North Atlantic treaty in April 1949, heralding the creation of NATO. For the Dutch government there was no doubt: the Americans had the power, the money and the nuclear capacity the Europeans were lacking. The build-up of an independent nuclear deterrent force in Western Europe was considered both unattainable and undesirable and NATO was therefore considered an attractive 'insurance agency' obtainable at relatively low costs. Some Dutch policy-makers realised that US nuclear hegemony was far from unassailable, but at the time a kind of wishful thinking prevailed that nothing serious would happen, as far as the security of Western Europe was concerned.

In reality, the government's position was rather awkward. In its first year of existence, NATO's military strategy was still the so-called peripheral strategy, meaning that in the event of a Soviet invasion of Western Europe, American and British troops would be withdrawn from Germany to the other side of the Pyrenees or overseas, to strike back at a later, more opportune moment. Because of the existing lack of depth in Western European defence and the geographical structure of the North-German lowlands, the Netherlands was an easy target for conventional attack from the east westwards. In those days, defence on the river Yssel was perceived as unfeasible and even the Rhine was still seen as a hardly tenable stronghold. On a domestic level, the government tended to play down the danger of a foreign invasion, realising that the only realistic strategy on offer those days was evacuation of a select number of prominent persons and valuable goods to safer parts of the world. Since such a policy was completely unacceptable for wider parts of the population, the government preferred to concentrate its efforts on the country's economic and financial recovery, to trivialise military dangers and to suspend the build-up of the army in a multilateral framework, particularly in the period until December 1949, when the colonial struggle in Indonesia was still in full blast.

Even after Indonesian independence, however, the Netherlands for some considerable time, refused to comply with international requirements to develop a standing army in either an Atlantic or European framework. Crucial here was the debate on German rearmament. The Hague was convinced that the country's above-mentioned strategic problems could be solved only by a German contribution to the defence of Western Europe. With German troops involved, it would be possible to abandon the scorned peripheral strategy, and move the allied defence line eastward, away from the Netherlands into Germany. From the summer of 1950, following the outbreak of the Korean War, the government openly advocated German rearmament and implementation of a forward defence on the river Elbe. This was considered attractive for both military-strategic and financial reasons. The more the Federal Republic was allowed and prepared to spend on combat-ready units, the less the Netherlands would have to worry about maintaining an expensive standing army at the frontline of NATO's defence. In all respects, West Germany constituted an ideal buffer for the security of the Netherlands. It was therefore not surprising, that, in all discussions on German rearmament the government came out in favour of equal rights for Germany and non-discrimination. At the same time, it was hoped that the re-establishment of commercial links between the two countries would soon produce results, the Dutch economy being in strong need of open export facilities to Germany.

This is not to say that so soon after the war the nation's confidence in Germany was completely restored. The government stipulated that German rearmament was to take place within an integrated Atlantic framework, with a strong US presence on German territory. The Hague therefore rejected any other option for German foreign policy: German reunification on a neutralist basis (only Drees supported this for a short while in 1953), a militarily independent Germany (possibly with its own nuclear weapons), or a European defence structure dominated by France and Germany (see under). To Dutch relief, the US administration held similar views, and from September 1950 Truman and Acheson spoke out in favour of German rearmament in NATO and a forward defence strategy. Washington also promised to send additional troops to Europe, to speed up equipment deliveries, and to appoint a Supreme Allied Commander Europe for operational leadership on the continent. In return, as a *quid pro quo*, the Americans urged the European governments to start building up their armies and armaments industries, to streamline their military organisations and, last but not least, to step up their defence budgets.

Despite US-Dutch agreement on the need for German rearmament and despite Dutch enthusiasm about the American commitment to the defence of Western Europe, the government hesitated in complying with the obligations laid down within the US package. Until March 1951, The Hague proved unwilling to respond to the pressure put on them by the NATO allies. This was caused by several reasons. Firstly, the government was still not fully convinced to what extent the allies would be willing to protect the country's territory in an emergency situation. The principle of forward defence had been accepted, but suspicions remained about the actual willingness of the partners to come to the rescue of the Netherlands. Moreover, the issue of German rearmament had come on the agenda but its practical realisation was still far away, especially after the initiation - in October 1950 - of the French European army plan, which was perceived in The Hague as a pretext for putting off the return of German soldiers. In those circumstances, the government questioned the benefits of building up the national army and increasing military expenditure. Secondly, Prime Minister Drees and Finance Minister Lieftinck, the most influential members of Cabinet, never made a secret of their real priorities: to secure the country's economic and social reconstruction in the post-war era and to alleviate the condition of the nation's finances. Extra spending on defence was incompatible with these priorities, because it would lead to higher taxes and lower consumption, heavy contraction in the civil sector and cuts in public and private investments. Drees and Lieftinck also pointed to the importance of the national navy and the shipbuilding industry, both of which absorbed a substantial part of the domestic defence budget and provided jobs to many people. Based on the balanced collective forces concept, NATO authorities urged The Hague to give precedence to the army build-up at the expense of the navy, but this was clearly contrary to Dutch national traditions and preferences. Thirdly, a substantial rift existed between civil and military authorities in The Hague, which manifested itself in continuous disagreements between Drees and Lieftinck on the one hand and the General Staff, headed by General Kruls, on the other. Kruls was highly frustrated by the lack of government support, both in material and psychological terms, and ventilated this by regular leaks of confidential information to foreign colleagues and the press. This angered the government, which was already alarmed by Kruls' self-willed behaviour at international conferences and his chaotic management at the level of the army. Until March 1951, Drees and Lieftinck dominated the scene and succeeded in keeping military expenditure at a relatively modest level. Within the Cabinet, Defence Minister Schokking proved unable to make his case for a higher national defence profile, both in terms of money and manpower. Schokking himself was probably too weak to get this done, but even the renowned Foreign Minister Stikker, Schokking's main ally in the Cabinet, was unable to stand up against the dominating duo Drees-Lieftinck. The chaotic state of the country's defence was illustrated most poignantly by the resignation of Schokking in October 1950, the dismissal of Kruls in January 1951 and the fall of the Cabinet, in the same month. The last two events took place shortly after a high-profiled visit of SACEUR General Eisenhower to The Hague. On that occasion, Eisenhower had not refrained from openly criticising the Dutch government for its complacency, lack of determination and inability to organise the army in a proper manner. Because of his war record and undisputed reputation, Eisenhower's words produced a severe shock in government circles and eventually proved to be the decisive push in the direction of a major policy change. Two months later, a new government (again headed by Drees) announced an ambitious defence programme, including a f 6 billion budget for a period of four years (1951-1954) and the build-up of an army corps of five divisions. Two years after the creation of NATO, the Netherlands had finally become a faithful member to the alliance.

In October 1950, when French Prime Minister Pleven launched his plan for an integrated European army inclusive of German units under the control of supranational institutions, the Dutch response was immediately negative. The Hague suspected that France looked for ways to postpone German rearmament and that the US would use the European army as a pretext to reduce its security commitment to Europe. This suspicion even increased in the summer of 1951, when the US administration made known that - in line with French preferences - it supported the elaboration of plans for a European Defence Community. Until then, The Hague had hoped that German rearmament would take place within the Atlantic framework, with a controlled German contribution to NATO, but following the American U-turn this hope was no longer realistic. This was also the reason why the government soon decided to give up the status of observer at the Paris conference on the European army and become a full participant. The Dutch delegation then discovered that, in the preceding months, the other participants, led by France and Germany, had succeeded in drafting an elaborate framework for the European Defence Community and it proved very difficult to put a distinctive Dutch stamp on the next stages of the negotiations. Far-reaching measures had already been taken on issues such as the composition of the proposed European army, institutional design, common budget and common armament programme. In those circumstances, delegation leader Van Vredenburch was left with the possibility of amending existing agreements, instead of introducing original proposals. This was a severe diplomatic set-back, but given that, it is remarkable how Van Vredenburch and his team managed to influence the subsequent discussions and, sometimes, succeeded to modify the achieved conclusions to Dutch advantage. This was mainly possible because of an unexpected revival of Benelux co-operation. After the early economic results of 1944 and 1948, Benelux had developed into a 'sleeping beauty' with little real impact, but the EDC negotiations of 1951-1952 witnessed a sudden re-emergence of Belgian-Dutch policy cohesion. In Paris, the Dutch delegation gratefully took advantage of fierce Belgian opposition to some essential supranational elements concerning the organisation of the proposed European army and eventually scored some results on issues like the constitution of the management board, the institutional link with NATO and the safeguarding of some degree of national control over the European budget and armament programme. During the EDC negotiations, the government chose for a distinctly intergovernmental approach, emphasising maintenance of national authority and freedom of action within the proposed European institutions. Even a European advocate as Agricultural Minister Mansholt was extremely reticent about his thoughts on the European army. The Hague's lack of federalist ambition in EDC matters was not so unique as sometimes assumed. Foreign Minister Stikker and his department were known to be decidedly hostile to supranational European experiments, especially if conflicting with the preferred Atlantic connection. Moreover, around the same time, ECSC negotiator Spierenburg successfully introduced the Council of Ministers as a watchdog of the national governments against a possibly dominating position by the supranational High Authority. Oddly enough, during the early period, it was not France that hampered the development towards further European integration, but the Netherlands and Belgium.

In May 1952, the EDC treaty was signed, but the government continued to be unhappy with the prospect of becoming involved in a European defence organisation, which included France and Germany while excluding the United States and Britain. For The Hague there was absolutely nothing attractive about such a continental constellation, with the tandem Paris-Bonn obviously in the driver's seat. Given that, it is rather surprising that the Netherlands, in January 1954, became the first of the six countries to ratify the EDC treaty. From the most outspoken adversary the country apparently had turned into the most dedicated adherent. How can we explain the Dutch 'conversion' in support of the EDC? Firstly, the appointment of Foreign Minister Beyen (in September 1952) as successor to Stikker played an important role. Soon after coming to power Beyen became a fervent supporter of regional economic integration and he considered the EDC to be one of the main instruments in strengthening cohesion among the countries of Western Europe. What Beyen basically wanted was the removal of internal trade barriers among the Six and he introduced a plan hereto at the negotiations on the European Political Community (EPC), which ran from 1952, as a consequence of a special provision pertaining to this in the EDC treaty. Political integration was not Beyen's priority, but because of the inherent connection between EDC, EPC and the Beyen plan, he came out in favour of speeding up the ratification process on the EDC treaty in the national parliament, hoping that the example set by the Netherlands would encourage the other participating countries to follow suit. For this strategy, he received support from two influential colleagues, Minister of Economic Affairs Zijlstra and Minister of Agriculture Mansholt. Although the latter two doubted the usefulness of the EDC, they agreed with Beyen on the necessity of regional trade liberalisation taking shape within an integrated European framework. Drees continued to be a qualified opponent of the EDC, but after the departure of Lieftinck and the emergence of the prominent trio Beyen-Mansholt-Zijlstra, the Prime Minister's position in the Cabinet had weakened. Secondly, the national parliament, known for its pro-European persuasion, was not an obstacle on the road to ratification. On the contrary, during the EDC negotiations, MP's had often criticised the government for being too reluctant and had pleaded for a more committed integrationist policy. The two most important political parties, KVP and PvdA, were in total agreement on this issue and stimulated the ratification process. Prominent MP's like Klompé

(KVP) and Van der Goes van Naters (PvdA), with their vast networks at the Council of Europe's Assembly in Strasbourg, regarded the EDC as an end in itself - serving the European ideal - rather than a necessary instrument in the development towards economic integration (Beyen's view). In general, the government's approach towards the EDC was much more pragmatic than that shown by parliament. Thirdly, two external factors - one French, the other American - influenced the Dutch position on ratification. After the signing of the Treaty, the government became increasingly aware of a deep French dislike of the obligations resulting from EDC membership. Especially after the Gaullist return to power in January 1953, The Hague realised that France would probably never be willing to present the Treaty to her own parliament, which would in fact mean the end of the EDC. In those circumstances, the government thought it wise to go ahead with the national parliamentary procedure, in the expectation that a constructive attitude would earn the country international prestige and recognition. Moreover, in case of a rejection of the EDC, the finger of blame could be clearly pointed in French direction. It was another sign that the diplomatic relations between Paris and The Hague were very distant in those days. The American factor concerned the extreme relevance, which the Eisenhower-Dulles administration had attached to ratifying the EDC treaty. Dulles even threatened with 'an agonizing reappraisal' of US policy towards Europe in case the European governments failed to deliver. Although the Dutch government felt that Dulles' threat was mainly used for tactical reasons to confront Paris, at the same time, it hoped that a co-operative stance would reap benefits in the form of US equipment deliveries and offshore orders. Also here was the adage: it does not hurt to ratify first.

In comparison with Britain, which was - in Ruane's analysis - highly alarmed by the 'agonizing reappraisal' policy and the US threat of withdrawing troops from Europe, the Dutch response was rather calm. For the Netherlands, the danger of a peripheral strategy had always been present, and it would remain so until after the rearmament of Germany in 1955; Dulles's threats were, in that respect, hardly a new source of concern.

Due to proper analysis and a pragmatic approach of the matter, the government was neither surprised nor hurt when the French *Assemblée* eventually refused to consider dealing with the treaty, which meant in essence the end of the EDC. Beyen was the only minister who voiced disappointment. He had hoped till the last moment that the Mendès-France government would drop its resistance and put its full weight behind the treaty. Other members of cabinet, Drees in particular, felt secretly relieved that the EDC had been finally removed from the agenda and that after four 'wasted' years, German rearmament within NATO had become a feasible option again.

During the entire period 1950-1954, the government was emphatically in the driver's seat as far as national EDC policy was concerned. The General Staff and the business community tried several times to leave their mark on the debate, but without satisfactory result. The Foreign Ministers Stikker and Beyen played a crucial role, as witness the strong impact of their respective stances on domestic policy-making regarding the European army. With Stikker in power, the Netherlands thwarted EDC development, but under the Europe-minded Beyen the government changed direction and became the first participant to ratify the treaty. Also Prime Minister Drees and Finance Minister Lieftinck were actively involved in determining the Dutch position on the EDC. Drees's prominent contribution to the debate formed another example of his genuine interest in international politics and European integration in particular. It would therefore be wrong to picture Drees, as sometimes done in the literature, as 'the alderman (*wethouder*) of the Netherlands', referring to a kind of narrow-minded, inward-looking approach to politics. In reality, the Prime Minister had a critical view on the EDC, but his input in the domestic debate testified to a broad, internationalist orientation.

The literature on post-war European policy in the Netherlands mentions three dominating features of this policy valid for the entire period until 1990: 1. The priority given to Atlantic co-operation in 'High Politics' matters, meaning a declared preference for US leadership and NATO membership to involvement in European defence frameworks; 2. The distinction made between political and economic integration, the government being a warm advocate of the latter but downright dismissive as concerns the former; and 3. The resistance offered to a formalised or semi-formalised Franco-German leadership of the European institutions. If we look to the country's defence policy in the period 1948-1954 and to its handling of the EDC project, we may conclude that the three characteristics are indeed applicable to the subject under study. The government clearly wanted German rearmament to take place in an Atlantic rather than a European constellation; it promoted the liberalisation of trade between the six countries, but rejected political and military integration on the continent; and it feared that France and Germany would dominate the EDC at the expense of the smaller countries. The Atlantic priority was undisputed.

In the end, The Hague got what it initially wanted and maybe even more than that. In 1955, the Federal Republic entered NATO and the remobilisation of German troops, coupled to a US-UK commitment to western security, made the long-awaited forward defence become reality. After a long period of uncertainty, The Hague could finally trust that the first defence line of Western Europe was to be the river Elbe in Germany, far away from home territory. The direct danger of invasion receded, when the Cold War entered a phase of relaxation after Stalin's death in 1953. Within NATO, under the undisputable supremacy of the United States, Franco-German claims for leadership were easily neutralised and a new European defence initiative was still long in coming. And finally, at the Messina conference of June 1955, the Beyen plan (in a new version) for opening the European borders to foreign trade, was brought back to the negotiating table and, as would turn out later, with considerable success. The Netherlands had lived through some stormy years, but the future looked bright again.

Appendices

I. Defence expenditure in the Netherlands, 1949-54

	Total expenditure (in mlns of guilders)	% of GNP
1949	680	4.5
1950	901	5.4
1951	1,060	5.6
1952	1,253	6.3
1953	1,333	6.3
1954	1,538	6.7

Source:
NATO Facts and Figures (NATO Information Service, Brussels, January 1976), pp.294 and 296.

In the NATO figures, expenditure on civil defence and on defence of overseas possessions is omitted.

II. Dutch army forces, 1949-54

1949:	50,000 men (incl. Air force, excl. Indon. soldiers);
1950:	39,000 men (incl. Air force);
1951:	53,000 men;
1952:	75,000 men;
1953:	92,000 men;
1954:	110,000 men.

These figures concern the regular, reserve and conscript personnel in active service.

III. National shares in NATO's defence expenditure, 1951-55

Percentage of total expenditure in constant prices and, exchange rates of 1973. Excl. US defence expenditure.

Country	1951-1955
Belgium	3.1
Canada	10.4
Denmark	1.2
France	22.6
Greece	0.8
Italy	6.7
Luxembourg	0.1
Netherlands	**4.1**
Norway	1.3
Portugal	0.7
Turkey	1.4
United Kingdom	30.9
West Germany	16.7
Total	100.0

Source: Stockholm International Peace Research Institute, *World Armaments and Disarmaments: SIPRI Yearbook 1973* (New York 1973).

IV. Total Defence Expenditure of the Netherlands, 1950-1980

Deflated by Index for Consumer Prices. In mlns of guilders (1975=100).

1950	2,694	1960	4,020
1951	3,008	1961	4,580
1952	3,861	1962	5,078
1953	3,793	1963	5,298
1954	4,285	1964	5,442
1955	4,578	1965	5,418
1956	4,684	1970	6,309
1957	4,405	1975	7,524
1958	3,879	1980	8,262
1959	3,642		

Source: J.G.Siccama, 'The Netherlands Depillarized: Security Policy in a New Domestic Context'. In: G.Flynn (ed.), *NATO's Northern Allies. The national security policies of Belgium, Denmark, the Netherlands and Norway*, New Jersey 1985, p. 144.

V. *Dutch Defence Firms and their Dependence on Military Orders*

(i) Firms, more than 90 percent dependent on military orders

NAME		MILITARY PRODUCTION	CIVIL PRODUCTION
1. Artillerie Inrichtigen NV,	Hembrug	Ammunition, weapon parts	Tool-machines
2. Ned. Springstoffenfabriek,	Amsterdam	Gunpowder	-
3. Organisch Chemische Ind.,	Ossendrecht	TNT	-
4. Hispano Suiza,	Breda	Ammunition, 20 mm guns	-
5. Nefra,	Leiderdorp	Cartridge-case for ammunition	-
6. Franex,	Woensdrecht	Labouring activities	-
7. Holland Signaal,	Hengelo	Fire-guidance	Textile-machines
8. Fokker,	Amsterdam	Aeroplanes	Overhaul
9. Aviolanda,	Papendrecht	Aeroplanes	-
10. Avio Diepen,	Ypenburg	Repair of aeroplanes	Repair of aeroplanes
11. Wilton Feyenoord,	Schiedam	40 mm guns, gun-barrels	-

(ii) Firms, 50-90 percent dependent on military orders

NAME		MILITARY PRODUCITON	CIVIL PRODUCTION
1. Van Doorne	Eindhoven	Lorries	Lorries
2. De Kruithoorn	Den Bosch	Ammunition	Sporting-cartridges
3. Verenigde Blikfabrieken	Doesburg	Various	-

(iii) Firms, 20-30 percent dependent on military orders

NAME		MILITARY PRODUCTION	CIVIL PRODUCTION
1. Philips Telecommunicatie,	Hilversum	Radio, radar and telephone equipment	Radio, radar and telephone equipment
2. Johan de Wit,	Dordrecht	Clock-work fuses for ammunition	Hot-air engines
3. Beckers Sons,	Brummen	Turnery for ammunition	Turnery-ware

(iv) Firms, less than 20 percent dependent on military orders

NAME		MILITARY PRODUCTION	CIVIL PRODUCTION
1. Van Heyst,	Den Haag	Projectiles	Various
2. Philips,	Eindhoven	Radio	Various
3. Van der Heem,	Den Haag	Radio	Various
4. Oude Delft,	Delft	Optical articles	Optical articles
5. Various Shipyards,	...	Ships	Ships
6. Vredestein,	Deventer	Field tyres	Motor Tyres
7. Hevea,	Haveadorp	Gas-masks	Various
8. Draka,	Amsterdam	Field-cables	Various

VI. Domestic Industry Involved in Defence Production and their Relative Importance to the National Budget (in mlns. of guilders)

Sectors of Industry	Appropriated 1951-54
Chemical	217.6
Metal	305.7
Shipbuilding	555.2
Transport	421.6
Aircraft	227.9
Electronics	325.4
Rubber	35.0
Textile	244.6
Leather	25.2
Wood	35.7
Building	995.8
Ammunition	727.8
Optical	17.1
Foodstuffs	187.3
Paper	16.3
Miscellaneous	139.8
Total	**4,478.0**

VII. Rhine-Yssel line

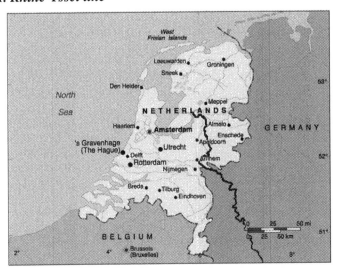

Archivalia

This thesis is based largely on research into Dutch central government archives. Below, an attempt has been made to describe the nature of the sources consulted in the period September 1983 to August 1986. After each description, details are given to locate the abbreviation employed in the text.

The level of policy with which this thesis is primarily concerned is that formulated by Cabinet. The minutes of the meetings of the full Cabinet are deposited in chronological order in the *Algemeen Rijksarchief,* under code 2.02.05.02.

Algemeen Rijksarchief, Notulen van de Ministerraad, Description of the document, date (ARA, MR, description, date).

The full Cabinet, however, rarely concerned itself with purely defence matters unless the latter had a clearly political dimension (e.g. the problem of German rearmament, the fixation of the defence budget and the EDC debate). The day-to-day discussions on military topics devolved to a cabinet sub-committee, the Council for Military Affairs of the Kingdom, whose membership included only the ministers most directly concerned, the General Staff and some top civil servants (the latter on an *ad hoc* basis). The minutes of the meetings of this Council are kept in chronological order at the Ministry of General Affairs, a ministerial department headed by the Prime Minister.

Ministerie van Algemene Zaken, Raad Militaire Aangelegenheden van het Koninkrijk, Minutes date (Min.AZ, Raad MAK, Notulen date).

From August 1952, the Council of Military Affairs of the Kingdom was renamed General Defence Council. In general, the activities of the latter were broader than those of the former. Files of the General

Defence Council are to be found in the Ministry of Foreign Affairs. They form part of the archive of the Directorate for Military Affairs.

Ministerie van Buitenlandse Zaken, Algemene Verdedigingsraad, archief Directoraat Militaire Aangelegenheden, Minutes date (Min.BuZa, AVR DMA, Notulen date).

In addition to the Cabinet and sub-committee minutes, the discussion papers (*bijlagen*) were also consulted: firstly, in their function as background papers to the Cabinet discussions, and secondly, because on many occasions, when Cabinet (or sub-committee) could agree to the recommendations without discussion, they are the only source of information on the policy decisions actually taken. The greater part of the discussion papers are collected in the *Algemeen Rijksarchief*.

Algemeen Rijksarchief, Notulen van de Ministerraad, Bijlagen, Description of the document, date (ARA, MR, Bijlagen, description, date).

In addition, to clarify certain points or to trace documents that proved exceptionally illusive, use was made of the archives of the ministerial departments themselves. The following list enumerates the various ministries and archives consulted. This list does not provide for classification details because of the highly divergent filing systems used by the ministries.

Ministry of Foreign Affairs (Ministerie van Buitenlandse Zaken, Min.BuZa):
Europese Defensie Gemeenschap (EDG), 1950-54; Directoraat Militaire Aangelegenheden (DMA), 1950-54; Directoraat-Generaal voor het Economische en Militaire hulpprogramma (DGEM), 1949-54; Privé-archief Van der Beugel (this archive has been transferred to the Algemeen Rijksarchief).

Ministry of Defence (Ministerie van Defensie, Min.Def.): Europese Defensie Gemeenschap (EDG), 1950-54; Kabinet van de Minister/Staatssecretaris van Oorlog, 1949-54; Hoofdkwartier Generale Staf, 1949-54; Comité Verenigde Chefs van Staven (Comité VCS), 1948-51; Kwartiermeester Generaal, 1948-1950; Legerraad, 1951-53; Materieelraad, 1951-52; Directie Administratieve Diensten (DAD), 1949-50; Directoraat Materieel Landmacht, 1951-54; Belgisch-Nederlandse militaire samenwerking, 1948-52.

For covenience sake, use has been made of the term 'Ministry of Defence', although the official term used at the time was 'Ministry of War and Navy' (Ministerie van Oorlog en Marine).

Ministry of Finance (Ministerie van Financiën, Min.Fin.):

Europese integratie algemeen, 1952-54; Directie Defensie Aangelegenheden (DDA), NATO + MHP, 1951-54.

Ministry of Economic Affairs (Ministerie van Economische Zaken, Min.EZ): Buitenlands Economische Betrekkingen (BEB), 1950-54 (this archive has been transferred to the Algemeen Rijksarchief).

All the archives mentioned above are located in The Hague.
Furthermore, the printed documents of the Foreign Relations of the United States (FRUS) have been consulted, particularly the volumes concerning Western Europe, 1948-54.

Finally, use has been made of some files of the political archive of the Ministry of Foreign Affairs in Bonn (nowadays in Berlin), Germany (Politisches Archiv des Auswärtigen Amts, PAAA Bonn): Europäische Verteidigungsgemeinschaft, 1950-54; Beziehungen zwischen der Niederlände und West Deutschland, 1948-54.

The writing of this thesis was only made possible by the exceptional help and co-operation I received from the staff in charge of the archives consulted. I take this opportunity of recording my thanks to all concerned and in particular to Messrs Bos and Poulisse (Foreign Affairs), Gans and Van der Valk (Defence), Plantinga (Algemeen Rijksarchief), Stegenga (Finance), Visser (General Affairs) and Weinandy (PAAA, Bonn).

Interviews

Dr. J. Linthorst Homan, Rome, 30 October 1985; Prof. dr. E.H. van der Beugel, The Hague, 4 December 1985; Prof. mr. W. Riphagen, The Hague, 5 December 1985; Mr. M.H.J.C. Rutten, The Hague, 2 June 1998; Drs. M. Kohnstamm, Brussels, 5 May 2000.

Bibliography

Atlantic and/or European co-operation

Baylis, J., 'Britain, the Brussels Pact and the continental commitment', *International Affairs* 60 (1984), pp. 615-629.

Beloff, M., *The United States and Unity of Europe* (Washington D.C. 1963).

Benthem van den Bergh, G. van (ed.), *Europa eenmaal andermaal, beschouwingen over veiligheid* (Amsterdam 1985).

Beugel, E.H. van der, *From Marshall Plan to Atlantic Partnership: European Integration as a Concern of American Foreign Policy* (Amsterdam 1966).

Borowski, H.R., *A Hollow Threat. Strategic Air Power and Containment before Korea* (Westport 1982).

Calandri, E., 'The Western European Union Armaments Pool: France's Quest for Security and European Co-operation in Transition, 1951-1955', *Journal of European Integration History* 1 (1995) 1, pp. 37-64.

Carlton, J.R., 'NATO Standardization: An Organizational Analysis', in: L.S. Kaplan and R.W. Clawson, *NATO after thirty years* (Wilmington 1981).

Deighton, A. (ed.), *West European Union, 1954-1997: Defence, Security, Integration* (Oxford 1997).

De Porte, A.W., *Europe between the superpowers: The enduring balance* (New Haven 1979).

Dockrill, S., *Britain's policy for West-German rearmament, 1945-1955* (Cambridge 1991).

Duchêne, F., *Jean Monnet. The First Statesman of Interdependence* (New York 1994).

Elgey, G., *La République des contradictions, 1951-1954* (Paris 1968).

Feis, H., *From Trust to Terror: The Onset of the Cold War, 1945-1950* (New York 1970).

Gillingham, J., *Coal, Steel and the Rebirth of Europe, 1945-1955: The Germans and French from Ruhr Conflict to Economic Community* (Cambridge 1991).

Gordon, L., 'Economic aspects of coalition diplomacy - The NATO experience', *International Organization* 10 (1956) 11, pp. 529-543.

Guillen, P., 'La France et la question de la défense de l'Europe occidentale du Pacte de Bruxelles au Plan Pleven', *Revue d'histoire de la deuxième guerre mondiale* 144 (1986) pp. 79-98.

Haas, E.B., *The Uniting of Europe. Political, social and economic forces, 1950-57* (London 1958).

Hellema, D., *Frontlijn van de Koude Oorlog. De Duitse herbewapening en het Atlantisch Bondgenootschap* (Amsterdam 1984).

Heller, F.H., and J.R. Gillingham (eds.), *NATO: the Founding of the Atlantic Alliance and the Integration of Europe* (New York 1992).

Herken, G., *The winning weapon. The atomic bomb in the Cold War, 1945-1950* (New York 1980).

Honig, J.W., *Defense Policy in the North Atlantic Alliance: the Case of the Netherlands* (Westport 1993).

Ireland, T., *Creating the Entangling Alliance: The Origins of the North Atlantic Treaty Organization* (Westport 1981).

Kaplan, L.S., *A Community of Interests. NATO and the Military Assistance Program, 1948-1951* (Washington D.C. 1980).

Kaplan, L.S., *The United States and NATO. The Formative Years* (Kentucky 1984).

Kaplan, L.S., 'Western Union and European military integration, 1948-1950', Conference paper Freiburg (Dec.1985).

La Feber, W., *America, Russia and the Cold War, 1945-1966* (New York 1967).

Loth, W., *Die Teilung der Welt, 1941-1955* (München 1980).

Lynch, F., 'The economic effects of the Korean War in France, 1950-1952', EUI Working Paper 86/253 (Florence 1986).

Melandri, P., *Les Etats-Unis face à l'Unification de l'Europe, 1945-1954* (Paris 1980).

Militärgeschichtliches Forschungsamt (ed.), *Von der Kapitulation bis zum Pleven Plan* (Vienna 1982).

Milward, A.S., *The European Rescue of the Nation State* (Londen 1994).

Milward, A.S., *The Reconstruction of Western Europe, 1945-1951* (London 1984).

Osgood, R.E., *NATO: The Entangling Alliance* (Chicago 1962).

Riste, O. (ed.), *Western Security: The Formative Years* (Oslo 1985).

Schwartz, T.A., *America's Germany. John J. McCloy and the Federal Republic of Germany* (London 1991).

Soutou, G., 'La France, l'Allemagne et les accords de Paris', *Relations Internationales* 52 (Winter 1987) pp. 451-470.

Spierenburg, D.P., and R. Poidevin, *Histoire de la Haute Autorité de La Communauté du Charbon et de l'Acier* (Brussels 1993).

Taviani, P.E., *Solidarietà Atlantica e Communità Europea* (Florence 1954).

Trachtenberg, M., *A Constructed Peace. The Making of the European Settlement 1945-1963* (Princeton 1999).

Urwin, D.U., *The Community of Europe. A History of European Integration since 1945* (London 1991).

Wall, I., *The United States and the Making of Post-war France, 1945-1954* (Cambridge 1991).

Warner, G., 'The United States and the Rearmament of Germany', 1950-54', *International Affairs* 61 (1984-85) 2.

Wiebes, C. and B. Zeeman, 'The Pentagon Negotiations, March 1948: The Launching of the North Atlantic Treaty', *International Affairs* 59 (1983) 3, pp. 351-363.

Willis, F., *France, Germany and the new Europe, 1945-1963* (New York 1968).

Yergin, D., *Shattered Peace. The Origins of the Cold War and the National Security State* (Boston 1977).

EDC

Bariety, J., 'La décision de réarmer l'Allemagne, l'echec de la Communauté européenne de défense et les accords de Paris du 23 Octobre vus du côté français', *Revue belge de philologie et d'histoire* 71 (1993) 354-383.

Baring, A., *Aussenpolitik in Adenauer's Kanzler-Demokratie. Bonns Beitrag zur Europäischen Verteidigungsgemeinschaft* (München 1969).

Clesse, A., *Le Projet de CED du Plan Pleven au "Crime" du 30 août* (Baden Baden 1986).

De Smet, A., *La Communauté Européenne de Défense. Expérience et Leçons* (Heule 1966).

De Vos, L. de., 'La CED, une occasion manquée', in: M. Dumoulin (ed.), *La Belgique et les débuts de la construction européenne* (Louvain-la-Neuve 1987) pp. 103-117.

Dumoulin, M. (ed.), *La Communauté Européenne de Défense, Leçons pour demain?* (Brussels 2000).

Frenay, H., *La Communauté Européenne de Défense. Réponse au Général De Gaulle* (Paris 1953).

Fursdon, E., *The European Defence Community. A History* (London 1980).

Guillen, P., 'Les chefs militairs français. Le réarmement de l'Allemagne et la CED (1950-1954)', *Revue d'histoire de la deuxième guerre mondiale* 129 (Jan 1983) pp. 3-33.

Harst, J. van der, 'The Pleven plan', in: R.T. Griffiths (ed.), *The Netherlands and the Integration of Europe* (Amsterdam 1990), pp. 137-164.

Harst, J. van der, 'The Netherlands and the European Defence Community', EUI Working Paper 86/252 (Florence 1986).

Kaplan, L.S., 'The United States, EDC and French Indo-China', Dienbienphu project center for NATO studies, draft Febr. 1986.

Kersten, A.E., 'Niederländische Regierung, Bewaffnung Westdeutschlands und EVG', in: MGFA (ed.), *Die Europäische Verteidigungsgemeinschaft. Stand und Probleme der Forschung* (Boppard am Rhein 1985) pp. 191-220.

Lapie, P.-O., 'La Communauté Européenne de l'Armement', *La Revue des deux mondes* (Sept. 1953) pp. 17-27.

Larminat, Gen. de, 'La Communauté Européenne de Défense. Les Données Techniques', *Politique Etrangère* 18 (1953) pp.149-160.

Legaret, J., and E. Martin-Dumesnil, *La Communauté Européenne de Défense. Etude Analytique du Traité du 27 Mai 1952* (Paris 1953).

Leites, N., and Chr. de la Malène, 'Paris from EDC to WEU', *World Politics* 9 (1957) 2, pp. 193-219.

Lerner, D., and R. Aron (ed.), *La Querelle de la CED* (Paris 1956); also published in English: *France defeats EDC* (New York 1957).

Manet, O., 'La CED. Les Données Politiques', *Politique Etrangère* 18 (1953) pp. 160-168.

Militärgeschichtliches Forschungsamt (MGFA) (ed.), *Die Europäische Verteidigungsgemeinschaft. Stand und Probleme der Forschung* (Boppard am Rhein 1985).

Militärgeschichtliches Forschungsamt (ed.), *Die EVG-Phase* (München 1990).

Noack, P., *Das Scheitern der Europäischen Verteidigungsgemeinschaft* (Düsseldorf 1977).

Pitman, P., 'Interested Circles: French Industry and the Rise and Fall of the European Defence Community (1950-1954)', in: M. Dumoulin (ed.), *La Communauté Européenne de Défense. Leçons pour Demain?* (Brussels 2000).

Poidevin, R., 'La France devant le problème de la CED: Incidences nationales et internationales (été 1951 à été 1953)', *Revue d'histoire de la deuxième guerre mondiale* 129 (Jan. 1983) pp. 35-57.

Ruane, K., *The Rise and Fall of the European Defence Community. Anglo-American Relations and the Crisis of European Defence, 1950-55* (London 2000).

Spits, F.C., *Naar een Europees Leger*, Ned. Raad der Europese Beweging (The Hague 1954).

Vial, Ph., 'Jean Monnet, un père pour la CED?' in: R. Girault and G. Bossuat (eds.), *Europe brisée, Europe retrouvée* (Paris 1994).

Walton, C.C., 'Background for the European Defence Community', *Political Science Quarterly* 68 (1953) 1, pp. 42-69.

Young, J.W., 'German rearmament and the European Defence Community', in: J.W. Young (ed.), *The Foreign Policy of Churchill's Peacetime Administration, 1951-1955* (Leicester 1988) pp. 91-108.

Netherlands

Barents, J., 'De internationale situatie en de Nederlandse landsverdediging', *Socialisme en Democratie* (April 1951) pp. 193-201.

Barents, J., 'De verdedigbaarheid van Nederland', *Socialisme en Democratie* (Nov. 1952) pp. 675-690.

Brakel, W., *De industrialisatie in Nederland na 1945* (Leiden 1954).

Brouwer, J.W.L., and C.M. Megens, 'Het debat in de ministerraad over de Nederlandse militaire bijdrage aan de NAVO, 1949-1951', *Bijdragen en Mededelingen betreffende de Geschiedenis der Nederlanden*, 112 (1992) 3, pp. 486-501.

Brouwer, J.W.L., '"De stem van de Marine in de ministerraad". Schout-bij-nacht H.C.W. Moorman als staatssecretaris van Marine in het kabinet-Drees-Van Schaik, 1949-1951', *Politieke Opstellen* CPG/KUN 9 (1989), pp. 29-56.

Brouwer, J.W.L., 'Om de doelmatigheid van de defensieuitgaven, 1948-1951', *Politieke Opstellen* CPG/KUN 10 (1990) pp. 85-108.

Campen, S.I.P. van, *The Quest for Security. Some Aspects of Netherlands Foreign Policy, 1945-1950* (The Hague 1957).

Daalder, H., and N. Cramer (eds.), *Willem Drees* (Houten 1988).

Duyverman, S.D., *Zijn wij met onze defensie-inspanning op de goede weg?* Brochure (The Hague 1953).

Eng, P. van der, *De Marshall-hulp. Een perspectief voor Nederland, 1947-1953* (Houten 1987).

Flynn, G. (ed.), *NATO's Northern Allies. The national security policies of Belgium, Denmark, the Netherlands and Norway* (New Jersey 1985) pp.113-170.

Govaerts, F., 'Belgium, Holland and Luxembourg', in: O. de Raeymaeker (ed.), *Small powers in alignment* (Louvain 1974).

Griffiths, R.T. and A.S. Milward, 'The Beyen Plan and the European Political Community', EUI Colloquium Paper, col. 1 (Florence 1986).

Griffiths, R.T., 'Economic Reconstruction Policy in the Netherlands and its international consequences, May 1945-March 1951', EUI Working Paper 76 (Florence 1984).

Griffiths, R.T. (ed.), *The Netherlands and the Integration of Europe, 1945-1957* (Amsterdam 1990).

Harryvan, A.G., J. van der Harst and S. van Voorst (eds.), *Voor Nederland en Europa. Politici en ambtenaren over het Nederlandse Europabeleid en de Europese integratie, 1945-1975* (Amsterdam 2001).

Harst, J. van der, 'Nabuurstaten of uniepartners? Aspecten van defensiebeleid van de Beneluxlanden, 1945-1954', in: E.S.A. Bloemen (ed.), *Het Benelux-effect* (Amsterdam 1992) pp. 129-142.

Hellema, D., *Buitenlandse politiek van Nederland* (Utrecht 1995).

Hoffenaar, J., and G. Teitler (eds.), *De Koude Oorlog. Maatschappij en Krijgsmacht in de jaren '50* (The Hague 1992)

Hommes, P.H. (ed.), *Nederland en de Europese eenwording* (The Hague 1980).

Hoogen, Th. J.G. van den, *De besluitvorming over de defensiebegroting. Systeem en verandering* (Leeuwarden 1987).

Jaquet, L.G.M. (ed.), 'European and Atlantic Cooperation. The Dutch attitude', special issue of the *Internationale Spectator* 19 (1965) 7, pp. 433-692.

Janssen, J.A.M.M., *De legerraad, 1945-1982* (The Hague 1982).

Kersten, A.E., 'In de ban van de bondgenoot', D. Barnouw, M. de Keizer en G. van der Stroom (ed.), *1940-1945: Onverwerkt verleden?* (Utrecht 1985) pp. 99-126.

Kersten, A.E., *Maken drie kleinen één grote? De politieke invloed van de Benelux, 1945-1955* (Bussum 1982).

Klein, P.W. (ed.), *Herrijzend Nederland in de periode 1945-1950* (The Hague 1981).

Kosman, H., 'Dutch share in Europe's Air Defense', *Aviation Age* 19 (May 1953).

Kruls, H.J. (ed.), *Five Years NATO. Special NATO issue under the auspices of the Royal Dutch Association 'Our Army'* (Amsterdam 1955).

Labohm, H.H.J. (ed.), *De waterdragers van het Nederlandse Europabeleid. Terugblik op 40 jaar DGES* (Den Haag 1997).

Leurdijk, J.H. (ed.), *The Foreign Policy of the Netherlands* (Alphen aan den Rijn 1978).

Lubbers, J.H., *Van overloop naar overheveling. Mogelijkheden tot vergroting van de doelmatigheid in het Nederlandse financiële defensiebeleid* (Leiden 1962).

Megens, C.M., *American Aid to NATO Allies in the 1950s. The Dutch Case* (Groningen 1994).

Megens, C.M., 'Militaire hulpverlening in de jaren vijftig - de Amerikaanse hulp aan Nederland', *Internationale Spectator* 36 (1982) 8, pp. 466-471.

Rozemond, S., *Nederland in West Europa. Een plaatsbepaling* (The Hague 1986).

Schaper, H.A., 'Van afzijdigheid naar bondgenootschappelijkheid', *Internationale Spectator* 32 (1978), pp. 324-336.

Schaper, H.A., 'Het Nederlandse Veiligheidsbeleid, 1945-1950', *Bijdragen en Mededelingen betreffende de Geschiedenis der Nederlanden* 96 (1981) 2, pp. 277-299.

Schulten, J.W.M., 'De wederopbouw van de Koninklijke Landmacht na de Tweede Wereldoorlog', *Militaire Spectator* 148 (1979) 9, pp. 452-460.

Schulten, J.W.M., 'Die militärische Integration aus der Sicht der Niederlande', in: MGFA (ed.), *Militärgeschichte seit 1945. Die westliche Sicherheitsgemeinschaft, 1948-1950* (Boppard am Rhein 1988) pp. 89-101.

Sectie Militaire Geschiedenis (ed.), *1 Divisie '7 December' 1946-- 1986* (Amsterdam 1986).

Staden, A. van, *Een trouwe bondgenoot: Nederland en het Atlantisch bondgenootschap, 1960-1971* (Baarn 1974).

Staf, C., *Nota inzake het defensiebeleid* (The Hague 1954).

Visser, A., *Alleen bij uiterste noodzaak. De rooms-rode samenwerking en het einde van de brede basis* (Amsterdam 1986).

Voorhoeve, J.J.C., *Peace, profits and principles. A study of Dutch foreign policy* (The Hague 1979).

Westers, M.F., *Mr. D.U. Stikker en de na-oorlogse reconstructie van het liberalisme in Nederland. Een zakenman in de politieke arena* (Amsterdam 1988).

Wiebes, C., and B. Zeeman. 'Stikker, Indonesië en het Noord-Atlantisch verdrag; of hoe Nederland in de pompe ging', *Bijdragen en Mededelingen betreffende de Geschiedenis der Nederlanden* 100 (1985) 1, pp. 225-251.

Wielenga, J.W.F., *West-Duitsland: partner uit noodzaak. Nederland en de Bondsrepubliek 1949-1955* (Utrecht 1989).

Zitzewitz, H. von, 'Der NATO Beitrag und die nationale Verteidigung der Niederlande', *Wehrkunde* 14 (1965), pp. 580-586.

Memoirs

Acheson, D., *Present at the Creation. My years in the State Department* (London 1970).

Adenauer, K., *Erinnerungen, 1945-1953* (Stuttgart 1965).

Alphand, H., *L'Etonnement d'Etre* (Paris 1978)

Beaufre, A., *NATO and Europe* (New York 1966).

Beyen, J.W., *Het spel en de knikkers. Een kroniek van vijftig jaren* (Rotterdam 1968).

Boon, H.N., *Afscheidsaudiëntie. Tien studies uit de diplomatieke praktijk* (Rotterdam 1976).

Drees, W., *Zestig jaar levenservaring* (Amsterdam 1962).

Eden, A., *Full Circle. The Memoirs of Sir Anthony Eden* (London 1960).

Ismay, Lord, *NATO. The First Five Years, 1949-1954* (Paris 1954).

Kruls, H.J., *Generaal in Nederland. Memoires* (Bussum 1975).

Linthorst Homan, J., *Wat zijt ghij voor een vent?* (Assen 1974).

Massigli, R., *Une Comédie des Erreurs* (Paris 1978).

Mendès-France, P., *Choisir* (Paris 1978).

Moch, J., *Histoire du réarmement allemand depuis 1950* (Paris 1965).

Monnet, J., *Mémoires* (Paris 1976).

Nutting, A., *Europe Will Not Wait: A Warning and a Way Out* (London 1960).

Spaak, P.-H., *Combats Inachevés* (Paris 1969).

Speidel, H., *Aus unserer Zeit. Erinnerungen* (Frankfurt 1977).

Stikker, D.U., *Men of Responsibility* (London 1965); also published in Dutch.

Vredenburch, H.F.L.K. van, *Den Haag antwoordt niet. Herinneringen* (Leiden 1985).

List of abbreviations

AI	Artillerie Inrichtingen
ALFCE	Allied Land Forces Central Europe
AMP	Adviesraad voor Militaire Productie
AOP	Artillery Observation Plane
ARA	Algemeen Rijksarchief (Dutch National Archive)
ARP	Anti-Revolutionaire Partij
AVR	Algemene Verdedigingsraad
AZ	(ministerie van) Algemene Zaken
Benelux	Belgium, the Netherlands and Luxembourg
BTO	Brussels Treaty Organisation
BuZa (BZ)	(ministerie van) Buitenlandse Zaken
CDI	Comité pour la Défense des Intérêts francais en politique étrangère
CDU	Christlich-Demokratische Union
CED	Communauté Européenne de Défense
CHU	Christelijk-Historische Unie
CNPF	Conseil National du Patronat Francais
CPN	Communistische Partij Nederland
DC	Defence Committee
DC	Democrazia Cristiana
DGEM	Directoraat-Generaal voor het Economische en Militaire Hulpprogramma
DMA	Directoraat Militaire Aangelegenheden
DPB	Defence Production Board
ECA	Economic Co-operation Administration
ECSC	European Coal and Steel Community
EDC	European Defence Community
EDG	Europese Defensie Gemeenschap
EDP	Emergency Defence Plan
EPC	European Political Community
ERP	European Recovery Programme
FEB	Financial and Economic Board
FN	Fabrique Nationale

FRG	Federal Republic of Germany
FRUS	Foreign Relations of the United States
GNP	Gross National Product
GS	General Staff
IMF	International Monetary Fund
JCS	Joint Chiefs of Staff
KMA	Koninklijke Militaire Academie
KNIL	Koninklijk Nederlands-Indisch Leger
KNP	Katholieke Nationale Partij
KVP	Katholieke Volkspartij
MDAP	Mutual Defence Assistance Programme
MP	Member of Parliament
MR	Ministerraad
MRP	Mouvement Républicain Populaire
MSA	Mutual Security Act
MTDP	Medium Term Defence Plan
NATO	North Atlantic Treaty Organisation
NCO	Non-Commissioned Officer
NLG	Netherlands (Dutch) Guilder
NSC	National Security Council
OEEC	Organisation for European Economic Co-operation
PAAA	Politisches Archiv des Auswärtigen Amts
PvdA	Partij van de Arbeid
QMG	Quartermaster-General
Raad MAK	Raad Militaire Aangelegenheden van het Koninkrijk
RDIARoyal	Dutch Indies Army
SACEUR	Supreme Allied Commander Europe
SGP	Staatkundig Gereformeerde Partij
SHAPE	Supreme Headquarters Allied Powers Europe
TAF	Tactical Air Force
TCC	Temporary Council Committee
UK	United Kingdom
UN	United Nations
US	United States
USSR	Union of Soviet Socialist Republics

VVD	Volkspartij voor Vrijheid en Democratie
WEU	West(ern) European Union
WU	Western Union

Index

336

Milton Keynes UK
Ingram Content Group UK Ltd.
UKHW011259251123
433259UK00001B/100